SHOW BOAT
The Story of a Classic American Musical

SHOW BOAT

The Story of a
Classic American Musical

MILES KREUGER

New York
OXFORD UNIVERSITY PRESS
1977

COPYRIGHT © 1977 BY MILES KREUGER

PRINTED IN THE UNITED STATES OF AMERICA

LIBRARY OF CONGRESS CATALOGING IN PUBLICATION DATA

Kreuger, Miles.
  Show boat, the story of a classic American musical.

  Bibliography: p.
  Filmography: p.
  Includes index.
  1.   Kern, Jerome, 1885–1945. Show boat.
2.   Hammerstein, Oscar, 1895–1960. Show boat.   3.   Mu-
sical revue, comedy, etc.—United States.   I.   Title.
ML410.K385K7   782.8'1'0924   76-51717
ISBN 0-19-502275-0

This book is for Grandma,
who took me to my first Broadway musical,
Knights of Song,
when I was only four.

CONTENTS

INTRODUCTION

I have loved **Show Boat** for so many years that it is impossible to recall my introduction to this remarkable work. Like so many children growing up during the 1940's, I discovered the beautiful Jerome Kern-Oscar Hammerstein II score through radio, in those days when many hours of network time were devoted to live broadcasts of civilized music. Later, I saw several theatrical revivals in New York City and the 1951 film version when it was released.

As a drama student at Bard College during the early 1950's, I upset some of my teachers by being more interested in Rodgers and Hart than Beaumont and Fletcher, more attracted to the wit of Cole Porter than Bulwer-Lytton (an easy choice!), and more beguiled by Burton Lane's melodies in **Finian's Rainbow** (1-10-47, 46th Street) than Vivaldi's **The Four Seasons,** which had just recently been rediscovered via the early long-playing record.

At that time, there was only one book on the American Musical Theatre, Cecil Smith's **Musical Comedy in America** (Theatre Arts, 1950). I carried it around like a Bible, reading it to the end and then starting at the first page all over again. Although I have come to learn that it abounds in factual flaws, it is still the best and most concise introductory narrative on the subject for a general reader.

Having learned from Smith and other sources that **Show Boat** marked a turning point in the maturing of the stage musical, I always hoped to write a book about this one work. While a production assistant on my first professional show, the **1955 ANTA Album** (3-28-55, Adelphi), I met Oscar Hammerstein II and, on several occasions during the next five years, asked him many questions about his career and his philosophy of musical theatre. There were more questions about **Show Boat** than any other single subject.

When Oxford University Press agreed to let me write a book honoring the fiftieth anniversary of **Show Boat** (December 27, 1977), I could hardly believe my ears. After two decades, my dream to document this historic musical was to come true.

The biggest problem was what to exclude to avoid a tome the length of **War and Peace.** I felt that all foreign-language versions should be left out, in addition to references to most of the countless American touring or regional productions that have appeared over the decades. The appendix does, however, contain complete casts and production staffs for all St. Louis Municipal Opera, Los Angeles Light Opera, and Dallas Summer Musicals productions.

Introduction

Similarly, references to the major British stage productions, all important radio versions, Kern's symphonic adaptation, "Scenario for Orchestra," the now-forgotten New York summer revival on Randall's Island (6-29-38, Municipal Stadium) with Guy Robertson, William Kent, and the Hall sisters, Bettina and Natalie, are all included in the appendix.

This book is not intended as a dewy-eyed valentine to **Show Boat,** but rather an analytical study that examines the work in all its forms: the Edna Ferber novel, the original 1927 stage version and its later revisions, and all three (and quite dissimilar) film adaptations. The strengths and weaknesses of all are pointed out in detail, along with a vast amount of background on each version.

The critical evaluations may sometimes seem harsh and at variance with popular criticism of the period, but critics have tended to be kind to **Show Boat,** despite occasional glaring inadequacies that come sharply into focus when one production is compared with another.

As this is (to my knowledge) the very first book to document the history of a single work of the American Musical Theatre, I have tried to broaden the scope to embrace theoretical observations about the differing aesthetics of stage and screen, and how these attitudes and forms have changed over the years. Presumably, such observations ought to hold true for any theatrical or cinematic work created under similar circumstances.

Like any major work of art, **Show Boat** is encrusted with lore, much of it pure myth. I have long known as Gospel that the musical had been "kicking around Broadway" for two or three years before Florenz Ziegfeld finally decided to produce it; and even then he never cared for the show. Rubbish! He was excited by the work from the very first week that Kern and Hammerstein purchased the stage rights from Edna Ferber.

It is carved on a tablet that **Show Boat** was scheduled to be the initial attraction at the Ziegfeld Theatre in early 1927, but that its long delay in writing forced the producer to open his theatre with Rio Rita (2-2-27, Ziegfeld) instead. Balderdash! **Rio Rita** was publicly announced as the theatre's premiere production even before construction was completed.

Dogma decrees that when **Show Boat** finally went into production, it was designed for the Ziegfeld Theatre. Nonsense! Until just two weeks prior to the New York opening, the production was being advertised for the Lyric Theatre on 42nd Street and was switched to the Ziegfeld as a last-minute decision.

Numerous books and articles mention that early in **Show Boat**'s post-Broadway national tour, its original Magnolia, Norma Terris, was replaced by her understudy, Irene Dunne. Drivel! Although Miss Dunne did in fact replace Miss Terris on Monday, June 3, 1929, at the Colonial Theatre in Boston, Miss Dunne was never an understudy to the role but was brought in expressly to replace her predecessor.

Even scholars of musical theatre disagree on whether or not Hammerstein had a hand in rewriting the 1918 Jerome Kern-P. G. Wodehouse song, "Bill," for its interpolation into **Show Boat.** Hammerstein himself credits Wodehouse as the sole author of the lyrics in an announcement in the playbill for the 1946 revival. Yet a comparison of the two versions reveals that both Kern and Hammerstein musically and lyrically rewrote the entire first half of the refrain (both choruses) for **Show Boat.** For the first time, the two versions of this song are printed together for comparison. My thanks to Dean Kaye of T. B. Harms, publisher of the **Show Boat** score, for permission to print both versions (and other lyrical examples as well).

In order to focus sharply on events as they actually took place, it was necessary to ignore virtually everything printed in books about **Show Boat** and to confirm in detail everything told during personal interviews. "Oral history," so fashionable now among collegiate and professional researchers, is an all-too-easy method of preserving on tape the voices of people who participated in important events; but the memories even of participants can often be faulty due to the passage of years.

Except for Philip Graham's **Showboats: The History of an American Institution** (University of Texas, 1951), used as a reference on the little-documented history of the show boat, all research materials were original resources: unpublished scripts and screenplays in varying stages of finality, piano vocal scores, sheet music, playbills, reviews, film studio production files, costume and scenic designs, production photographs, newspaper accounts with heavy emphasis upon the weekly reports in *Variety*, private memos and correspondence, and many other items of the original periods.

One fascinating aspect of **Show Boat** is that, unlike most major musicals, it has never had an official script or

Introduction

score. Following the 1932 Broadway revival, Hammerstein himself and later his son William and others began to alter the work in small, but often significant, ways: sometimes for length, sometimes to trim some of the comedy sequences originally intended simply to cover long scene changes, sometimes to reflect the nation's changing racial attitudes.

The vastly altered English script was published (by Chappell & Co. Ltd.) but never an American version. Yet I was able to draw from a manuscript of the 1946 version given to me by Oscar Hammerstein, and several others made available by William Hammerstein, who also opened up the **Show Boat** legal files, his personal address book for contacts, and his memory of the 1946 revival (for which he was a stage manager) and all important subsequent productions. Without Billy Hammerstein's enthusiastic support, this book could not have been written; and I cannot express strongly enough my gratitude for his warmth and informed assistance.

As there was no known print of the 1929 film version during the writing of this book, it was necessary to use the files at Universal Pictures: production sheets, articles in the studio's internal house organ *Universal Weekly*, and other reference materials. These were made available by the studio's superb research department, headed by Andy Lee, with his staff: Margaret Ross, George Neill, and Sherri Seeling. Stanley Newman made a special microfilm print-out of the original screenplay, and Peg Shillito of the *Miami Herald* provided information about the film's bizarre world premiere. As a result of this book, MGM, which now owns the screen rights to **Show Boat**, is currently preparing a new silent print of the 1929 version for its first public screening in roughly four decades.

Countless hours of fruitful research were spent in one of New York's most important institutions, the Theatre Collection, Library and Museum of the Performing Arts at Lincoln Center, a division of The New York Public Library. My gratitude is most profound for the patience, help, and resourcefulness of curator Paul Myers, Dorothy Swerdlove, Roderick Bladel, Donald Fowle, Betty Wharton, Monty Arnold, David Bartholomew, Maxwell Silverman, and others on staff. From the library's Rodgers and Hammerstein Archives of Recorded Sound, I want to thank David Hall, Sam Sanders, and J. Peter Bergman; and also Richard Jackson of the library's Music Collection.

It was necessary to acquire newspaper reviews and theatre programs from many cities outside New York, and I found that many new and old friends were willing to help. I am most grateful to Mary Edson, librarian at Knights Landing, California, who sent me numerous photo copies of articles documenting the location shooting of the 1929 film, during the summer of 1928. In addition, she was kind enough to gather a collection of snapshots taken by local townspeople who had been drafted as extras. Pictures (appearing on page 80) were provided by her neighbors Charles V. Hooper and Mr. and Mrs. Mervin Springer.

Many friends, professional colleagues, and others helped to fit the pieces together. In alphabetical order, I should like to thank Wade Alexander (Stanyan Records), Hartney Arthur, Tom Barensfeld (*Cleveland Press*), Dr. Barry Brooks, Alexander Crosby Brown, Corinne and David Chertok, Jean Dalrymple, Ursula Deren (BBC), Daniel Dietz, Mrs. Charles Ellis, Kelle Eubanks (*Goldenrod* show boat), Hugh Fordin, Gail Freunsch (Library of Congress), Roberta Gerry (Fawcett Publications), Herbert G. Goldman, Stanley Green, E. Y. Harburg, Hanna Henner (APCO), Edward Jablonski, David A. Jasen, Leonard Josephson, Manny Kean (Kean Archives, Philadelphia), Ardie L. Kelly (The Mariners Museum), Jacques Kelly (Baltimore *News-American*), Abigail and Robert Kimball, Hilary Knight, Don Koll, Diane and Richard Koszarski, Don Krim (UA-16), H. Pierson Mapes, Samuel Marx, Frank McGlinn, Betty Kern Miller, Norman Miller, Roger Mohovich, Sally Pavetti, Harriet Pilpel, Thomas Reynolds Jr. (*Majestic* show boat), Saul Richman, Paul Robeson Archives, Leo Robin, Roger Robles, Harold Rome, Axel Rosin (Book of the Month Club), Julius Rutin, Mildred Sale (Dallas Summer Musicals), Allan Salyers, Phil Scales (*Majestic* show boat), Mrs. Joseph Schildkraut, Sylvia Schulman, Nat Shapiro, Martin Shwartz (Los Angeles Civic Light Opera), Richard Siegel, Alfred Simon, Romano Tozzi, Lars Walldov, Ray Wile, John Willis, Alice and James Wilson (The Steamship Historical Society of America), and individuals from several organizations: American Society of Composers, Authors and Publishers (ASCAP)— Walter Wager, Sara Kerber, and Patricia Sniffen; Belwin-Mills Publishing Co.—Martin Winkler, Dan Gendason, Nick Russo, and Bill Collins; Columbia Broadcasting System (CBS)—Betsy C. Broesamle and John Behrins; Columbia Records—Tiny McCarthy, Eugene Kraut, Fred Swanson, and Josephine Mangiaracina; Col-

Introduction

umbia University Libraries Special Collection Division—Bernard Crystal and Mary Bowling; Doubleday—Ken McCormick, Joan Ward, and Dorothy Harris; Long Island Park and Recreation Commission—Elaine Lawlor and Bud Latham; Lynn Farnol Group—Alice Regensburg and Elissa Zimet; National Broadcasting Co. (NBC)—Merle S. Rukeyser Jr., Joseph Riccuiti, Audrey Halbig, Marilyn Dean, and Catherine Lim; St. Louis Municipal Opera—Jerry Berger and Ann Marie Skinner; and the Ziegfeld Club—Doris Vinton and Harriet Waldron. A special nod of thanks to Martin Grebler, Bill Pagan, and the staff of Ad-Link, Inc., for their extraordinary photo reproduction service.

I am particularly grateful to Lester Glassner for providing very special help, and to my grandmother, mother, Kay and Neil Harris, and Albert Husted for being there when I really needed them.

I was privileged to draw from the reminiscences of several **Show Boat** alumni: Norma Terris, who created the role of Magnolia; Robert Russell Bennett, who orchestrated the score; Leighton K. Brill, Oscar Hammerstein's long-time assistant; Eva Puck, Phil Sheridan, and Rose Mariella of the original and 1932 productions; Laura La Plante, who starred in the 1929 film; Gladstone Waldrip, who played in the 1932 revival and, in the 1933 tab version, took over the role of Steve under the amusing pseudonym "Stoney Wahl," devised by his close friend Helen Morgan; Freita Shaw, whose vocal group appeared in the 1933 West Coast production; Carl Laemmle Jr., who produced the 1936 film; Irene Dunne and Allan Jones, who starred in it; Lucinda Ballard and Howard Bay, who designed the costumes and settings, respectively, for the 1946 revival; and Jan Clayton and Pearl Primus from its cast. Harry Fender provided a remarkable letter from Ziegfeld, demonstrating that he was the producer's first choice for the role of Ravenal.

It must be clear that **Show Boat** has become something of a way of life for me. For that, I want to thank James T. Maher for bringing me to Oxford, Sheldon Meyer for having faith in my work, my editor Leona Capeless for tolerating my pedantic use of the comma to set off transposed adverbial phrases, art director Frederick Schneider for allowing me to crop and size my pictures and assist in the book's design, and all the other members of the Oxford family who have welcomed me into the fold.

MILES KREUGER
New York City
August 15, 1977

SHOW BOAT
The Story of a Classic American Musical

CHAPTER 1

1926
The Ferber Novel

AS AMERICA pushed its borders westward during the nineteenth century, its nomadic players were not far behind the earliest settlers. Hardy bands of actors from the East and even from England toured the pioneering communities and often established primitive repertory companies that combined drama with song-and-dance.

Along the great river arteries of the Mississippi, Ohio, Kanawha, Allegheny, Monongahela, Missouri, and the bayous of Louisiana sprouted dozens of little hamlets, from which farm produce and manufactured goods were put aboard steam-powered paddle wheelers. Excursion packets too brought travelers leisurely along the winding paths of the inland waterways. The Mississippi River, with its deceptively shallow bottom, concealed a tangle of submerged, fallen tree branches, sharp enough to puncture the hulls of passing boats. Yet the river was a marvel of power and beauty and became a way of life, providing trade, relaxation, travel, and, in time, entertainment.

In 1815, an Albany-born actor named Noah Ludlow set out with his troupe to bring the art of theatre to Frankfort, Kentucky, which he had decided (presumably accurately) was starved for enlightened play-acting. Upon arrival, he found an indifferent public, so the group purchased a keelboat for two hundred dollars, christened it *Noah's Ark,* and sailed up and down the Mississippi River, looking for theatres in which to perform. As the only places of amusement in many towns were raffish saloons, it is believed that Ludlow and his troupe occasionally performed aboard the boat itself. If this is so, show boats were modestly introduced in 1817.

The first craft expressly designed as a show boat was the *Floating Theatre,* created by the English actor William Chapman Sr. Launched in the summer of 1831, the *Floating Theatre* carried Chapman's wife and grown children, all veterans of distinguished companies in London, New York, or Philadelphia. Chapman had built a crude hut 100 feet long and 14 feet wide atop the hull of an ordinary barge. His plan was to start his annual season at Pittsburgh and float

downstream to New Orleans. There, the troupe would take a steamboat home at the end of the season, and a new craft would be built the following year.

The prosperity and quality of the Chapman troupe soon inspired imitators. The strong moral character of many of the family-operated boats tended to dispel the conservative, midwestern impression that actors were all libertines; and the frequent visits of floating theatres became welcome events in most towns. By the 1840's, the rivers were swarming with show boats, many of which held lectures on phrenology, mesmerism, and other subjects that fascinated simple audiences. Still others housed freak shows and other special attractions.

After a mere quarter of a century, this first phase of the show boat came to an abrupt end due to the Civil War. The great flowering of the show boat age began in 1869, when Dan Rice launched the *Will S. Hays*, a steamboat that carried an exhibition of his marvels.

Show boating was dominated for the last quarter of the old century by a flamboyant impresario who called himself Augustus Byron French. In the course of his career, French owned five boats (of increasing size and pretentiousness), all called French's *New Sensation,* and numbered more or less according to appearance.

Contrary to a popular misconception, show boats were *never* self-powered. The image of a show boat fitted out with smoke stacks and huge side or rear paddle wheels is entirely spurious. Show boats were flat-bottom barges that rarely drew more than 2½ feet of water.

Although show boats developed in form over the years, the classic prototype of the late nineteenth and early twentieth centuries had three decks. Audiences would board the lowest or main deck at the bow end. They would buy tickets from a window at the front of the cabin and enter the auditorium with its long central aisle that ran down to the stage toward the rear. The auditorium itself comprised the entire width of the boat, with a narrow balcony along the sides generally reserved for Negro patrons. Small staterooms aft and sometimes toward the bow served the troupe as combination sleeping quarters and dressing rooms.

A narrow, exterior second deck generally ran around the entire boat, with the top deck sometimes called the roof and sometimes the Texas.

HISTORIC SHOW BOATS

1. Perhaps the finest show boat of them all had eight names during its long career. Built in 1889 as C. F. Breidenbaugh's *Theatorium,* it is seen here at the Monongahela River landing in 1898 as French's *New Sensation No. 1* (his third boat of that name). Better known in later years as the *Water Queen,* it sank in 1936 amid spring ice floes near the mouth of the Kanawha River.

2. Eugene Robinson's *Floating Palace* (built in 1893) seated 759. As French's *New Sensation No. 2* (his fourth boat of that name), it burned in 1900 at Elmwood Landing, Louisiana.

3. French's *New Sensation,* his fifth and final boat with that name, was built in 1901 to seat 960 patrons. As a sentimental tribute to the boat's heritage, its later captain, Bill Menke, kept the *New Sensation's* name and traditions intact until the craft's demise during a storm in 1930. The name *New Sensation* had been a river landmark since French launched his first boat of that name in 1878.

4. The largest of all show boats, W. R. Markle's *Goldenrod,* was built in 1909 to seat no fewer than 1400 patrons in a richly carpeted, fully mirrored, gilded auditorium. After a long and distinguished career on the rivers, the boat was permanently moored in 1937 at St. Louis, Missouri. The *Goldenrod* continues to thrive today as a dinner theatre that seats 400 patrons.

5. Capt. Tom Reynolds' trim little *Majestic,* built in 1923, seated only 450 and could float on a mere twelve inches of water. With its family management and low overhead, it managed to survive the Depression. Today, it belongs to the city of Cincinnati, Ohio, where it is permanently moored. The boat is operated by the University of Cincinnati, whose drama students present full seasons of plays and musicals for the general public.

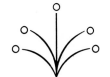

HISTORIC SHOW BOATS

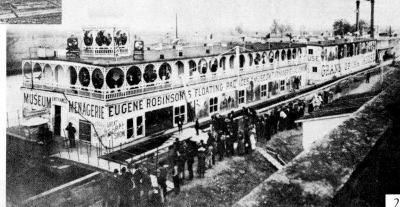

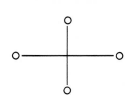

Goldenrod audiences used to hoot, stomp, and talk with members of the cast.

Because staterooms on steamboats were named for the states in the Union, the largest stateroom on the upper deck was appropriately called the Texas. This name was often carried over to show boats, although show boats rarely had rooms on the top deck.

Although some of the small, early show boats relied on the Mississippi's turbulent current to carry them downstream, the postwar crafts were always powered by small, twin-stack steamboats called towboats. These were tightly lashed to the rear of the show boat and, despite their name, did not tow, but rather pushed the clumsy show boat barges along their way. It was the towboat's pilot, rather than the show boat's captain, who was largely responsible for navigating these curious crafts through the winding and dangerous rivers.

The calliope, a steam-driven pipe organ that heralded the arrival of show boats and could be heard for miles, was invented in 1853 by Joshua C. Stoddard of Worcester, Massachusetts. The units were fitted on the roof of either the show boat or the towboat, with steam generally drawn

from the boiler of the latter. In 1882, the first electric open arcs were used for illumination, mainly as search or cargo lights; and incandescent light bulbs made their show boat debut in 1901.

Typical show boat fare consisted of a popular melodrama, in which virtue invariably triumphed over the forces of evil, or an occasional light and innocent comedy. If show boats intended to remain at a particular town for several days, a different play had to be performed each night to bring the patrons back. It was customary to conclude the evening's entertainment with the olio, a frequently spontaneous musical program, in which various members of the acting troupe would step out of character to perform popular songs, clog dancing, blackface routines, or other specialties. For twenty-five cents, the hard-working farm hands, miners, and tradesmen could buy a few hours of escapist, yet thoroughly moral, diversion.

As river towns like St. Louis and Natchez grew in size and developed their own local theatrical entertainments, show boats tended to ply

1926—The Ferber Novel

their trade in the smaller communities. They thrived until around 1915, when motion pictures began to supplant them in even the most rural villages.

To accommodate changing tastes, some captains converted their boats into floating cinemas. Others beached their crafts and used them as movie houses or dance halls, while the fate of most was sealed by a jagged snag on the river's bottom or a sudden flash fire.

By 1925, this once thriving medium of entertainment had all but disappeared. There were only fourteen boats left on the Mississippi-Ohio system. Some canny captains continued to perform the old-fashioned melodramas of yesteryear but intentionally overacted them for the purpose of parody. The few surviving boats remained as nostalgic souvenirs of a bygone era.

One spring afternoon, author Edna Ferber found

herself strolling through Washington Park in Chicago. She noticed on a nearby bench three old gentlemen discussing the ways of the world with animation and conviction. She remembered this little scene and soon after created what she always regarded as one of her finest short stories, "Old Man Minick." Published in 1922, this was the tale of an old man who meddles in the affairs of his son and daughter-in-law. It is set on the south side of Chicago, in an apartment overlooking Washington Park.

George S. Kaufman, who had collaborated on several plays with Marc Connelly, approached Miss Ferber to work with him on a stage adaptation of "Old Man Minick." Despite her conviction that the material could not be adapted easily to theatre, she acquiesced.

The play was produced by veteran theatre manager, Winthrop Ames, a New Englander, who had begun his career back in 1904, when he took over the Castle Square Opera House in

Virtue triumphs on the *Goldenrod*.

EDNA FERBER

WINTHROP AMES

1926—The Ferber Novel

Boston. In New York, he had managed the cavernous New Theatre on Central Park West and later ran the Little Theatre and the Booth.

Ames spent much of the summer of 1924 honing the play into shape by touring it like a summer-stock package throughout much of New England and upper New York. After several successful two-night stands in small Connecticut towns, **Old Man Minick** opened on Wednesday, August 20, in New London, at the venerable Lyceum Theatre, which had known some of the greatest nineteenth-century actors in the days when stars toured to even the tiniest hamlets.

By August 1924, however, local audiences had vacated the Lyceum in favor of the nearby movie houses. The ancient odeum, now usually dark, was dusted off to await its first-nighters. The audience was seated; the house lights dimmed; and, suddenly, hordes of bats, who claimed the theatre as their home, came swooping down on the patrons and caused havoc. Although the performance continued, it was hardly received with ardent enthusiasm.

After their dismal premiere, the company joined Ames in his hotel suite for snacks and coffee. Trying to cheer his crestfallen mummers, Ames told them that next time he would not bother with out-of-town tryouts, but would simply rent a show boat and drift down the river, playing the towns as they appeared.

An ad for **Minick** after it moved from the Booth to the Bijou Theatre. Pictured is Phyllis Povah with Frederick Burt (left) and O. P. Heggie.

1926—The Ferber Novel

When Edna Ferber asked what a show boat was, Ames began to explain that they were floating theatres on which the company lived and acted. The country people would come from miles around when they heard the call of the calliope.

According to her autobiography, **A Peculiar Treasure** (Doubleday Doran, 1939), Miss Ferber suddenly sprang to life, forgetting all about bats, the Lyceum, and even **Old Man Minick.** She wanted to know more about show boats, a nearly forgotten bit of Americana filled with adventure and romance and period charm.

As soon as her play, its title shorted to **Minick** (9-24-24, Booth), had safely opened (and was finally selected by Burns Mantle as one of the season's ten best plays), Miss Ferber began hungrily to seek out all she could learn about show boats.

She heard about the *James Adams Floating Theatre,* a family-operated show boat that served the coastal tidewaters of Chesapeake Bay and the Albemarle and Pamlico sounds. In October, not stopping to realize that the show boat season was drawing to a close, she dashed down to "Little" Washington, North Carolina, where a young Negro in a Ford drove her thirty miles to the landing.

Sensing that the boat was about to depart, she rushed up to a tall, thin, young man and introduced herself as Edna Ferber, a writer: she wanted to meet the owner.

Surprisingly, the man immediately recognized her name as the author of the Emma McChesney stories, and he rushed to get his wife. Thus Miss Ferber met Charles Hunter and his wife Beulah, known professionally as the "Mary Pickford of the Chesapeake" and sister of James Adams, who owned the show boat. Not only had the Hunters read the McChesney stories, but they were in fact Ferber fans and had read many of her works. Unfortunately, the season had ended, so the Hunters invited her to join them the following April at Bath, North Carolina, their very first stop for the season.

Back in New York, Detective Ferber began to seek out every available scrap of information about show boats. She met several people who had worked on them, including actor Wallace

Ford and an editor of *The Billboard,* then a major theatrical trade journal. There was even a reference, albeit a brief one, in David Graham Phillips' novel, **Susan Lenox: Her Fall and Rise.**

The following April, she returned to Bath, on the Pamlico River. Although the town had once served as the governor's seat before the Revolution, it had become pathetically run-down, its population reduced to just a few hundred. Miss Ferber received a message that the boat, which wintered in Elizabeth City, would be delayed by one or two days. Seeking lodging, she found that the one-time governor's mansion, a fine brick house, now accepted lodgers. Inside, she was shown a room smelling of mice and mold. The landlady was annoyed that Miss Ferber actually expected fresh sheets on her bed and was quick to point out that it was her own daughter who had slept on these sheets, and only once.

After a sleepless night and an inedible breakfast, Miss Ferber was happy to learn that the *James Adams Floating Theatre* had arrived. Built in 1914, the craft contained 700 seats. It was 122 feet long and 34 feet wide, and bore little physical resemblance to the more ornate Mississippi show boats.

For the next few days, Edna Ferber was in Heaven. The Hunters gave her their own bedroom, and the company regaled her with show boat lore. She learned that a typical show boat company consisted of a romantic leading man and woman, in this case the Hunters themselves. There were the ingenue and juvenile leads, a character team, a general business team, a heavy, and a general utility man. The towboat crew members often doubled in the band. The Negro cook and her husband, who served at table for the company, were soon to be transmuted into Queenie and Jo in Miss Ferber's novel. After a few days of frantically taking notes on a thinning yellow pad, traveling from town to town with the troupe, and steeping herself in the life style of a floating theatre company, Miss Ferber returned to New York.

Without ever having seen the Mississippi, she left for Europe early in the summer of 1925, intent upon writing her show boat novel. She settled in a spacious and sunny hotel room overlooking the Bay of Biscay in the tiny Basque

Charles M. Hunter.

His wife, Beulah Adams,
the "Mary Pickford of the Chesapeake."

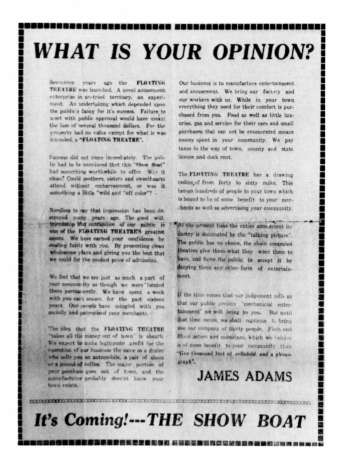
village of St. Jean de Luz, in the French border district Basses Pyrénées. The sounds of bathers, ice cream venders, and music from the orchestra at the casino provided a tranquil setting for putting ideas to paper. She continued to write in Paris and finally finished the book in New York.

Show Boat first appeared in serial form in the April through September 1926 issues of *Woman's Home Companion.* After just a few installments, film offers began to appear, but Miss Ferber felt she should wait until book publication before making a decision.

In August 1926, the novel was published in book form by Doubleday, Page & Co. It was dedicated "To Winthrop Ames, Who First Said Show Boat to Me." An instantaneous success at $2.50 a copy, it was chosen the September selection of the recently formed Book of the Month Club, which had been launched in April. Book club sales alone amounted to about 25,000 copies. In her autobiography, Edna Ferber claims that by 1939 the sales totaled 320,000 copies in the United States, and that the book had been

translated and published in one dozen European countries.

In nineteen chapters and 398 pages of text, **Show Boat** traces the lives of its characters for half a century, from the late 1870's until the time of the book's publication.

Chapter One opens aboard the *Cotton Blossom Floating Palace Theatre* during a violent storm early one April morning in 1889. A baby girl is being born to Magnolia Ravenal, whose parents, Captain Andy and Mrs. Parthenia Ann Hawks, own the boat. Because they happen to be just south of Cairo, where Kentucky, Illinois, and Missouri come together, the baby is named Kim, an acronym for the three states.

Through a series of references to recent events, we learn that this is the maiden trip of the new *Cotton Blossom,* which Andy had ordered from a shipyard in St. Louis. We are introduced to Mark Hooper, pilot of the towboat *Mollie Able,* and Gaylord Ravenal, Magnolia's husband and show boat leading man.

Chapter Two is a flashback, in which we learn

that Parthy had been a Massachusetts school teacher, keeping house for her henpecked father. She met perky, little Andy when he drifted into the area one summer to visit his fishermen kin. His real name is André, and he is descended from a long line of Basque fishermen from the vicinity of St. Jean de Luz. (Where do writers come up with such ideas!)

After their marriage, Andy and Parthy moved to the little Illinois town of Thebes on the Mississippi. Their lot improved as he went from pilot to river captain to owner and captain of the steamer *Creole Belle,* accommodating both passengers and freight.

For years Andy could not get Parthy to take a trip on the boat. When she finally did so with baby Magnolia, she created havoc by complaining about the filthy kitchen and the drinking and gambling she saw. Magnolia, however, was entranced by the river. Parthy's zeal for reform was so great that she remained on board and soon began to reform Andy out of business by reviling the "sinful" travelers.

In Chapter Three, Andy's steamboat business begins to fail, not only because of Parthy's interference but because of competition from railroads, which provided swifter travel for people and goods alike. Andy sells the boat and buys the *Cotton Blossom,* an old show boat he has read in a newspaper is for sale.

In Chapter Four, Parthy is enraged by the purchase and for three days refuses to speak to him, but "sends messages" through nine-year-old Magnolia. With his boat overhauled, Andy invites Parthy to inspect the transformation. Reluctantly, she agrees and examines the auditorium, the galley beneath the stage, and the bedrooms with their crisp curtains and cozy charm.

Just then, there is a visit from several company members: Elly Chipley, the ingenue lead (known on the bills as Lenore La Verne); Julie Dozier, female half of the character team; and Doc, advance man who posts the bills and arranges for landing sites.

Chapter Five is an atmospheric description of

life on the *Cotton Blossom* as Magnolia grows up. We meet Elly's husband, Schultzy (called Harold Westbrook on the bills); Queenie, the cook, and her husband Jo; Julie's husband Steve, who is tall, handsome, and a rather poor actor; Mr. and Mrs. Means, the general business team; Frank, the heavy; and Ralph, general utility man.

We witness the *Cotton Blossom*'s arrivals at river towns, Andy's ballyhoo, the calliope, and a typical performance. We learn how much the plays mean to simple audiences and to young Magnolia, who begs her mother to let her watch just the first acts. For an extra fifteen cents, a viewer is allowed to stay on after the play for the olio and its musical entertainment.

Chapter Six continues the sketch of show boat life, with emphasis on the troupe's routine following a performance: the quiet conversation, coffee, comments by the director, Schultzy, the cold supper, a pianist trying out new songs for Elly or Schultzy or Ralph, in preparation for the next day's concert.

We learn that Elly is fastidious and has "a knack with the needle." Julie is lazy, and her husband Steve jealous of any man who looks at her. He is particularly wary of Pete, engineer of the *Mollie Able,* who frequently sends her presents and openly tries to court her. Although Julie always gives the gifts to Queenie, Steve and Pete have a brawl in which the latter is tossed into the river and threatens retribution.

In the kitchen, Magnolia learns spirituals from Jo and cooking from Queenie. Over the years, Parthy has grown increasingly tyrannical but can never impose her will on Julie, who casually ignores her, much to Parthy's wrath.

Chapter Seven. On the day the *Cotton Blossom* is to play Lemoyne, Mississippi, Julie Dozier becomes ill and refuses to go on or to see a doctor. Schultzy appears in her doorway and mentions that Julie must have an admirer, for her picture has been stolen from the billboard.

Parthy reminds Andy that Julie became sick in the same town the year before, and Magnolia announces that the second picture Schultzy put up has also been taken. Windy, the pilot, says that Pete is up to something, for he saw Pete take the second picture after Steve removed the first one. When Steve asks why he would re-

move his wife's picture, Windy replies simply to prevent anyone in the town from recognizing her.

As Pete is discovered coming across the levee with Sheriff Ike Keener, Julie springs from her bed. The troupe watches in awe as Steve produces a large clasp knife, runs its blade firmly across the tip of Julie's forefinger, and presses his lips to the wound to suck her blood.

The sheriff confronts Julie and claims that she is half Negro. Her marriage to Steve constitutes miscegenation, a crime in Mississippi. Steve meanwhile swears that he has Negro blood in him at that very moment, a statement with which the entire troupe concurs. Annoyed that he has been given what seems to be false information by Pete, Keener warns that the troupe had better not give a performance in this town with a company of mixed blood. Julie agrees to leave the boat at once, but Steve asks if Andy will wait until the next day to let the two off at another town.

The following day, Julie is surprised that her dear, young friend, Magnolia, has not come to see her off. Steve and she carry their luggage onto the levee and begin to disappear over a hill. From her room, Magnolia looks out and screams. She slaps her mother, who has not told her of Julie's departure, and rushes after her friends. Julie pretends not to hear the child's calls, until Magnolia falls sobbing. She then runs back to embrace the little girl.

Chapter Eight. After three years of finding fault with river life, Elly has deserted Schultzy for a gambler from Mobile. Magnolia, now sixteen, has replaced her as the troupe's ingenue. The Soapers are the character team that has replaced Julie and Steve.

During Magnolia's first appearance in the melodrama **The Parson's Bride,** a rough backwoodsman in the left upper box begins to aim his rifle at Frank, who, in the role of the villain, has begun to throttle the girl. Frank gingerly releases her and turns his wicked expression into one of love and gentleness. The curtain is dropped, and Schultzy explains that the villain has been suddenly taken ill, and a free concert will now be given.

When the *Cotton Blossom* arrives at New Or-

Original endpapers of the Edna Ferber novel.

leans, Schultzy informs Andy that he must leave the troupe long enough to go to Elly, who has been deserted and is now hospitalized without money. He adds that he has spoken to a fellow down on the wharf who claims to have been an actor and would like to replace him. Andy peers through a pair of binoculars at a graceful figure of a man, lounging against a huge packing case on the wharf. Despite Parthy's wariness, she recognizes the company's need for a leading man and advises Andy to interview this prospect.

Thus, in Chapter Nine, Gaylord Ravenal, twenty-four-year-old river boat gambler, becomes leading man of the *Cotton Blossom* company. Although he appears a gentleman when viewed from a distance, his shoes are cracked and his suit a trifle shiny. In fact, he has never acted before, but was informed by Chief of Police Vallon that he has to leave New Orleans in twenty-four hours for having once shot and killed a man, though in self-defense.

The young man introduces himself to Andy as Gaylord Ravenal of the Tennessee Ravenals. When the Captain offers him fifteen dollars a week and a chance to see the world, Ravenal spies Magnolia on the upper deck and, learning that she is Andy's daughter and his potential leading lady, accepts at once.

Females in the audience are taken by Gay's charm and good looks, and they sense that the

love-making between him and Magnolia may not be confined to the stage. This enrages Parthy, who, when the troupe returns to New Orleans, confirms her suspicions. She and Frank learn that Gay once killed a man in self-defense. Andy takes the information quite calmly, while his wife faints.

In Chapter Ten, as the love between Gay and Magnolia develops, Parthy grows increasingly protective of her daughter. Gay takes Magnolia to a Tennessee graveyard, where he shows her an old Bible that once belonged to the Ravenal family. Parthy dismisses his claim to the gentry by saying to Andy that she could claim her name was Bonaparte and show him Napoleon's tomb, but that wouldn't make Napoleon her grandfather.

At one town, the young lovers visit a church and are quietly married amid the Easter decorations that are still up.

Chapter Eleven is a succession of flashbacks, in which we learn that during their first year of marriage, the Ravenals visited Chicago, which Magnolia found noisy and ruthless. Gay has begun to reveal his true nature as a gambler, by being alternately broke and rich.

Andy has ordered a new *Cotton Blossom* to be built with newfangled gas lights instead of kerosene. Both the boat and the Ravenal baby are expected to arrive in April 1889; and it is on the new boat's maiden trip that Kim is born.

One of her youthful memories is that of being awakened one night, wrapped in a blanket, and never again seeing her grandfather, for during a storm, Andy is swept overboard and drowns.

In Chapter Twelve, Parthy continues to run the new *Cotton Blossom* after Andy's death. Unwilling to work under a woman, Windy quits. Frank, who had harbored an unspoken love for Magnolia, left after she married Gay. Following a succession of arguments with Parthy, Gay takes his wife and daughter to live in Chicago, amid the tearful farewells of the company.

In Chapter Thirteen, Gay takes little more than a year to dissipate Magnolia's small fortune, her share of Andy's estate, including an interest in the *Cotton Blossom*. Although they had lived in the elegant Sherman House, visited the world's fair in all their finery, and known the smartest people, the Ravenals are now reduced to a humble boarding house on Ontario Street.

Chapter Fourteen. Having little money, Magnolia takes Kim on long walks and tells her stories of life on the show boat. She teaches the ten-year-old some of the old songs, as the family's financial state grows increasingly precarious.

Chapter Fifteen. With a favorable turn of the cards, Gay is able to take Magnolia to a smart restaurant, where they encounter a cheery, tipsy party of Gay's friends. Magnolia happily agrees to play "Deep River" on the banjo and sings for the group, despite Gay's objections. It is the first of two songs, and she is roundly applauded by the party.

With increasing concern for Kim's future, Magnolia hints to Gay that she might return to the stage.

Chapter Sixteen. Magnolia enrolls Kim in St. Agatha's Convent School on Wabash Avenue South. At the same time, a reform movement begins to close down all of Chicago's gambling dens, thereby diminishing Gay's already speculative financial resources. When they learn that Parthy is coming for a visit and expects them to be staying at the Sherman House, Magnolia asks Gay to borrow some money.

He returns home late that night, drunk, and with two thousand dollars: one thousand borrowed from the notorious madam Hetty Chilson, the second thousand won at roulette. At dawn, when he falls asleep, Magnolia dresses, counts out one thousand dollars, and leaves the house.

Chapter Seventeen. Magnolia goes to Hetty Chilson's house to return the borrowed money. The woman summons her secretary, Jule, a gaunt, grey-haired wraith, who comes down the stairs and hands Magnolia a receipt. It is only when the secretary returns up the stairs that Magnolia realizes she has just seen her beloved childhood friend, Julie Dozier.

She cries out to Julie, but in vain. The butler firmly shows her out, and Magnolia wanders around the city somewhat dazed. She finally goes to Jopper's Varieties, a basement cabaret on Wabash. She explains to a young man that she sings Negro songs with a banjo but has no instrument with which to audition. A hoarse-voiced man who has just been turned down of-

fers her his instrument, and she begins to sing and is engaged.

She returns home to find a farewell note and six hundred dollars from Gay. Although he claims he will be gone for only a few weeks, she will never see him again.

Resolutely, she goes to a nearby pawn shop and purchases a banjo.

Chapter Eighteen. Time has passed. Kim Ravenal, now married to a successful producer named Kenneth Cameron, is a Broadway star like her mother before her. Kim is granting a backstage interview, when her maid hands her a telegram informing her that Parthy has died in Cold Spring, Tennessee. Kim goes on to play her third act.

Magnolia comes to Kim's dressing room after the performance and, learning of her mother's death, takes the train that evening for Tennessee.

Upon her arrival, she is surprised to see how many people have come to pay their respects to Parthy, who had become something of a legend along the river. That night, Magnolia sleeps on the *Cotton Blossom*, which now has electricity and other modern conveniences.

Chapter Nineteen. Kim has written ten letters in one month to urge her mother to return home to New York. Instead, Magnolia feels that the *Cotton Blossom* is home. There is even a familiar face, for Elly and her new husband, Clyde Mellhop, are the current general utility team. Schultzy has been dead for quite some time, and Elly decided to return to the boat.

Not even an unexpected visit in June from Kim and Kenneth succeeds in persuading Magnolia to leave her river. The river was never really part of Kim's world, but it is Magnolia's. As Kim leaves, she looks back to see Magnolia on the upper deck, silhouetted against the sunset, one arm raised in farewell.

Like many of Edna Ferber's novels, **Show Boat** spans many decades and is filled with numerous references to specific famous people and places. Although it is quite frankly escapist romance with no hidden social meaning, the book touches upon so many varied ways of life, with such great detail, that it is ironically a most persuasive social document of a vanished time in America. Because of the author's gift for characterization, the reader comes to know Magnolia and her family and finds himself deeply involved in all the events of her life, however improbable some of them may be.

If Miss Ferber's greatest strength as a writer is characterization, her greatest weakness, at this point in her career, is an inconsistent narrative technique. Chapter Eleven, for example, is so confused with flashbacks and comments about events yet to come that one can hardly follow what is happening. Yet Chapter Twelve, by startling contrast, is simple and touching. Perhaps the two best chapters are Five and Six, which contain almost no action at all, but rather a deeply loving sketch of life aboard the *Cotton Blossom*.

In a curious way, Edna Ferber's style is often more that of an oral storyteller than a writer. She will frequently interrupt her own sentences with a dash and interject a totally new thought, as if she could not bear to wait until she had finished one thought before going on to the next.

Because events past and future are mixed in almost equal proportion with what is currently happening in the story, the reader is led to feel that, although he is reading the book for the first time, he has already experienced its story and is nostalgically reliving it. It is a fascinating literary device and may account for the ardent following of Miss Ferber's work. There is something warmly conforting about familiarity, even the first time around.

CHAPTER 2

1927
The Ziegfeld Production

EARLY in October 1926, Alexander Woollcott received a phone call from an excited Jerome Kern, who had just read **Show Boat** and thought it to be the perfect subject for a musical. Had Woollcott read it? He had. Did Woollcott know Edna Ferber personally? He did, and they were close friends. Would Woollcott agree to write Kern a letter of introduction? The idea that the foremost composer of the American Musical Theatre would seek a letter of introduction to one of America's most popular novelists amused the drama critic of the *New York World,* and he of course agreed to prepare such a document.

On the very evening that Woollcott finished the letter, he accompanied Edna Ferber to the opening of Charles Dillingham's latest musical, **Criss Cross** (10-12-26, Globe), starring the beloved comedian Fred Stone. By coincidence, the composer was Jerome Kern.

During intermission, Woollcott drifted away from Ferber and bumped into Kern. Across the lobby, the waggish Woollcott raised his voice and called to his guest. In the following mo-

ment, an introduction was made, and so was theatre history.

At first, Ferber thought the idea of adapting **Show Boat** to the musical stage was preposterous. Not only did the story sprawl over a fifty-year time span, but it dealt with miscegenation and a wife's desertion by her ne'er-do-well husband. The usual 1920's musical was invariably light-hearted fare about comic events at a college, country club, or Long Island estate. The most serious issues generally dealt with how a humble chorus girl might become a star, or how sweethearts from differing social stations could be united without the wealthy one being disinherited.

Kern, however, believed that a suitable libretto could be prepared by a thirty-one-year-old alumnus of Columbia University, Oscar Hammerstein II. The composer felt that because Hammerstein had collaborated on the book and lyrics of several successful shows in the preceding three years, he was ready to strike out on his own. Among the writer's more notable achievements had been **Wildflower** (2-7-23,

Oscar Hammerstein II and Jerome Kern in 1932.

Casino) with music by Vincent Youmans and Herbert Stothart, **Rose Marie** (9-2-24, Imperial) with music by Rudolf Friml and Stothart, and **Sunny** (9-22-25, New Amsterdam), which Kern himself had composed. On all three productions, Hammerstein had collaborated with veteran librettist Otto Harbach. The latest Hammerstein-Harbach collaboration, **The Desert Song** (11-30-26, Casino), with music by Sigmund Rom-berg, was proving a great hit in its pre-Broadway tryouts and was bound to enhance Hammerstein's reputation.

On November 17, thirteen days before the Broadway opening of **The Desert Song,** Ferber signed a contract giving Kern and Hammerstein the "dramatico-musical rights" (as they are called) to **Show Boat,** "the said play to be writ-ten immediately and to be ready for delivery to

the Producer on or about January 1, 1927." Although Kern and Hammerstein had no arrangements with a specific producer at the time, the contract authorized them "to make and enter into a contract with Mr. Florenz Ziegfeld, or any other responsible theatrical producer," and that upon such an agreement, Miss Ferber will receive a royalty advance of $500 from that producer, in addition to 1½% of the gross weekly box office receipts. This contract would be terminated if "the said play is not produced on or before April 15, 1928."

Kern and Hammerstein plunged into work at once. On Friday, November 26, they performed part of the score for Ziegfeld. The following day, the producer wrote to tenor Harry Fender, ". . . last night I heard the first act of the Show Boat, and Jerome Kern's music. This is the best musical comedy I have ever been fortunate to get hold of; it looks wonderful, and there are two of the greatest parts that have ever been written. I don't know if you have read the Show Boat by Edna Ferber, but the gambling lover is a part I think you can play. . . . This show is the opportunity of my life, and is an opportunity that comes once in a lifetime for the man and woman who play the two parts I mentioned above, and it would be a shame for you to throw such an opportunity away. . . . I can get somebody else to play the part if you can't so I must know immediately whether you are going to play it. If your health is such that you cannot, I will have to contract with the other party. In my opinion, there are only two men who can play this part, you and this other man, and I can get him. Think it over carefully, talk it over with your doctor and let me know Monday at the latest without fail, if you want it. I want to give you this opportunity, and it is up to you and your health." The letter is signed, "Kindest regards, Sincerely yours, Ziegfeld."

Harry Fender had made his Broadway debut as a dancer in **Follow the Girl** (3-2-18, 44th Street Roof) and was later under contract for several years to the Shuberts. He finally attained considerable popularity as the singing juvenile lead in Ziegfeld's **Kid Boots** (12-31-23, Earl Carroll) starring Eddie Cantor and **Louie the 14th** (3-3-25, Cosmopolitan) starring Leon Errol. Handsome,

urbane, and the darling of high society, Fender was a perfect choice for the dashing Gaylord Ravenal.

However, Fender had begun to develop, during the run of **Louie the 14th,** a curious fear of appearing onstage. Although his career was just beginning to break, and the role of Ravenal would have virtually assured stardom, he chose to give up the stage and instead become a patrolman on the police force in St. Louis, where, many years later, he was to emerge as a familiar local radio and television personality, mostly on talk shows.

From the outset, Kern felt that Paul Robeson was the only person to introduce "Ol' Man River." Having learned of his whereabouts from Woollcott, Kern visited the Negro singer in his Harlem flat. After Robeson sang the piece from Kern's handwritten lead sheet, the composer was so excited that he wanted Robeson to accompany him downtown immediately to perform the number for Hammerstein.

Woollcott reported in his book **While Rome Burns** (Viking Press, 1934) that the singer turned to his wife, who was half Jewish and held "custody of the privy purse," and asked for two dollars for taxi fare. Knowing that her husband was being driven downtown by Kern and would need fare only for the ride back, she offered him just one dollar, whereupon, according to Woollcott, Robeson said, "Aw, go on, be all nigger and give me two."

Although Robeson was indeed first choice for the part of Joe, the yearlong delay in mounting **Show Boat** prevented his taking the role, due to other commitments.

For quite some time, Flo Ziegfeld had been battling with his longtime partners, Marc Klaw and Abe Erlanger, with whom he shared an interest in the New Amsterdam Theatre on 42nd Street. Ziegfeld felt that it was time for him to have his own theatre, a temple of beauty to be the perfect setting for the lavish productions that he enjoyed mounting. With the financial support of William Randolph Hearst and Arthur Brisbane, two prominent newspapermen, the producer finally achieved his dream, the Ziegfeld Theatre, on Sixth Avenue at the northwest corner of 54th Street.

1927—The Ziegfeld Production

FLORENZ ZIEGFELD

For its design, Ziegfeld turned to Joseph Urban, the brilliant Viennese architect, interior decorator, and scenic designer, whose sense of color, lighting, and form had enriched the producer's shows since the **Ziegfeld Follies of 1915** (6-21-15, New Amsterdam).

Urban chose a light tan stone and modern style for the building, with a slightly bowed façade that suggested the auditorium within. In most novel fashion, the auditorium was a perfect oval, its front end cut off for the stage. With side walls and ceiling curved into an ellipse, and the complete elimination of all angles and gingerbread detail, the only decoration was a huge mural that covered the entire interior of the house. Designed by Urban's pupil, Lillian Gaertner, the tapestry-like mural, called "The Joy of Living," was a brilliantly colored fantasy of medieval figures, harlequins, lovers, cupids, stags, etc., in a modernistic treatment. The opening night program claimed this to be the world's largest oil painting, "the one in the Sistine Chapel being nearest it in dimensions." The mural's glitter of varied colors was contrasted with the stately, massive proscenium, finished simply in gold.

During a public ceremony heard on radio and attended by more than 800 persons, including dozens of notables, Ziegfeld, on Thursday afternoon, December 9, 1926, at precisely 2:47, put

21

JOSEPH URBAN

JOSEPH·URBAN·ARCHITECT·EXECUTED·BY·JOSEPH·URBAN·THOMAS·W·LAMB·ARCHITECTS

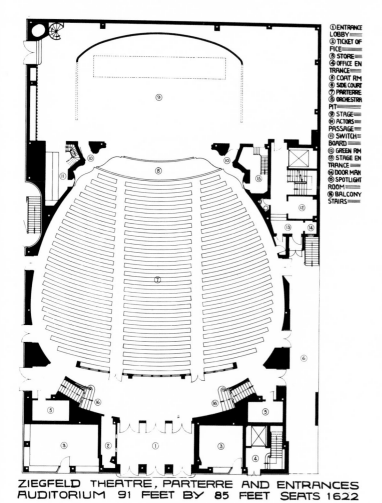

① ENTRANCE LOBBY ② TICKET OF FICE ③ STORE ④ OFFICE ENTRANCE ⑤ COAT RM ⑥ SIDE COURT ⑦ PARTERRE ⑧ ORCHESTRA PIT ⑨ STAGE ⑩ ACTORS PASSAGE ⑪ SWITCH BOARD ⑫ GREEN RM ⑬ STAGE ENTRANCE ⑭ DOOR MAN ⑮ SPOTLIGHT ROOM ⑯ BALCONY STAIRS

ZIEGFELD THEATRE, PARTERRE AND ENTRANCES
AUDITORIUM 91 FEET BY 85 FEET SEATS 1622

⑨ STAGE ⑰ BRIDGE ⑱ DRESSING ROOMS ⑲ CLEANER'S CLOSET ⑳ LIGHT COURT ㉑ TRUNK RM ㉒ UTILITIES RM ㉓ STAIRS TO ORCHESTRA FLOOR ㉔ BALCONY CROSSOVER ㉕ FIRE ESCAPE ㉖ TO SPOTLIGHT ROOMS ㉗ OFFICE STAIR

ZIEGFELD THEATRE GALLERY LEVEL 772 SEATS
SCENERY LOFT WITH TYPICAL DRESSING ROOMS

① ENTRANCE LOBBY ⑧ ORCHESTRA PIT ⑨ STAGE ㉘ FAN ROOM ㉙ REHEARSAL ROOM ㉚ OFFICE ㉛ PRIVATE OFFICE ㉝ CHORUS ㉞ BALCONY FOYER ㉟ USHERS ROOM ㉟ LOUNGE ㊱ PLENUM CHAMBER ㊲ CYCLORAMA SIDE DROPS ㊳ CYCLORAMA

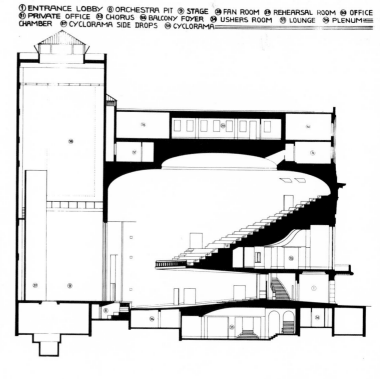

ZIEGFELD THEATRE: THE SECTION SHOWS THE CLEAR CORRESPONDENCE BETWEEN INTERIOR OF AUDITORIUM AND FACADE. THE MAIN PROMENADE ON THE SECOND FLOOR IS EXPRESSED OUTSIDE BY THE MARQUISE AT THE FLOOR LEVEL AND THREE TALL WINDOWS. AS SHOWN IN THE SECOND FLOOR PLAN THE OVAL OF THE AUDITORIUM PROJECTS ON THE FACADE IN A BAY. A BOLD CORNICE MARKS THE TOP OF THE GALLERY ON THE EXTERIOR. ABOVE IT A CHANGE IN SCALE IN THE FACADE EXPRESSES TWO FLOORS OF OFFICES. SIMPLICITY OF THE AUDITORIUM FORM, SUPPRESSION OF THE PROSCENIUM AND USE OF ACTORS DOORS ON THE APRON HELP, BY PLACING PERFORMER AND AUDIENCE IN THE SAME ROOM TO ESTABLISH GOOD THEATRICAL CONTACT.

ZIEGFELD THEATRE: MURAL AND DOOR ON ACTORS' APRON. THE SCHEME IS GOLD AND BLACK WITH MULTICOLOURED FLOWERS AND COSTUMES WOVEN INTO THE DESIGN

the cornerstone into place, and his house was complete. Not only did newspapers the following day report that the theatre was likely to open with **Rio Rita,** as it did on February 2, 1927, but that players from several current and future Ziegfeld productions, including **Show Boat,** were present at the ceremony.

Thus two persistent and wholly false theatre legends are disproved. In many reference works one reads that Ziegfeld had planned to open his new house with **Show Boat,** but when that work was not ready, he instead gave **Rio Rita** the honor: yet it is clear that **Rio Rita** was the first choice from the outset. Second, one hears how reluctant Ziegfeld was to attempt producing a show as serious in theme as **Show Boat,** one that would offer very few opportunities to present the lines of chorus girls for which the producer was

24

FROM ROMANCES OF ALL TIME AND MYTHS OF ALL AGES WERE DRAWN THE SUBJECTS TO GIVE THE LIVELINESS OF COLOUR AND FANTASY OF PATTERN TO THE SIMPLE DOMICAL ENVELOPE OF THE AUDITORIUM

famed. Yet the producer's enthusiastic letter to Harry Fender, written immediately after a first hearing of only part of the score, belies this myth. In addition, **Show Boat** was casually referred to as a Ziegfeld production merely twenty-two days after Kern and Hammerstein first obtained rights to create the musical. Furthermore, a brief item in the November 28, 1926, *New York Telegraph* mentions that Elizabeth Hines was scheduled to appear in Ziegfeld's **Show Boat** production. Either the authors were particularly persuasive, or the stories of Ziegfeld's doubts are startlingly exaggerated.

In any case, on Saturday, December 11, Ziegfeld signed separate contracts with Kern and Hammerstein to present the musical that was to become the crowning achievement of the manager's long career. Upon signing, Kern received

25

1927—The Ziegfeld Production

an advance of $1500 and Hammerstein $1000. Kern was to obtain a royalty of 4½% of the weekly gross, of which he was to pay Edna Ferber her 1½%. Hammerstein would receive 2½% when the weekly gross exceeded $30,000, or 2% if the gross merely reached or dipped below that figure. A script was to be delivered to Ziegfeld by January 1, 1927 (or only 21 days from the signing of the contract), "in a sufficiently completed form" so that rehearsals could begin at that time. In turn, Ziegfeld agreed "to produce the play on or before the first day of April, 1927."

While it may seem preposterous for him to have assumed that Kern and Hammerstein could actually complete a score and book to a work as complex as **Show Boat** in such a short time, it must be remembered that Ziegfeld was used to working with writers like William Anthony McGuire and J. P. McEvoy, who were old pros at turning out vaudeville routines and light comedy sketches at an hour's notice. Frequently, Ziegfeld had gone into rehearsal for a book show that had only its first act finished. While the first act was being staged, the authors would huddle in a hotel room and invent a wildly improbable second act finish. The formula had worked before, so there was little reason for Ziegfeld to assume it would not work again.

What he had not taken into consideration was the ardent dedication that both Kern and Hammerstein felt toward **Show Boat.** This was not to be a typical Ziegfeld girlie show, with extravagant routines for scantily clad show girls, and with scenes so casually sketched that the comics could interpolate their specialty routines. This was to be a tightly written musical play with devotion to character development, with songs that grew meaningfully out of the plot, with spectacle and dance only when spectacle and dance seemed appropriate to the story. In short, **Show Boat** was to be something the American Musical Theatre had never before experienced.

In some ways, Ziegfeld clearly lacked the capacity to understand fully the extent of his commitment. He announced that rehearsals were to begin early in the spring with the roles of Magnolia, Ravenal, and Joe played by Elizabeth Hines, Guy Robertson, and Paul Robeson, respectively. The opening night program for **Rio**

Rita (2-2-27, Ziegfeld) contains a full-page portrait of Miss Hines with the caption "Elizabeth Hines, to play 'Magnolia' in Mr. Ziegfeld's production of the 'Showboat', from the book of Edna Ferber. Book by Oscar Hammerstein. Music by Jerome Kern."

When the writers claimed that the work was simply not ready for production, the performers were released. Robertson promptly went into the Shubert production of the Emmerich Kálmán operetta, **The Circus Princess** (4-25-27, Winter Garden), while Robeson continued his concert career.

Miss Hines, however, decided to sue Ziegfeld for approximately $200,000 for breaking the contract she claimed the manager had signed with her on October 30, 1926. She claimed **Show Boat** was to open in January 1927, and, if it did not, she would be assigned another property. When she lost her suit in the Supreme Court, Miss Hines went into George White's production **Manhattan Mary** (9-26-27, Apollo), but left the cast after its tryout opening night, September 5, 1927, at the Nixon Theatre, Pittsburgh. No doubt she found comfort in what had been a secret wedding on August 18 to banker Frank Rigg Warton.

Ziegfeld loved to send lengthy telegrams to almost everyone about almost everything. On March 3, he complained bitterly in a wire to Kern that Hammerstein's libretto "has not got a chance except with the critics." He felt that because "Hammerstein never did anything alone," he ought to accept the advice of Dorothy Donnelly "or anyone you suggest or Hammerstein suggests." Ziegfeld's particular complaint was that following Ravenal and Magnolia's wedding, Hammerstein's "present layout too serious not enough comedy."

It is fortunate indeed that Ziegfeld was forced to wait, for during the unusually lengthy gestation period of this play, Oscar Hammerstein developed from a promising musical comedy librettist into a superb one. Early versions of his script reveal that his regard for Ferber's novel was so great that he tended to place on the stage almost every key incident in the book, even if such scenes distracted seriously from the main dramatic line. In addition, early scripts demonstrate

1927—The Ziegfeld Production

Elizabeth Hines. Ziegfeld's first choice for Magnolia, in a portrait
from the Ziegfeld Theatre opening night souvenir program.

Hammerstein's seeming unawareness that the great appeal of **Show Boat** as a stage piece tends to lie in its period sequences rather than the up-to-date situations toward the end.

In one early script, Act Two, Scene Seven is laid in Kim's apartment, a typical drawing room of Manhattan's east fifties. A party is taking place; and at rise a composer, George, is seated at a baby grand piano playing the finish of the "Rhapsody in Blue." The girls in the crowd swoon. Just then, Kim makes a grand entrance, and all her partying friends line up in "conventional musical comedy formation" to sing a "lyric typical of those used to build up a star's entrance." They all laugh when she tells them that now that her show has finally closed, she and her mother are planning to take a sleeper to Natchez to return to their show boat.

When an amiable drunk asks what a show boat is, Kim snaps back, "Now listen, moron—d'ya mean to tell me you haven't read Edna Ferber's book?" To illustrate her point, she sings an old show boat song first in its original style and then in a more modern fashion. Everyone

1927—The Ziegfeld Production

Show Curtain   DESIGN BY JOSEPH URBAN

joins in a big dancing number. Blackout. Mercifully, this scene was deleted even before the out-of-town tryouts.

Another excess dropped early was a lengthy and exceedingly banal chorus number on the subject of the new year, to be sung in an interlude immediately preceding the Trocadero sequence, in which Magnolia makes her night club debut. Not all such excisions were made prior to the world premiere on November 15, 1927, at the National Theatre in Washington, for **Show Boat** underwent a Broadway musical's typical out-of-town pruning and refashioning before exploding on Broadway December 27, at the Ziegfeld Theatre. By the time the musical reached Broadway, its tale was told in two acts, with eight scenes in the first, and nine in the second.

Act One, Scene One is set on the levee at Natchez, about 1890. It is a brilliant blending of period spectacle, character and situation exposition, and memorable music. Upstage, we see the exteriors of the towboat *Mollie Able* and the *Cotton Blossom*. Negro stevedores are piling up cotton bales, while singing ("Cotton Blossom"). Windy (Allan Campbell), the old pilot, looks on, as Steve (Charles Ellis), the troupe's leading man, enters from the show boat and sets up the company's framed pictures. Pete (Bert Chapman), engineer and bandman, enters from the towboat. He sees that Queenie (Tess Gardella), the Negro cook, is wearing a brooch and demands to know where she obtained it, but she refuses to tell him.

As the stevedores continue to sing, a group of dainty, beruffled young ladies and their beaux enter and admire the pictures, all in song.

Presently, Cap'n Andy (Charles Winninger) and the troupe's brass band enter with the acting company following behind. One by one, Andy introduces his players to the crowd: Miss Ellie May Chipley (Eva Puck), the toast of Cairo, Illinois; Frank Schultz (Sammy White), the

1927—The Ziegfeld Production

villain, who is "stuck on Ellie" (The two perform a brief buck-and-wing dance, ending in a nautical pose.); Rubber Face Smith (Francis X. Mahoney), a toothless codger who can twist his face into knots; and Julie La Verne (Helen Morgan) and Steve Baker, the romantic leads, who are also husband and wife.

As Julie stands to one side, Pete reviles her for giving the brooch he had given her to "a nigger." Julie rebuffs his advances with a warning that Steve is very jealous. When Steve sees Pete forcing himself on his wife, he attacks Pete and knocks him down. To pacify the crowd, Andy quickly pretends the whole matter has been a scene from one of the company's melodramas, but Pete mutters that he will get even.

When Andy fires Pete and tells him he must never return to the *Cotton Blossom*, Parthy (Edna May Oliver) turns her anger on Julie for

enticing him. Julie's only concern is that Magnolia was not present to witness such an ugly scene, but Parthy warns the actress to stay away from her daughter. Ellie, seizing on the situation, swiftly offers to assume the romantic leads herself and is gently discouraged from all such hopes by the good captain, who exits.

Ellie turns and sees a handsome and dapper stranger, Gaylord Ravenal (Howard Marsh), and slyly drops her handkerchief. Amused, Ravenal returns it. Just then, Sheriff Vallon (Thomas Gunn) enters to remind Ravenal that he can remain in town for only twenty-four hours.

Left alone, Ravenal sings "Where's the Mate for Me?" in which he expresses that he is guided by chance and does not care where life leads him. He hears Magnolia (Norma Terris) off-stage artlessly practicing a tune on her piano. When she appears on an upper deck, he is smit-

Act One, Scenes One and Eight

DESIGN BY JOSEPH URBAN

ten by her loveliness. Although shy, she is so taken by the young man that she dares to speak first. She tells him that she is not an actress on the show boat, even though her father owns it, but she dreams of acting one day, because an actress "can make believe so many wonderful things that never happen in real life." In a situation reminiscent of the **Romeo and Juliet** balcony scene, Ravenal suggests that the two suppose they have fallen in love at first sight ("Make Believe").

Joe (Jules Bledsoe), carrying a sack of flour, enters and witnesses Vallon's request for Ravenal to come with him, because the judge wants to talk with him. When the two men leave, Magnolia with youthful ardor tells Joe she cannot wait to ask her friend Julie what she thinks about the gentleman she has just met.

With the cynicism of experience, Joe mutters to himself that she ought to ask "old man river what he thinks—he knows all 'bout dem boys." Joe sits on a box, takes out a knife, and idly starts to whittle, as he sings "Ol' Man River." A group of Negro barge men (and the black Jubilee Singers*) join him on the middle section of the song, as the curtains close behind them to allow for a change of scene.

In one economically written scene, Hammerstein has managed to present a lively and innovative opening number, featuring both a black and white chorus singing in counterpoint, all of the show's principal characters, two of the score's major song hits, a character soliloquy not unlike the kind he would later write with Richard Rodgers, and two of the basic plot threads: the love of Magnolia and Ravenal, and the vicious jealousy of Pete.

Scene Two takes place in the kitchen pantry of the *Cotton Blossom* a half-hour later. While Queenie is preparing biscuits, Magnolia excitedly tells Julie she has fallen in love. Julie cautions that he may turn out to be a "no-account river feller," yet in her heart she knows that whatever a man is, you can't stop loving no matter how he behaves. Julie begins to sing "Can't Help Lovin' Dat Man" but is interrupted

---

*The show's vocal arrangements were made by Will Vodery, a gifted Negro musician, who worked for Ziegfeld on many productions.

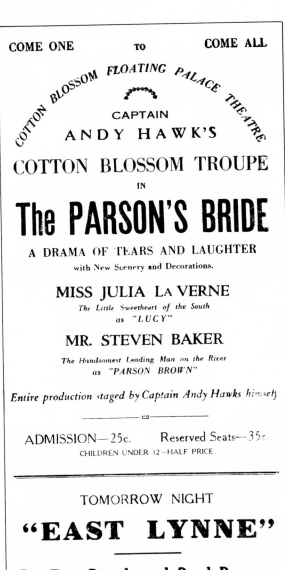

Handbill inserted into each souvenir program.

by Queenie, who is surprised to hear a white person sing that song. Although an expression of terror sweeps over Julie's face, she defiantly returns to the verse when Queenie asks if she

1927—The Ziegfeld Production

Tess ("Aunt Jemima") Gardella

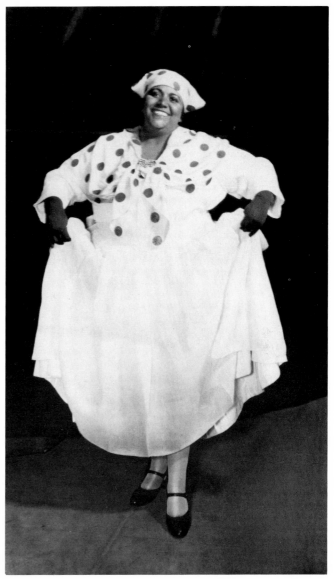

COSTUME BY JOHN HARKRIDER

COSTUMES BY JOHN HARKRIDER

Sammy White and Eva Puck

31

Act One, Scene Two   DESIGN BY JOSEPH URBAN

knows the entire song. Both Queenie and Joe (who enters) join Julie's vocal, while Magnolia gets into the joyous spirit of the song and starts to imitate a Negro shuffle dance, much to the amusement of the others.

Scene Three, its action simultaneous with Scene Two, is laid outside a riverfront gambling saloon. Vallon warns the Faro Dealer (Jack Wynn), who is standing with a group of men, not to deal Ravenal any cards if he shows up, for the young gambler has to leave town in twenty-four hours. Ellie and Frank enter, and she pretends to faint to keep him from going into the saloon. When Ellie enters a notions shop to buy some thread, Pete approaches Frank and asks him if it is not against the law "in this state for a white man to be married to a nigger wench." He adds that there is "a case of it right on the *Cotton Blossom.*" Pete produces a photo of Julie and explains that she is passing herself off as white. Although Frank urges him not to do anything with this information, Pete stops Vallon and takes Frank and the sheriff into the saloon.

Ellie emerges from the shop and is stopped by admiring ladies of the town, all eager to know about the exciting world of theatre. Ellie ex-

plains that the theatre is not everything it seems ("Life on the Wicked Stage"). They exit.

A Gambler (Phil Sheridan) and his friend enter. When the latter inquires about Gaylord Ravenal, the Gambler reveals that about a year ago he killed a man but claimed it was done in self-defense and got off. However, he has been told that he can stay in Natchez for only twenty-four hours during each visit. Gay enters, and, with his gambling cronies, he sings a ballad of the carefree adventurer, "Till Good Luck Comes My Way."

Although the first two scenes are as tautly constructed as possible, Scene Three is a typical sequence from a 1920's musical, though somewhat better written than most. It is a scene of convenience. Either lacking confidence in his own writing or his audience's ability to read between the lines, Hammerstein feels he must demonstrate the exact moment in which Pete confirms that miscegenation is illegal in Mississippi and then obtains the sheriff's willing ear to wreak his vengeance. Further, the young writer creates two bit-roles just to explain Ravenal's obligation to leave town in twenty-four hours: this information could certainly have been fitted

1927—The Ziegfeld Production

more subtly into Vallon and Ravenal's dialogue in the opening scene.

These two segments, in addition to Frank and Ellie's comic banter—a classic of 1920's boy-girl patter—tend to show that Hammerstein's own roots were still firmly planted in musical comedy traditions of the time. On the other hand, the scene skillfully allows the introduction of two fine songs of contrasting style, each designed to show off the talents of two of the play's principals.

In Scene Four, one hour later, a rehearsal of the melodrama, **The Parson's Bride,** is taking place in the *Cotton Blossom* auditorium. With Magnolia playing piano accompaniment, Andy is directing Julie and Steve and trying to organize the technical cues with Rubber Face, while Parthy sits on the side sewing costumes.

Frantically, Ellie rushes in. She bounds onto the stage and whispers into Steve's ear. Dazed,

he continues to act, but in turn he whispers something to Julie, who swoons and weakly claims that she cannot perform that evening. Windy enters and tells the group he knows that Pete is up to something, because he saw him remove Julie's picture; and now Pete and Vallon are coming along the levee toward the *Cotton Blossom*.

Just then, Steve whips out from his pocket a large clasp knife and snaps it open. All the women scream but Julie. Andy springs at Steve but is shaken off. Steve takes his wife's hand and runs the blade across the tip of her finger, throws the knife upstage, bends his head, and, pressing his lips to the wound, sucks it greedily. Julie falls back onto a bench.

Vallon enters, followed by a group of curious Negroes. The sheriff claims he has been informed that there is a case of miscegenation on the boat, that a Negress named Julie Dozier is

Act One, Scene Three

33

1927—The Ziegfeld Production

Act One, Scenes Four and Six

DESIGN BY JOSEPH URBAN

Curtain for *Cotton Blossom* auditorium

DESIGN BY JOSEPH URBAN

1927—The Ziegfeld Production

married to a white man, Steve Baker. His information is that Julie's father was white and her mother black. Julie admits that this is so. Vallon is about to arrest the couple, when Steve asks if Vallon would call a man white "that's got Negro blood in him." Vallon replies that "one drop of nigger blood makes you a nigger in these parts." Steve then claims to have more than a drop of Negro blood in him and says that everyone present will swear to that fact. Somewhat skeptical at first, Vallon is convinced when the venerable Windy steps forward and confirms what Steve has said.

With no law broken, Vallon prepares to retreat, but offers the advice that the troupe had better not attempt to play with a racially mixed cast in this town, or there might be trouble.

As the black chorus softly incants the melancholy "Mis'ry's Comin' Aroun'" theme, Steve tells Andy that he and his wife will leave the company. They go to their rooms to pack. When Magnolia calls to Julie and begins to follow her, Parthy summons her back, suggesting to Andy that show boat life has ruined the girl. Andy staunchly defends his daughter's character and then announces, despite his wife's objections,

Act One, Scene Four: Julie swoons. Francis X. Mahoney, Charles Ellis, Helen Morgan, Norma Terris, Eva Puck, Charles Winninger, Edna May Oliver

1927—The Ziegfeld Production

Act One, Scene Five

DESIGN BY JOSEPH URBAN

that Magnolia will have to play the ingenue leads until another actress can be found.

Frank enters and mentions that there is a fellow whom he met in town waiting outside to inquire whether or not the *Cotton Blossom* would take him on as a passenger. When he adds that the fellow is good-looking, Andy's curiosity is aroused; and he asks Frank to have the man come in.

The stranger introduces himself as Gaylord Ravenal—"of the Tennessee Ravenals." Parthy sniffs loudly with contempt, as the young man offers to pay for his board. Andy promptly asks if he has ever acted and offers Ravenal fifteen dollars a week as leading man, and a chance to see the world. When Magnolia re-enters, and she and Gay see each other again, his fate is sealed.

Meanwhile, Julie and Steve are ready to depart. With deep emotion, Andy bids them farewell and presses some money into Steve's hand. Magnolia runs to kiss her friend, who pulls her head away but does promise to write. She and Steve walk up the aisle and away, as the entire company, including Joe, looks on.

Andy now must return to the business at hand. He gives Ravenal a script and asks him to read a love scene with Magnolia. As this occurs, Joe, very wise in the ways of the river, knows the significance of the change that is taking place in life on the *Cotton Blossom.* Philosophically, he begins to sing "Ol' Man River" quietly, as the new leading players of the troupe begin their dialogue. When Andy urges Ravenal to express more feeling, the young man flings the script aside and recites his protestations of love with a bit more fervor than Parthy wants to hear. She jumps up and down, stamping her feet, as Joe, watching all, concludes his refrain, his face

framed by a pin spot, after the lights have faded on the rest of the scene.

At the rise of Scene Five, Ellie is sellling tickets in the box-office on the foredeck. In the three weeks since the previous scene, Gay and Magnolia have become stars along the river. Frank, watching a group of girls and boys ogling photographs of the new leading players, is annoyed that he has been acting for twelve years, and nobody ever heard of him; but Ravenal is a star in three weeks. Ellie explains that audiences can tell that he and Magnolia are really in love.

Just then, a rough Backwoodsman (Jack Daley) enters and buys a ticket for himself and his friend Jeb (Jack Wynn). He pays for his two thirty-five-cent tickets with Confederate coins, claiming that they are still in use in the mountains. He informs Ellie and Frank that he and Jeb are coming to the theatre that night with their guns, his inquiry about any objections sounding more like an order. When the pair exit, Frank warns Ellie that she needs a man to protect her ("I Might Fall Back on You"). They exit.

Parthy enters and tells Andy that she objects to the attention Ravenal is paying to Magnolia. She has received a letter from Pete, who has something of interest to tell Andy about Ravenal. Pete is now in Fayette, a two-hour side trip from Natchez, to which the *Cotton Blossom* returns the following day. When Andy declines to go, Parthy says she intends to see Pete.

When Parthy storms off in her perpetual rage, Queenie enters and tells Andy that he does not know how to sell tickets to the local black community. She proceeds to take matters into her own hands by singing a rousing ballyhoo that recounts in song the plot of a typical melodrama ("C'mon, Folks").

Scene Six takes place during the third act of **The Parson's Bride** performance that evening. The audience sits on rows of benches, with Negroes in the balcony, and the Backwoodsman and Jeb in an upper stage box. Andy is playing Lange's "Flower Song" on the violin, while Ellie and Magnolia, and later Ravenal, are emoting on the stage. When Frank, as the drunken, mustachioed villain, enters and begins to throttle poor Magnolia, the Backwoodsman picks up his pistol and gruffly orders Frank to let the girl go. In terror, Frank releases the girl and begins to pat her with an outpouring of sudden affection. Meekly, he crawls off the stage. Ravenal, not knowing what has happened, enters as the hero to confront the villain, but finds him missing.

Just then, Andy calls for the curtain to be lowered. He turns to the audience and explains that Mr. Schultz has been suddenly taken sick. Scampering onto the little stage, its curtain now rolled up again, Andy begins to act out what the audience would have seen had the play continued. He gives the lines for all the characters, struggling with himself as both villain and hero, swinging at an imaginary foe, and whacking himself on the jaw so hard that he knocks himself down. He wrestles with himself on the floor, while continuing to revile himself with declamatory dialogue, begs as the heroine for mercy from the villain, enters with a mincing step as the foster sister, and, in that role, smashes a rubber water pitcher on the imaginary head of the villain. He explains that he has succeeded in killing the "dirty rascal deader'n a door nail." And that is what the audience would have seen if Mr. Schultz had not become ill.

Following this show-stopping comic turn, easily the highlight of Charles Winninger's entire career, Andy introduces the olio. The first number is a soft-shoe dance by Mr. Schultz, who, now safely out of character, has had a surprisingly swift recovery.

The dance is performed "in one," thereby providing the time to set up for Scene Seven, the upper deck, later that night. It is a love scene, in which Ravenal proposes marriage and claims that it was Andy's idea to perform the ceremony in Natchez the next day, while Parthy is off in Fayette for the afternoon. Gay promises to show Magnolia the world, claiming that he thought he had seen everything until he looked into her eyes ("You Are Love").

Scene Eight is the same levee that opened the play, but there is now some impromptu decoration for a wedding, about which the townspeople have assembled to sing ("Happy the Day"). The dancing and gaiety are suddenly interrupted by Parthy, who enters shrieking that Ravenal is a murderer and must not be allowed to speak with

Act One, Scene Six: The Backwoodsman
aims his pistol. Norma Terris, Sammy
White. In foreground, Charles Winninger.
In box, Jack Daley, Jack Wynn, Edna May
Oliver.

Act One, Scene Six: Andy acts out **The Parson's
Bride.** Charles Winninger. In box, Jack Daley, Jack
Wynn, Edna May Oliver.

1927—The Ziegfeld Production

Act One, Scene Seven

DESIGN BY JOSEPH URBAN

her daughter. Vallon explains that the crime was determined to be self-defense. With mock bravado, Andy proudly confesses that even he once killed a man when he was nineteen; and, furthermore, Magnolia is about to marry Ravenal. When Parthy faints, Andy announces that the wedding can continue. On a reprise of the last few lines of "Can't Help Lovin' Dat Man," the bride and groom embrace and happily march off stage with the crowd. Curtain.

Act Two opens on the midway plaisance at the 1893 World's Columbian Exposition in Chicago. As the barkers excite the crowd with promises of thrilling displays of feminine beauty, including the hootchy kootchy dance of La Belle Fatima (Dorothy Denese), Magnolia tries to pacify Parthy, who is growing impatient that Ravenal is late in joining Andy and the two women. Despite Parthy's repeated inquisitions, Magnolia refuses to divulge her husband's source of income. Her mother snarls, "How I hate not

to know things," a line that always brought down the house for Edna May Oliver.

When Gay finally arrives with an Old Sport (Bert Chapman), it is revealed that he has had a winning streak and is prepared to treat his party to a stylish evening on the town. Happily, he and Magnolia sing "Why Do I Love You?"

When the group leave the stage, the Dahomey villagers, supposedly a horde of wild African natives, emerge from their pavilion and proceed to chant in native lingo. When the crowd exits in fear, the villagers suddenly begin to sing in perfect English that they are happy to see the white folks go and cannot wait to return to Avenue A in old New York ("In Dahomey").

Scene Two is the interior of a room in a typical second-class boarding house on Ontario Street in Chicago in 1904. At rise, Ethel (Estelle Floyd), a Negro cleaning girl, is tidying up and softly singing "Good Morning, Carrie" to herself.

39

NORMA TERRIS
in Magnolia's wedding gown.

Act One, Scene Eight: "Happy the Day," sung by the chorus.

Act Two, Scene One   DESIGN BY JOSEPH URBAN

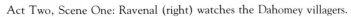

Act Two, Scene One: Ravenal (right) watches the Dahomey villagers.

Act Two, Scene One: Ravenal and companions at the world's fair, in front of the portal to the Streets of Cairo side show. Dorothy Foster, Rose Gallagher, Howard Marsh, Dinorah Castillo, Annette Harding.

An Irish Landlady (Annie Hart) enters and shoos Ethel out, in order to show the tiny apartment to Frank and Ellie, now working vaudeville hoofers and vulgarly overdressed to prove it. The Landlady begins an improbably long narrative about the current tenants, a gambler and his wife, who, for ten years, have been moving back and forth between here and the fancy Sherman House, depending upon his fortunes. First, his fancy cane went, then her diamond ring, then her fur coat, and this winter the poor thing has only an old woolen coat. Suddenly, Magnolia enters and is overjoyed at the surprise of seeing her two old friends, but embarrassed by the surroundings.

She unconvincingly explains that she stays in these humble quarters to help out Mrs. O'Brien, who promptly exits with a sneer. Magnolia shows them a photo of her daughter Kim, now eight years old and enrolled in St. Agatha's Convent School. She adds that Gay is doing quite well, a statement that proves pathetically

false a moment later, when Ethel brings in a letter from him. Magnolia is afraid to read it and asks Ellie to do so. Gay writes that he has nothing left to pawn and no more friends from whom to borrow. Thus he is enclosing two hundred dollars to complete Kim's school term: after that she and Magnolia can return to the *Cotton Blossom*.

Relieved that she no longer has to pretend to her friends, Magnolia confesses what life has been like for ten years. Frank suggests that, if she wants a singing job, he thinks he can arrange one at the Trocadero, where he and Ellie open on New Year's Eve. They leave Magnolia to her tears.

Following the bright and colorful spectacle of Act Two's first scene and its optimistic, dream-like mood, the grimness of the next sequence is most affecting. Yet one cannot help but wish that the Landlady's long tale of Magnolia's dwindling fortunes, a typical expository narra-tive of the period, might have been omitted, for as soon as Magnolia breaks down and tells the truth to Ellie and Frank, we hear the same story all over again and more persuasively from the lips of the character who has lived through it all. It is hard to believe that audiences were ever so slow that such expositions were really necessary, but they do possess in retrospect a certain an-tique charm. Perhaps their need is no more im-probable than the once prevailing ideas that au-tomobiles had to be cranked and that tomatoes were poisonous.

Scene Three, two weeks later, is a rehearsal room at the Trocadero, about five in the after-noon. Jim (Jack Daley), the manager, watches the girls dance, as Jake (Robert Faricy) bangs out "The Washington Post March" on an upright piano. Seated on the side is Julie, looking con-siderably older and sadly worn. She is wearing too much make-up, and her hair is dyed red.

Act Two, Scene Two

DESIGN BY JOSEPH URBAN

1927—The Ziegfeld Production

Act Two, Scene Three: Helen Morgan
sings "Bill."

From time to time, she furtively takes a drink from a pint flask she keeps in her handbag. At Jim's urging, she reluctantly agrees to try out a new song. Julie goes to the piano and, sitting atop it, sings "Bill." When she exits, Jim observes how quickly she fell apart when her husband deserted her.

Next, a man with a guitar (Ted Daniels) is about to audition, but Jim claims there were too many guitars at the world's fair and prepares to leave. He is stopped by Frank, who introduces Magnolia. She says that she sings Negro songs while accompanying herself on the guitar, and, borrowing the rejected applicant's instrument,

44

she begins to sing "Can't Help Lovin' Dat Man."

As she does so, Julie enters quietly, passing behind the piano. Recognizing Magnolia, she begins to step forward to greet her, then stops as if arriving at a decision. Julie makes a shy, hesitant gesture of throwing a kiss and swiftly, silently slips away.

Jim is impressed by Magnolia's voice but feels her song is not up-to-date enough. Just then, Charlie (J. Lewis Johnson), the doorman, runs in with the news that Julie has left to go on a spree. She said that if Jim needed a girl, he should hire the one who was just singing. Jake decides Magnolia's song can be improved by "ragging" it and plays it in fast tempo. As he pounds away on the keys, Frank tap dances at furious speed to help the girl get into the spirit and finally collapses from exhaustion, his body and legs still twitching with the music.

In the brief Scene Four, which takes place simultaneously, Ravenal has gone to St. Aga-tha's Convent to pay Kim (Eleanor Shaw) a final visit. He tenderly sings her a variant version of "Make Believe," which he offers as his system of enabling her to have anything she wants.

When one considers how seriously both Gay and Magnolia have been hurt by the song's philosophy of fantasying as a way to obtain life's goals, it is grimly ironic that Ravenal is now offering the same advice to his own daughter.

Scene Five is a corner of the lobby of the Sherman House on New Year's Eve. Parthy and Andy have come to town seeking Magnolia and Ravenal. Parthy decides to go to her room, but Andy plans to celebrate. With his wife gone, he turns to three attractive cocottes, Lottie (Tana Kamp), Dolly (Dagmar Oakland), and Hazel (Maurine Holmes), whom he finds lingering about, and escorts them to the Trocadero.

Scene Six is the interior of the Trocadero, gaily decorated for the holiday. On the stage, Jim introduces the acts, first the Apache, a Pari-

Act Two, Scene Four

DESIGN BY JOSEPH URBAN

1927—The Ziegfeld Production

Act Two, Scene Six

DESIGN BY JOSEPH URBAN

sian novelty danced by the Sidell Sisters, then a sprightly cakewalk, "Good-bye, Ma Lady Love," performed by Frank and Ellie.

Feeling chipper, Andy cries out with a tipsy "Ha-a-a-apy New Year." Frank sees him and, following his act, joins the captain at his table. Frank explains that Ravenal has deserted Magnolia, who is making her debut this very evening; and he points out that her whole future depends on how well she performs.

When Jim announces that a new singer is to replace Julie, her fans grow vocally abusive. A frightened Magnolia steps out to sing the old favorite, "After the Ball." She begins timidly, amid catcalls from the audience. Just then, Andy rises from his table and begins to advance slowly toward the stage, calling to his little girl to smile. Seeing him and heeding his advice, she regains her confidence and completes the refrain with the ardent approval of the crowd. The

scene ends on an exultant second chorus, sung by the patrons as Andy and his daughter waltz gaily around the stage.

Scene Seven is a drop depicting the street in front of the office of the *Natchez Evening Bulletin.* It is now 1927, the change of era denoted by a bulletin heralding Lindbergh's arrival in Mexico City. Joe, now grey-haired, is seated on a box before the window, still whittling, and singing a reprise of "Ol' Man River." Queenie enters in a fancy dress that she tells a friend was given to her by Kim, whom she calls "the finest actress in New York City." Turning to Joe, Queenie offers some modern, jazzy musical advice on how to catch a man ("Hey, Feller!).

Until theatre stagecraft was streamlined in the late 1940's, scenes like this were written not so much because of their dramatic value, but rather as an expedient method of preparing the larger stage setting of a scene to follow. Often such

46

Act Two, Scene Seven: Tess Gardella sings "Hey, Feller!"
COSTUME BY JOHN HARKRIDER

Act Two, Scene Seven   DESIGN BY JOSEPH URBAN

scenes were played "in one," or in front of the bank of drops nearest to the audience.

Scene Eight is a small part of the upper deck of the new *Cotton Blossom*, freshly painted. Andy, now a sprightly eighty-two, and Ravenal, a dignified sixty-five, are seated, while listening to Magnolia sing "Can't Help Lovin' Dat Man" on a radio. Ravenal's return, timed perfectly for a happy ending to the musical, is explained away when Andy casually remarks, "It seems like fate my bumping into you at Fort Adams yesterday." Andy has sent Magnolia a telegram to return to Natchez, though Ravenal fears that perhaps a reunion is unwise. With fatherly advice, the old captain tells his son-in-law not to blame himself because he happened to be unlucky. Instead of trying to be a gentleman, Gay should have remained an actor and might have become a big Broadway star. When the old man leaves at

Parthy's call, Ravenal nostalgically sings a partial reprise of "You Are Love."

Scene Nine is the Natchez levee in 1927, with the modern *Cotton Blossom*, decorated with electric lights, in the background. Parthy enters with the grown Kim (Norma Terris), who has made her grandmother wear a modish frock and a boyish bob. At Parthy's urging, Kim shows a young female admirer how she sings her mother's old song, "Why Do I Love You?" with vocal impressions of Ethel Barrymore, Beatrice Lillie, and Ted Lewis. After she leaves, Constance McKenzie and Una Val continue the reprise by performing an eccentric and a tap dance respectively.

By a startling coincidence, Frank and Ellie have dropped by Natchez, although they now live in Hollywood, where little Frankie Schultz is the boy wonder of the screen.

Act Two, Scene Nine

DESIGN BY JOSEPH URBAN

Act Two, Scene Nine: Jules Bledsoe as old Joe.

Magnolia and Ravenal then enter, an embarrassing silence between them. An old lady (Laura Clairon) breaks the mood by saying that she attended the wedding of the two, and it is such a comfort to learn that the marriage has turned out so well that the two are still together. Slowly, Magnolia and Gay come toward each other and kiss. As they walk toward the boat, Magnolia looks up and says, "Look, Gay—there's Kim." Joe and the chorus swell a final reprise of "Ol' Man River," as the curtain slowly falls.

In transferring Edna Ferber's novel to the stage, Hammerstein and Kern were forced to tighten the chronological span of the story by a decade, simplify its details, and eliminate a number of characters. There is no depiction of Parthy and Andy's early years of marriage or of Magnolia as a child or of Kim's dramatic birth. Julie's departure, which occurs in the book during Magnolia's childhood, is therefore advanced until the girl is grown and quite capable of replacing her friend as leading lady.

Although members of the troupe come and go in the novel, as they might in real life, the musical presents the same company of actors throughout. Therefore, many minor players, including Mr. and Mrs. Means, the Soapers, Doc, and Ralph, in addition to the pilots Mark Hooper and Mr. Pepper, Kim's husband Kenneth Cameron, and many others are deleted entirely.

Hammerstein also blends several Ferber characters to create new ones for the stage.

Frank Schultz of the musical is a combination of Frank, the *Cotton Blossom* heavy, who harbors an unspoken love for Magnolia, and Schultzy, Elly's husband and the troupe's juvenile lead and director. In the musical, Frank Schultz is both the heavy and the husband of Ellie, whose name is now spelled differently.

Ike Vallon, the sheriff of Natchez in the musical, is Ike Keener in the book, and the town is Lemoyne, Mississippi. Vallon in the book is the police chief of New Orleans. Similarly, Elly Chipley's professional name as the ingenue lead in the book is Lenore La Verne. Hammerstein took the last name and gave it to Julie in the musical.

Because Hammerstein omits the character of Hetty Chilson and thereby Magnolia's encounter with Julie as Hetty's wan secretary, Julie in the musical is brought back in a far more natural setting for one who has been a performer: as a singer in a cabaret. In addition, her silent act of sacrifice for the little girl who once loved her is an ingenious invention of Hammerstein's and substantially improves on the situation in the book.

Generally, however, the fate of the principals is somewhat more logical in the novel than in the show. By the time the novel ends, Andy, Parthy, and Schultzy are dead; other characters, including Jo and Queenie, have been forgotten; and the focus sharpens on Magnolia and Kim. To provide a traditional musical comedy ending, Hammerstein not only keeps everyone alive, but contrives a remarkable reunion at Natchez that brings back Ellie and Frank from Hollywood, Magnolia and Kim from New York, and even long-lost Gaylord Ravenal from wherever he has been roaming for the past twenty-three years.

There is simply no way to rationalize the return of Ravenal. It is clearly an immature concession to musical comedy convention that in days to come Hammerstein himself would help abolish. It is very likely that, had **Show Boat** been adapted for the stage one decade later, Hammerstein would have adhered to Miss Ferber's elimination of the gambler and not permitted him to reappear.

If one regards the continuity of life and tradition as important themes in **Show Boat,** then it is imperative that the story move from the turn of the century up to modern times. Yet the charming period scenes provide most of the work's great appeal: this is a difficult conflict to resolve.

In his earliest scripts, Hammerstein devoted an enormous amount of time to Kim and her career as a Broadway star, most of which was cut out by the time the show opened in Washington. Curiously, in Hammerstein's screenplay for the 1936 film version, he restored some of this material (in somewhat variant form), but much was deleted by director James Whale. In the 1951 film version, on which Hammerstein did not work, the story remains in the past; and Kim never grows beyond childhood. Since Hammerstein's death in 1960, several revivals have omitted Kim altogether.

The triumph of **Show Boat** is certainly its first act, which in a sense forms its own complete story. The lovers meet, fall in love, resolve their problems, and marry at the final curtain. In addition, all the major songs, except for "Why Do I Love You?" and "Bill," occur in the first act. It is significant too that most of the changes during out-of-town tryouts were made in the second act.

The legendary opening night, Tuesday evening, November 15, 1927, took place at the National Theatre in Washington. Leonard Hall in *The Washington Daily News* described the event.

Charles Winninger appeared before the curtain... and in the name of Florenz Ziegfeld bespoke the patience of the audience on behalf of the new opera about to begin. Mr. Ziegfeld, said his principal comedian, proposed to present every rehearsed scene, sans cut or slash, if we didn't get out of the trenches till Septuagesima. After a little amiable back-tickling concerning the good taste and discernment of the Washington audience, Mr. Winninger bowed and withdrew, and the curtain went up.

The first act rang down at 10:30, and the final curtain fell not before 12:40 in the morning. Harold Phillips in *The Washington Times* commented, "It was 12:50 by the Postoffice clock when a cheered, but slightly enervated, audience emerged into the night."

The critics praised everything they saw and

singled out "Can't Help Lovin' Dat Man," "Make Believe," and particularly "Ol' Man River" as potential song hits. They all agreed that drastic pruning was in order.

The surgery began the following morning, with some of its results discernible at the Wednesday matinee that afternoon. The simplest cut was a ballet that had opened the Trocadero scene. Its principal dancer, Madeline Parker, who had been featured in the ads, was dropped from the cast.

Act One, Scene Four, the rehearsal sequence, originally opened with a lengthy concerted piece known as "Mis'ry's Comin' Around." It is a Negro lament, sung by the Jubilee Singers, as they spruce up the auditorium. The lyric, led by Queenie and Julie, is a foreboding of death and tragedy. As a mood piece, it is one of Kern and Hammerstein's most original and exciting conceptions; but it ran nearly ten minutes and had to be sacrificed. Happily, the entire selection has been preserved in the original 1928 piano vocal score, published by T. B. Harms Co. In addition, a brief fragment remains during the miscegenation scene.

Scene Five now opens with Ellie and Frank chatting about the great success of Ravenal and Magnolia. Originally, the curtain went up on "I Would Like To Play a Lover's Part," in which the town's boys and girls are ogling photos of Magnolia and Gay. Frank steps forward to inform the ladies that leading men are fickle and unheeding men. The girls should be interested in a "wealthy clubman type" like him. By the song's end, the girls have grown angry at the crudeness of their escorts and revile them for their checkered suits and call them silly oafs and mad galoots. After a dance, the boys appease their sweethearts by buying tickets for the show. The scene then continued as it does today.

Early in tryouts, Frank and Ellie's specialty at the Trocadero was Joseph E. Howard's "Hello, Ma Baby." This was soon replaced by the same composer's "Good-bye, Ma Lady Love." Even in rehearsal, there had been a similar change. Norma Terris recalls that she had been assigned "Ta-Ra-Ra-Boom-der-é" as Magnolia's debut song at the Trocadero. While the sprightly air was suitable for New Year's Eve, it lacked the

poignance needed within the plot itself; and someone wisely substituted "After the Ball."

By the time the show moved the following week to the Nixon Theatre, Pittsburgh, on Monday, November 21, the major changes had been made. However, only the elimination of the Trocadero ballet is reflected in the playbill, which had to be printed while the show was still undergoing changes in Washington.

If most of the alterations in Washington had consisted of cuts, one major addition took place in Pittsburgh: "Why Do I Love You?" Because the song is performed twice in the second act, it actually replaced two other songs, first "Cheer Up" in the world's fair scene, and later a jazzy tune called "It's Getting Hotter in the North," which was performed by Kim in the closing sequence. The latter comments on the craze for hot, southern dances that have taken over "the levees of Broadway," an obvious reference to the popular Negro-originated "Charleston" and "Black Bottom."

Show Boat began its third week on Monday, November 28, at the Ohio Theatre, Cleveland, where audiences heard Magnolia, Andy, and Parthy sing a new, perky little ditty called "Be Happy, Too" in the first act. Somehow the tune seemed more suited to Ellie and Frank, so, with different lyrics, it emerged in Philadelphia as "I Might Fall Back on You."

Another late addition was "Hey, Feller!" which was given to Queenie in the second act, when her specialty spot, consisting of two old coon songs, "Coal Black Lady" and "Bully Song," was dropped.

Show Boat was such a success at the Erlanger Theatre in Philadelphia, where it opened Monday, December 5, that it remained there three weeks and closed Christmas Day.

Despite a myth that persists even till today, the musical was never scheduled to open in New York at the Ziegfeld Theatre, because **Rio Rita** was still playing there quite successfully. An ad in the December 12 Erlanger program clearly states, "The show opens in New York at the Lyric Theatre on Monday night, December 26th."

As a last-minute decision, Ziegfeld moved **Rio Rita** to the Lyric on 42nd Street and brought

1927—The Ziegfeld Production

Cartoon by Charles Bell, *Philadelphia Inquirer.*

Cartoon by Bert Link, *Pittsburgh Press*, November 22, 1927.

Show Boat, which he billed "An All American Musical Comedy," into the glorious 1632-seat temple of beauty that bore his own name. The double move required that the opening be postponed by one day, thus marking Tuesday, December 27, 1927, as the Broadway opening of **Show Boat.**

That same evening, Philip Barry's play, **Paris Bound** (12-27-27, Music Box), opened and went on to be acclaimed by Burns Mantle one of the season's ten best plays. Regarding the Barry opening as the more prestigious, several top newspaper critics chose to attend **Paris Bound** instead of **Show Boat.** One of these was Brooks Atkinson, who finally got around to documenting his impressions of the Ziegfeld production in the January 8, 1928, *New York Times.* His enthusiastic Sunday report began:

Shortly after the opening of "Show Boat" at the Ziegfeld Theatre, the henchmen of the press were privately and publicly acclaiming it as the "best musical show ever written." To one who inadvertently missed Lydia Thompson's "Ixion" on that showery September evening in 1868, this superlative praise of "Show Boat" does not seem excessive. Faithfully adapted from Edna Ferber's picturesque novel, set to an enchanting score by Jerome Kern, staged with the sort of artistry we eulogize in Reinhardt, "Show Boat" becomes one of those epochal works about which garrulous old men gabble for twenty-five years after the scenery has rattled off to the storehouse.

After a most complimentary report on individual aspects of the production, Atkinson singled out for praise each of the principals. He then remarked, "They blend into the sort of joined, harmonized performance that we extravagantly commend in good dramatic productions." It is significant of the era that Atkinson's highest praise for acting in a musical is to compare it to acting in a nonmusical.

Every so often, a Broadway musical opens with a cast that remain permanently identified with the roles they create. However frequently **Show Boat** may have been performed over the years, its original cast members continue to hover over the proceedings as theatre legends.

In 1927, the two best-known players were Edna May Oliver and Charles Winninger, both long-time theatrical favorites. Oliver, with her horse-face, had made a specialty of playing imperious dowagers and crusty spinsters and could not have been a better choice for the domineering Parthy. Winninger, with his impishness, boundless vitality, and skill at turning pratfalls and cartwheels into gestures of comic brilliance, was Oliver's perfect foil.

Norma Terris and Howard Marsh were the romantic Magnolia and Ravenal. Marsh had created the tenor leads in two of the decade's most popular operettas, **Blossom Time** (9-29-21, Ambassador) and **The Student Prince in Heidelberg** (12-2-24, Jolson's 59th Street), both produced by Ziegfeld's rivals, the Shubert brothers. For Miss Terris, **Show Boat** was to be the role of a lifetime. She had started in vaudeville with her first husband, Max Hoffman Jr., and then played in a few minor productions. She too was a Shubert alumna, having been most recently seen in **A Night in Paris** (1-5-26, Casino de Paris) and **A Night in Spain** (5-3-27, 44th Street), both revues.

The comic leads of Ellie and Frank went to the married song-and-dance team, Eva Puck and Sammy White, vaudeville hoofers recently featured in Rodgers and Hart's **The Girl Friend** (3-17-26, Vanderbilt).

Two supporting characters who appear briefly but whose presence pervades the entire musical are Julie, the tragic mulatto, and Joe, the ship's hand and husband of Queenie, the cook. Although Helen Morgan had been in Broadway shows since her first appearance as a chorus girl in Ziegfeld's **Sally** (12-21-20, New Amsterdam), she was better known as the singing queen of the speakeasies. Her crooning of sad songs while seated on an upright piano, today regarded as one of the symbols of New York during the roaring '20's, was already a familiar signature by the time of **Show Boat.** Although only twenty-seven, Miss Morgan's dissipation from brandy had already given this former beauty queen a somewhat worn quality. Her voice, far from that of the husky altos who usually sang torch songs, was a delicate, high-pitched soprano. The vulnerability suggested by both Miss Morgan in reality and Julie onstage blended so thoroughly that in retrospect it is impossible to think of **Show Boat** without Julie without Helen Morgan.

In the novel, Jo (as Miss Ferber spells his

name) is only vaguely sketched and does little but serve meals on the *Cotton Blossom*. Although little dialogue was given to Joe in the musical, he appears during all the critical moments of the *Cotton Blossom* section of the show. When the lovers first meet, Joe is there: when Magnolia gleefully tells Julie she is in love, Joe is there: and finally, when the entire story has been concluded, Joe is there to sing the last notes of the score.

It is his song, "Ol' Man River," that weaves through the entire play as a haunting *leit motif*. The lyric's tribute to the wisdom and eternity of the river assumes the stature of a hymn. Despite its familiarity, one rarely stops to notice the song's revolutionary construction; for example, in its twelve-line refrain there is only one true rhyme, "cotton" and "forgotten."

Ol' man River,
Dat ol' man River,
He mus' know sumpin',
But don't say nothin',
He just keeps rollin',
He keeps on rollin' alon'.
He don't plant 'taters,
He don't plant cotton,
An' dem dat plant 'em
Is soon forgotten,
But ol' man River,
He jes keeps rollin' alon'.

As Hammerstein's most mature lyric up to that time, its rare power is heightened by the complete absence of the clichéd thirty-two-bar popular song structure of the period.

The song's creator, Jules Bledsoe, was one of the most distinguished Negro baritones of the 1920's and 1930's. Although he made a critically acclaimed appearance in the unsuccessful musical **Deep River** (10-4-26, Imperial), most of his career was spent touring the world in recitals and grand opera. Plagued by poor health, Bledsoe died July 14, 1943, at the age of forty-four.

Queenie, oddly enough, was not played by a Negro actress at all, but rather by the rotund, Italian Tess Gardella, who always appeared in blackface in her characterization of Aunt Jemima. It was the character Aunt Jemima, not Miss Gardella, who was credited in the program for the role of Queenie. Her hardy voice was given ample expression in two solos and her section of "Can't Help Lovin' Dat Man."

Down to the tiniest roles, Ziegfeld populated his cast with first-rate players, many of whom had been headliners in earlier days. Charles Ellis (Steve), in his first musical, had distinguished himself in **Desire under the Elms** (11-11-24, Greenwich Village) and other important dramatic plays. Allan Campbell (Windy), Thomas Gunn (Vallon), Annie Hart (Landlady), and Laura Clairon (Old Lady on Levee) were all prominent around the turn of the century. Even beautiful Dagmar Oakland, in the tiny role of Dolly, had begun as a pre-teenage dancer in the **Ziegfeld Follies** and later played principal roles in many musicals. She was originally cast as Hetty Chilson in **Show Boat,** but this role had been reduced by Hammerstein to an atmospheric bit at the world's fair, where she and her girls encounter Ravenal. The part was eliminated shortly after tryouts began, and Miss Oakland was given the equally brief, but amusing, bit as Dolly, one of Andy's three New Year's Eve flames.

It is difficult to write about Jerome Kern's contribution to **Show Boat** without the aid of recordings or printed musical examples. Perhaps his great contribution to musical theatre history is best given by Arthur B. Waters in his extraordinarily perceptive **Show Boat** review in the December 16, 1927, *Philadelphia Public Ledger*.

Just where the highest honors are to be bestowed we are not certain, but, without doubt, Mr. Kern, as the composer of the score . . . should come in for first mention. A few years ago we were second to none in our admiration of Kern for his musical-comedy contributions. What other song writer, for example, had such an array of successes to his credit as "Oh, Boy," "Leave It to Jane," "Oh, Lady, Lady," "Sally" and "Good Morning, Dearie," to mention but a few of the more striking ones? Then, it seemed to us, Mr. Kern went to the inspirational well too often and except for the exceptionally noteworthy score he provided for "Dear Sir," his work suffered. The music of "Sunny" we still insist was but a faint echo of, let us say, that of "Sally," and when "Lucky" came around last season, a low ebb had been reached.

In "Show Boat," however, Mr. Kern accomplishes a superb about face. In it he has put all the tuneful-

1927—The Ziegfeld Production

Ziegfeld and his **Show Boat** principals, seen immediately following a performance. Notice how many players are wearing the old-age make-up and 1920's costuming of the final scene.
Annie Hart, Charles Ellis, Tess Gardella, Thomas Gunn, Laura Clairon, Eva Puck, Sammy White, Howard Marsh, Helen Morgan, little Eleanor Shaw, Florenz Ziegfeld, Norma Terris, Charles Winninger, Edna May Oliver, Jules Bledsoe, musical director Victor Baravalle.

ness that marked the old Princess Theatre hits, plus a more mature musicianly quality than was first noted in "Dear Sir" and a remarkable fidelity to the spirit and atmosphere of the subject in hand. Here he has blended the Negro spirituals of the Southland with jazz of today. What is even more noteworthy, he has caught the subtle distinction that exists between jazz and the ragtime of twenty or twenty-five years ago, and several of his numbers of the last-named category are amazingly characteristic of the early years of the present century.

Throughout the whole play he has interwoven a magnificent motif number, "Old Man River," which is in itself a most happy inspiration in view of the fact that Miss Ferber in writing the story expressed in words the same idea of the unchanging qualities of the majestic Mississippi, that flowed on, inscrutable and eternally while birth and death and human dramas were being enacted along its banks.

There is also a note of the spiritual in another of Mr. Kern's numbers, "Can't Help Lovin' That Man."

On the other hand, there is the tinkling melody of a more conventional present-day sort in "Why Do I Love You?" which enters the later developments of the action in the second act. For a romantic love ballad there is "You Are Love" and the possibly more human "Only Make Believe," both of which are ex-

ceptionally good. "Cotton Blossom" is a vigorous ensemble, with a tricky, impudent, haunting little refrain concerning the talents and personal qualifications of "Cap'n Andy." For comedy, there is the delightful "Life on the Wicked Stage," which possesses some clever lyrics.

Then there are the several songs of old-time vintage which are introduced, such as "After the Ball," which provides one of the most vivid and pathetic moments of the play; "Good-by, My Lady Love," which permits Sammy White and Eva Puck to indulge in a capital cakewalk.

We know of no musical comedy in recent years at any rate, which has so uniformly high-grade a score in which the usual "fillers" of such offerings are distinguishable by their total absence.

While most Broadway composers staunchly hold to the standard contract clause that forbids producers to interpolate musical selections by other composers into their own scores, Jerome Kern over the years frequently chose to use the work of other songwriters, usually for period or atmospheric flavor. **Very Good Eddie** (12-23-15, Princess), **Leave It to Jane** (8-28-17, Long-

Original sheet music cover, published November 30, 1927, two days after the Cleveland opening.

Standard sheet music cover, which soon replaced the lyre cover, and which remains in use today.

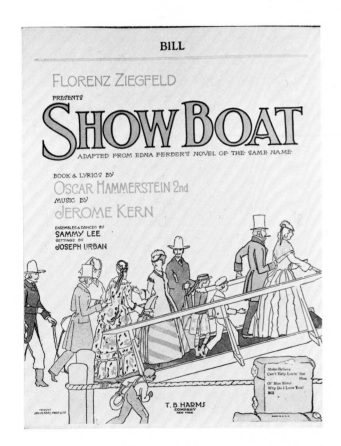

1927—The Ziegfeld Production

acre), **Sally,** and **Sunny** are but a few Kern scores that contain interpolations. **Show Boat** is no exception.

In the Trocadero scene, for example, there is music throughout but not a note of Kern. John Philip Sousa's "The Washington Post March" is used as a bridge from the previous lobby scene. The sequence then opens with an Apache, featuring Offenbach's familiar "Valse des Rayons" from his ballet, **Le Papillon.** This is followed by the cakewalk which combines a vocal of Joseph E. Howard's "Good-bye, Ma Lady Love" and an instrumental of Kerry Mills' "At a Georgia Camp Meeting." The scene builds to Magnolia's rendition of "After the Ball" by Charles K. Harris, and it concludes with a rousing instrumental of "A Hot Time in the Old Town Tonight" by Theodore A. Metz. There is another non-Kern vocal of sorts in the Ontario Street boarding house scene, in which the cleaning girl, Ethel, softly sings "Good Morning, Carrie" by Cecil Mack and Tim Brymn.

Other non-Kern tunes are heard instrumentally throughout. When Andy makes his first entrance with the *Cotton Blossom* band, they are playing an old Bohemian air. His violin accompaniment to **The Parson's Bride** includes Lange's "Flower Song" and "Pop Goes the Weasel." Then too there is the popular hootchy kootchy dance music for La Belle Fatima at the world's fair. This was actually composed for the seductive dancer Little Egypt by one of the fair's publicists, Sol Bloom, later congressman from New York.

Kern even turned to himself as a source for two interpolations. In the Kern–P.G. Wodehouse Princess Theatre show, **Oh, Lady! Lady!!** (2-1-18, Princess), Vivienne Segal had a song about a boy she loved whose name was Bill (played by Carl Randall). The song was deleted, although a fragment remained in the first act finale. Over the years, Kern tried to place it in other productions without success. Finally,

given the need to create a show-stopping torch song for Helen Morgan in the second act of **Show Boat,** Kern dug "Bill" out of the trunk.

The song has two verses and choruses. Hammerstein retained both of Wodehouse's verses and the last eight bars of his refrains. However, he and Kern rewrote both music and lyrics for the first eight bars of the two choruses. In the playbill of the 1946 revival, Hammerstein, with customary modesty, insisted on setting the record straight.

I am particularly anxious to point out that the lyric for the song "Bill" was written by P. G. Wodehouse. Although he has always been given credit in the program, it has frequently been assumed that since I wrote all the other lyrics for "Show Boat," I also wrote this one, and I have had praise for it which belongs to another man.

In fact, the first half of each refrain is entirely Hammerstein's.

The little tune that Magnolia struggles to play on the piano just before she first meets Ravenal is another Kern-Wodehouse interpolation. It is part of the first act entrance scene from their English musical, **The Beauty Prize** (9-5-23, Winter Garden, London), and was sung by Vera Lennox in the role of Kitty.

What lovelier things a bride could adorn
Upon her happy wedding morn?
Now here is one
The fairies might have spun.

THE BEAUTY PRIZE
Copyright © 1923 T.B. Harms Co. Copyright Renewed.
All Rights Reserved. Used by permission.

This author had the privilege of spending the afternoon of Wednesday, August 3, 1960, with Oscar Hammerstein at his Manhattan town house. Certain that he was dying of cancer, Hammerstein left with his wife, Dorothy, late that afternoon for their farm in Doylestown, Pennsylvania, where he passed away on Tuesday, August 23.

Sensing his illness but not its severity, I asked

ON THE FOLLOWING PAGES, THE ORIGINAL 1918 WODEHOUSE-KERN "BILL"

from **Oh, Lady! Lady!!,** and the familiar version revised by Hammerstein and Kern for **Show Boat.** For the first time, the two versions can be easily compared. Despite Hammerstein's later disclaimer to having worked on this song, his contribution is clearly evident.

Bill.

Lyric by
P. G. WODEHOUSE.

Music by
JEROME KERN.

came 'round my way.   I al-ways used to fan - cy then, He'd be
men that I know.   He is-n't tall and straight and slim, And he

one of the god - like kind of men, With a gi - ant brain and a
dress - es far worse than Ted or Jim, And I can't ex - plain why

no - ble head Like the he - roes bold in the books I read.
he should be Just the one, one man in the world for me.

Chorus.

But a long came Bill Who's quite the op - pos - ite of all the
He's — just my Bill He has no gifts at all: A mo - tor

men — In sto-ry books. In grace and looks I know that Ap - po - lo, Would
car — He can-not steer; And it seems clear When - ev - er he dan-ces, His

beat him all hol-low, And I can't ex-plain It's sure-ly not his brain That
part-ner takes chan-ces, Oh I can't ex-plain It's sure-ly not his brain That

makes me thrill. — I love him — Be - cause he's
makes me thrill. — I love him — Be - cause he's

won-der - ful — Be-cause he's just old Bill. — But a Bill. —
I don't know — Be-cause he's just my Bill. — He's — Bill. —

BILL

Words by
P.G. WODEHOUSE and
OSCAR HAMMERSTEIN IInd

Music by
JEROME KERN

came 'round my way. I al-ways used to fan-cy then He'd be
men that I know. He is not tall and straight and slim, And he

one of the God-like kind of men With a gi-ant brain and a
dres-ses far worse than Ted or Jim; And I can't ex-plain why he

no-ble head Like the he-roes bold in the books I read;
should be just The—— one, one man in the world for me;

Burthen

But a-long came Bill, Who's not the type at all, You'd meet him on the street and nev-er
He's just my Bill, An or-di-nar-y boy, He has-n't got a thing that I can

not-ice him; His form and face, His man-ly grace Is not the kind that you Would
brag a-bout And yet to be Up-on his knee So com-fy and room-y Feels

find in a sta-tue And I can't ex-plain, It's sure-ly not his brain That
nat-ur-al to me And I can't ex-plain It's sure-ly not his brain That

makes me thrill.— I love him — Be-caue he's
makes me thrill.— I love him — Be-caue he's

2nd time

colla voce

won-der-ful,— Be-cause he's just old Bill. He's Bill.—
I don't know,— Be-cause he's just my

1.

2.

Ped.

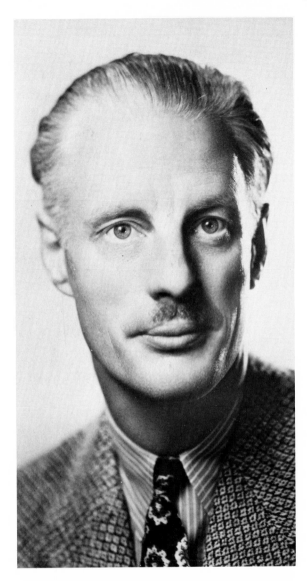

ROBERT RUSSELL BENNETT

mechanism rolling smoothly. Hammerstein added that with Colvan gone, he could admit that it was he who actually directed the book, with the close participation of Kern and Ziegfeld. This statement has been confirmed by Norma Terris and orchestrator Robert Russell Bennett, two of the few survivors of the original production.

Until **Show Boat,** Ziegfeld had been famed as the "glorifier of the American girl." In all his revues and loosely constructed book shows alike, there were numerous situations in which beautiful girls had the opportunity to parade before the "bald heads in the first row." Except for the Congress of Beauty in the world's fair scene, **Show Boat** afforded no such situations.

More than a mere musical comedy, **Show Boat** was a musical play, a drama-with-song that could not help but touch upon the life of any American who viewed the work. The depiction of the innocent South of the nineteenth century, the roistering gaiety of old Chicago with its world's fair, smart hotels, and colorful cabarets, and the depiction of the modern theatre all rang true, because they were sketched without the exaggeration and superficiality theatregoers of the 1920's had come to expect.

Then too there is the remarkable role of Magnolia, who appears to be the first character in the entire literature of the American Musical Theatre to change and mature before the audience's eyes. At the outset, she is a dewy-eyed innocent, easily awed by one as handsome as Gaylord Ravenal. Slowly, subtly, she gains in strength as the burden of Gay's weakness is shifted to her shoulders. With the cathartic conquering of a rude New Year's Eve audience, one has the feeling that Magnolia now can conquer the world, or at least the theatrical world. And this she does with ease. Despite the brilliance of Bledsoe's "Ol' Man River" and Morgan's "Bill," it was Norma Terris' subtle shading of Magnolia that provided the original production with overall continuity. Blessed with a strong presence and a radiantly clear voice, it was her intelligent playing of the heroine's growth that brought Magnolia and this **Show Boat** dramatically to life.

Until Ziegfeld saw long lines queuing up for

him a number of questions about his career. In relation to **Show Boat,** I wanted to know how the most important musical of the 1920's could have been directed by someone whose name, Zeke Colvan, was so thoroughly unfamiliar.

Hammerstein replied that in fact Colvan did not really direct **Show Boat** but rather was its production stage manager. Because of the vastness of the cast and complexity of the many scene, costume, and technical changes, it was agreed that Colvan should be rewarded with credit as director for his ability to keep the

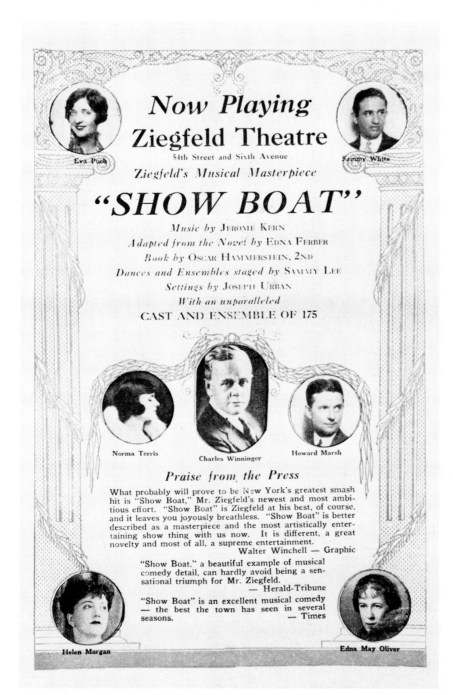

Advertising flier

tickets in front of his theatre when the morning reviews appeared, he was skeptical of **Show Boat.** To him, perhaps the most uncharacteristic aspect of the production was its dancing. Instead of a succession of specialties and ensemble routines, choreographer Sammy Lee had staged only the kind of routines that grew naturally out of the plot. During the pseudo-Negro folk tune, "Can't Help Lovin' Dat Man," Magnolia glides into a languorous shuffle. Frank and Ellie do a vaudeville dance to "I Might Fall Back on You" and a cakewalk to "Good-bye, Ma Lady Love,"

65

Cartoon by A. Birnbaum, *New York Evening Post*, December 31, 1927.

Charles Winninger, Edna May Oliver and Howard Marsh in the New Musical Offering at Ziegfeld's Theatre

From the New York Mirror, Jan. 2, 1928.

'Show Boat' Touches the Heart, Says Fay King

By FAY KING

The other day I read a small item in the paper saying that a show boat down South had struck a snag and was sinking.

This meant nothing in my life. I've never been South. I've never seen a show on a boat.

But if I had read it today, it would have had a very different meaning to me. For since spending at the Ziegfeld Theatre, an afternoon with Cap'n Andy Hawks' little troupe of players on his Cotton Blossom Floating Palace Theatre, anything about Show Boats will be news of great importance to me in the future.

In presenting a musicalized adaptation of Edna Ferber's book, "Show Boat," Flo Ziegfeld has struck a new and more wonderful note than ever before. He has blazed a trail beyond the eye and the ear and has reached the HEART!

In "Show Boat," Ziegfeld glorifies emotion!

Oh! You will love "Show Boat!" It will shake you with laughter. It will tickle your toes, it will make you burst into song—but it will also make you choke a little and wipe away a tear.

The two big acts of "Show Boat," with 18 different scenes, carries you along with Cap'n Andy's little troupe from 1890 to 1928, closely following the times and fads. To the older members of the audience, it will bring back many pleasant memories. To the younger members it is a peep into those "good old times" we hear so much about.

"Show Boat" is really the biography of Magnolia, Cap'n Andy's pretty daughter. And right here I want to say that Norma Terris gives one of the finest, most versatile performances that has ever been given on Broadway!

David Belasco would pin a medal on her I know!

The cast of "Show Boat" is gigantic! The costumes, the scenery, the music, the dancing—all is perfection!

It's different from anything you have ever seen! Don't miss it! And don't forget your handkerchief!

"Show Boat" will linger in your memory—not for a day, or a year—but always!

66

Cartoon from *The New York Times*.

Nell Brinkley drawing from souvenir program centerfold.

Nell Brinkley's Impressions of Ziegfeld's "SHOW BOAT"

67

MARILYN MILLER
adorns the **Show Boat** souvenir program cover.

A typical **Show Boat** souvenir program.

Ad from the back of a souvenir program. Mr. Ziegfeld died in 1932 from pleurisy, a lung ailment.

both of which are relevant to their character and the era. From the robust Dahomey dancing of the black ensemble to the refined steps allocated the Natchez beaux and belles in the first act opening and finale, Sammy Lee broke fresh ground in musical comedy dance direction.

Attention to period detail was particularly evident in the costumes of John Harkrider and the settings by Joseph Urban, both of whom avoided the lure of designing artificially theatrical trappings. Instead, meticulous attention was paid to the subtle use of materials and color to evoke mood.

Audiences responded to the beauty, cast, strong story, and melodic riches of **Show Boat** by keeping it running until Saturday, May 4, 1929. **The Best Plays** annual gives the number of performances as 572, though *The Billboard,* possibly more accurately, says 575.

With a potential box-office gross of $55,000 a week, the production averaged around $50,000. Ziegfeld claimed, however, that hardly any money was made on the massive presentation because his operating expense was around $31,000, with an additional cost of $16,800 for the staff of 110 employees in both the front of the house and backstage.

With **Show Boat** set for a long run, Ziegfeld enjoyed the greatest theatrical success of his career. Only fourteen days after its opening came a charming Ruritanian romance, **Rosalie** (1-10-28, New Amsterdam), with a score by George Gershwin and Sigmund Romberg and starring the lovely Marilyn Miller. Two months later, Ziegfeld presented Dennis King and an all-star cast in Rudolf Friml's **The Three Musketeers** (3-13-28, Lyric). The year came to a rousing conclusion with one of the producer's favorite shows, the wild-west romp, **Whoopee** showboat 40
Ruth Etting, and Ethel Shutta. All three productions ran well over three hundred performances, an impressive feat during the 1920's.

Ziegfeld was so pleased by the popularity of **Show Boat** that, in February 1928, he actually announced his plan to form a second New York company to play in another theatre. Raymond Hitchcock as Cap'n Andy, Paul Robeson as Joe, and Libby Holman as Julie were mentioned as

Cartoon by Firestone, *Brooklyn Eagle,* December 23, 1928.

possible cast members. The plan, of course, never came to pass.

One sad note during the Broadway run was the sinking of the show boat that had given Edna Ferber her inspiration. During the summer of 1928, a fire began in the hold of the *James Adams Floating Theatre,* and while the crew fought vainly to stem the spread of flames, the acting troupe gathered some belongings and rowed safely to shore. From the embankment, the actors watched their home sink to the muddy bottom of the Pamlico River in North Carolina. The ship was salvaged, however, and managed to survive sinking in the Dismal Swamp in November 1929 and being broken up during a hurricane off Gwynn's Island in August 1933. It was finally destroyed by fire on November 14, 1941, in the Savannah River in Georgia.

Throughout **Show Boat**'s long run, most of the original cast remained intact, although Edna

IRENE DUNNE,
dressed for Act One, Scene Two.
COSTUME BY JOHN HARKRIDER

Cartoon by Keenan, *Chicago Herald*, October 20, 1929.

TheatreRoyal DruryLane

LONDON 1928

"Can't Help Lovin' Dat Man." Norris Smith, unidentified player, Paul Robeson, Alberta Hunter, Edith Day, Marie Burke, unidentified player, John Payne, unidentified player.

The miscegenation scene. Henry Thomas, Viola Compton, Edith Day, Dorothy Lena, Marie Burke, Colin Clive, Cedric Hardwicke, Jack Martin, Percy Parsons. On balcony, Paul Robeson.

PAUL ROBESON

The Parson's Bride. Howett Worster, Edith Day. In box,
Roy Emerton, Gordon Crocker, Viola Compton.

Finale Act One. Left: Paul Robeson, Alberta Hunter. Right: Howett Worster, Edith Day, Leslie Sarony, Dorothy Lena,
Cedric Hardwicke.

1927—The Ziegfeld Production

May Oliver and Jules Bledsoe were briefly replaced in August 1928 by Maude Ream Stover and Daniel L. Haynes. It was the Broadway cast that took **Show Boat** to the road.

On Monday, May 6, 1929, two days after the Broadway closing, the entire show, with all its major players, reopened at the Colonial Theatre in Boston. When the theatre season ended, Saturday, June 1, Norma Terris, Edna May Oliver, and Helen Morgan all left to make films. Lorraine Weimer took over the role of Parthy, and Margaret Carlisle that of Julie. The pivotal character of Magnolia was given to Irene Dunne (her name still being spelled without the final e).

An alumna of an earlier Kern musical, **The City Chap** (10-26-25, Liberty), Miss Dunne had made her Broadway debut in **The Clinging Vine** (12-25-22, Knickerbocker), followed by a succession of musicals. Contrary to yet another **Show Boat** myth, Miss Dunne had never been Norma Terris' understudy but was brought in expressly to replace the original Magnolia. Both women recently confirmed this.

After closing in Boston on June 15, **Show Boat** took a summer lay-off and resumed on Monday, September 23, at the Shubert in Newark. This one-week stand was arranged to help whip the show back into shape. Miss Oliver returned to the cast, and Julie was now being played by Kathryn Manners. Miss Carlisle returned to the role the following week, however, when **Show Boat** opened for a sixteen-week engagement at the Illinois Theatre in Chicago, Tuesday, October 1. Then there followed seven one-week stints at the American, St. Louis (1-20-30), Davidson, Milwaukee (1-27-30), Wil-30), Nixon, Pittsburgh (2-17-30), National, Washington (2-24-30), and finally Ford's, Baltimore (3-3-30).

It was during the Baltimore engagement that scouts from RKO Radio Pictures discovered Irene Dunne and swiftly signed her for the film version of Rodgers and Hart's musical **Present Arms** (4-26-28, Mansfield), known on the screen as **Leathernecking** (RKO, 1930). Her second picture, Edna Ferber's **Cimarron** (RKO, 1930), was her first dramatic role and the turning point of what proved to be one of the screen's most distinguished careers.

During **Show Boat**'s long Broadway run, there were several productions abroad, produced by arrangement with Ziegfeld. Most notable was the English version (5-3-28, Theatre Royal Drury Lane, London), directed by Felix Edwardes, choreographed by Max Scheck, conducted by Herman Finck, and produced by Alfred Butt.

The distinguished cast featured Cedric Hardwicke as Andy, Colin Clive as Steve, Viola Compton as Parthy, and three of the London musical theatre's most popular players, Edith Day (an American), Howett Worster, and Marie Burke as Magnolia, Ravenal, and Julie.

Most impressive was the casting of Paul Robeson, finally playing the role of Joe, which had been created for him. Normally staid British audiences were thrilled by the massive physical presence of this dignified and soft-spoken black, and the thunderous power that he brought to "Ol' Man River" became the talk of London.

Robert Russell Bennett recently explained that Robeson sang this piece in the key of B flat major, one tone lower than Jules Bledsoe's key of C major. This allowed Robeson to reach a bottom note of low F, rather than Bledsoe's low G, thereby imparting a more dramatic air. Norma Terris, who eventually appeared with both baritones, claimed "Robeson was a brooding 'Ol' Man River,' while Bledsoe was a happy 'Ol' Man River.'"

Kern and Hammerstein wrote a new song for Robeson called "Me and My Boss," but this was never performed. To fill the spot in which Norma Terris had done her impressions to a reprise of "Why Do I Love You?" the authors simply made a brief cut for Irene Dunne. For Edith Day, however, a completely new song, "Dance Away the Night," replaced the original one.

Shortly after the London opening, several other changes were made. The convent and Sherman House lobby scenes were cut out, along with Queenie's "Hey, Feller!"; and "Good-bye, Ma Lady Love" was replaced with an early Kern hit, "How'd You Like To Spoon with Me?" The production ran for an impressive 350 performances.

In 1929, the musical was presented in Australia, and also in Paris under the title **Mississippi**, its French lyrics translated by Lucien Boyer.

1927—The Ziegfeld Production

Cover of the original English piano vocal score, published in 1928.

The first American production not presented by Ziegfeld was given at the huge outdoor amphitheatre, the St. Louis Municipal Opera, which had been a home to operetta since its inception in 1919. **Show Boat** was the final offering of the 1930 Muny season and played two weeks, from Monday, August 11, through Sunday, August 24. During this period, the 10,000-seat theatre (later enlarged to 12,000 seats) was being operated by the Shubert organization, with Milton I. Shubert in charge.

Far from the usual modest summer stock production, cast with unknowns or stars beyond their prime, the Muny presentation was headed by one of the country's most prominent comedians in the role of Cap'n Andy: W. C. Fields, who received $4000 for his appearance. Guy Robertson, whom Ziegfeld had first announced as Ravenal, finally had his chance to play the role; and Puck and White re-created their original parts

of Ellie and Frank. Maude Ream Stover and Margaret Carlisle, both veterans of Ziegfeld's national tour, played Parthy and Julie. Others in the cast included Charlotte Lansing (Magnolia), Lois B. Deppe (Joe), Mammy Jinny (Queenie), Leonard Ceeley—husband of Margaret Carlisle (Steve), Frank Horn (Pete), and Hal Forde (Windy). The Fisk University Male Octette sang during the changes in scene.

No professional company has been a greater champion of **Show Boat** than the St. Louis Municipal Opera, which has presented the work no fewer than ten times during the last half century: for two weeks in 1930, 1934, 1938, 1942, 1947, 1952, and 1958, and for a single week in 1964, 1968, and 1976. Featured players have included Norma Terris, Allan Jones, Kenneth Spencer, and others associated with the work on Broadway or in films.

CHAPTER 3

1929
The First Film Version

IF ONE CAN regard a major Hollywood film version of a literary work as a reward for a fiction writer, then Edna Ferber is one of the most generously rewarded of all American novelists. Almost all her novels have been filmed, many of them more than once. **Show Boat** has been presented on the screen in no fewer than three versions with varying artistic and commercial success.

Screen rights to the novel were purchased by Universal Pictures on October 26, 1926, only two months after the book's publication. The sale price of $65,000 seems modest even by standards of that time, when one considers the enormous popularity the book was enjoying.

The chore of preparing a first screen treatment was assigned to Winnifred Reeve, who completed a fifty-two-page version on December 14. The material was then turned over to Charles Kenyon, who finished his own fifty-eight page treatment on January 13, 1927. Between March 26, 1927, and April 19, 1928, Kenyon prepared no fewer than ten continuity scripts for the property; and it was he who was finally credited with having written the film's scenario.

Universal was still being run by its founder,

Carl Laemmle, who was affectionately known in the industry as "Uncle Carl." Laemmle was born in Laupheim, Germany, on January 17, 1867, and came to the United States in 1884. In New York City, Chicago, and Oshkosh, he worked at various odd jobs, but, in 1906, upon his return to Chicago, he developed an interest in the infant industry of motion pictures. On February 24, 1906, he opened his first theatre, the Whitefront, on Milwaukee Avenue, and a second a few months later on Halsted Street.

In 1907, he formed the Laemmle Film Service and established a chain of distribution exchanges in about a dozen northern and midwestern cities. In June, he returned to Germany and brought back an experimental talking picture system, the Synchroscope, which was marketed with only modest success.

In 1909, Laemmle broke with the patents companies that held a monopoly stranglehold on the film industry. He formed the Independent Motion Picture Company, known as IMP, and released its first picture, **Hiawatha** (IMP, 1909), on Monday, October 25, 1909, his father's birthday. After a successful battle with the patents companies, Laemmle formed Universal

Pictures in 1912, and in March 1915 formally opened Universal City, which remains today the world's largest movie studio facility.

By the late 1920's, Universal had attained a secure position in the industry. Its most successful films included Lon Chaney in **The Hunchback of Notre Dame** (Universal, 1923) and **The Phantom of the Opera** (Universal, 1925), and the first four pictures directed by Erich von Stroheim, including **Blind Husbands** (Universal, 1919) and **Foolish Wives** (Universal, 1921).

Although Universal was noted chiefly for unpretentious westerns and domestic dramas, the studio's stable of contract artisans included several sensitive and artistic directors, among them Paul Fejos, Paul Leni, and Clarence Brown. Its cinematographers Hal Mohr and Gilbert Warrenton were experimenting with inventive and mobile camera techniques, often resulting in images and sequences of startling beauty. Warrenton, for example, shot three of Universal's most stunningly attractive (though totally different in style) features, **The Cat and the Canary** (Universal, 1927), **The Man Who Laughs** (Universal, 1928), and **Lonesome** (Universal, 1928), the first two directed by Leni, the third by Fejos. Warrenton was assigned to shoot **Show Boat.**

One of the studio's major releases late in 1927 was a silent version of the Harriet Beecher Stowe classic, **Uncle Tom's Cabin** (Universal, 1927), directed by Harry A. Pollard. Because of Pollard's experience in depicting the Old South, Laemmle handed the forty-five-year-old, hard-drinking director the assignment of "megaphoning" the Ferber work.

Born in Republic, Kansas, on January 23, 1883, Pollard had acted in almost five hundred roles, many of them romantic leads, in various stock and touring companies, including the legendary company run by Frederick Belasco at the Alcazar Theatre in San Francisco. He entered films as an actor for the Selig company but soon turned to direction. His forte was light comedy; and his two-reel series **The Leather Pushers** (Universal, 1922–24) and the comedy **The Cohens and the Kellys** (Universal, 1926) proved particularly appealing to the general public.

Laemmle's assignment of Pollard to **Show Boat** surely represents a considerable act of faith, for, except for **Uncle Tom's Cabin** and the director's first-hand familiarity with old-fashioned, melodramatic acting styles like those to be depicted during the river boat presentations, very little in Pollard's background suggested that he might be able to cope with the exacting task of making a coherent photoplay from an episodic novel that rambles over half a century and is set against a wide variety of backgrounds.

By spring 1928, the production pieces were beginning to be assembled. There were casting rumors that suggested Magnolia would be played by Mary Philbin, Universal's popular leading lady of **The Phantom of the Opera,** Captain Andy by Jean Hersholt, Parthy by Belle Bennett, and Julie by Estelle Taylor, then married to former heavyweight champ Jack Dempsey. Later, Barbara Kent and Reginald Denny were announced for the leads. However, not even one of these Universal contract players appeared in the picture.

While Pollard and Kenyon continued to refine the script, scouts were sent to find locations along the Ohio, Mississippi, and Sacramento rivers, suitable to suggest the Mississippi of the 1880's. Martin F. Murphy, general production manager, supplied complete lists of sets and locations, including interiors, exteriors, miniatures, etc., to Technical Director Archie Hall, Art Director Charles Daniel (Dan) Hall, Chief Studio Electrician Frank Graves, and Chief of Props Russell Gausman. Johanna Mathieson, head of the wardrobe department, was faced with preparing costumes for four distinct periods: 1885, 1896, 1905, and what was then the present. Universal dubbed its super productions "Jewels"; and **Show Boat** was to be a jewel of jewels, with no expense spared in bringing Ferber's Mississippi saga to life on the silent screen.

By early June, the studio announced Emily Fitzroy as Parthy and Alma Rubens as Julie. Not long after Mary Philbin was cast in another film, Laura La Plante was announced as Magnolia. Miss La Plante, a cheery-faced blonde who specialized in light drama and comedy, was Universal's most popular leading lady and, with the addition of a dark wig, a natural choice for such an important role. Character actors Otis Harlan,

Carl Laemmle

THE man who made *SHOW BOAT*—the picture which marks a new era in entertainment.

The man who, for the first time in show business history, combines a best-selling novel with a tremendous musical comedy success and blends the two into the most gigantic screen entertainment ever dreamed of—

The man who gives every theatre in the land the opportunity of presenting, at popular prices, the cream of a $7.70-per-seat stage production *plus* a romantic drama that has swayed the nation's millions.

Truly—Carl Laemmle Shows the Way!

CARL LAEMMLE'S
SHOW BOAT

Jack McDonald, and Neely Edwards were cast as Captain Andy, Windy, and Schultzy, respectively. Negro performers Stepin Fetchit and Gertrude Howard were to be seen as Joe and Queenie. Child actress Jane La Verne would play both the young Magnolia and her daughter Kim.

The dashing role of Gaylord Ravenal went to Joseph Schildkraut, the stylish Broadway leading man who had distinguished himself in **Liliom** (4-20-21, Garrick), **Peer Gynt** (2-5-23, Garrick), and **The Firebrand** (10-15-24, Morosco), among dozens of plays in which he had appeared since his 1913 professional debut in Berlin under the great Max Reinhardt. During his intermittent screen career, Schildkraut had attracted attention as Chevalier de Vaudrys in D.W. Griffith's **Orphans of the Storm** (UA, 1921) and Judas in Cecil B. DeMille's **The King of Kings** (Pathé, 1927).

According to Schildkraut's autobiography, **My Father and I** (Viking Press, 1959), he was about to depart Hollywood to appear in the Broadway production of **Death Takes a Holiday** (12-26-29, Ethel Barrymore), when he learned that Universal was searching through a huge roster of screen lovers to find a suitable Mississippi gambler. Without notifying his agent, he hopped

into a car and burst onto the Universal stage where Pollard was shooting tests. "You don't know me, Mr. Pollard, and I don't know you. But you probably know me by name and I know you by name. I am Joseph Schildkraut, the only actor who can play Gaylord Ravenal." Pollard looked at the short, unshaven actor, dressed in casual sports clothes, and, removing his pipe, said softly, "I don't think so."

With the aid of Hollywood's well-known tailor Eddie Schmidt and the Western Costume Company, Schildkraut bought himself a dashing period costume, built-up shoes to raise his height, and a smart pearl-grey top hat to add even more inches. With a beautiful cane given by his actor-father, Rudolph Schildkraut, he once again bounced into Pollard's studio, brazenly twirling his cane before the director, who was watching John Gilbert make a test. An hour later, Schildkraut was signed for the plum role,

and the part of Ellie was given to his wife, Elise Bartlett.

Actual production on the picture began July 16, 1928, with parts of a melodrama among the first sequences shot. On July 31, 1928, the entire company went up north to the tiny Sacramento River community of Knights Landing, California. There, and at Hood and Sacramento, several weeks were spent shooting all the Mississippi exterior scenes. In Sacramento, a full-sized floating show boat was constructed with a working calliope, and residents of Knights Landing and neighboring Woodland were pressed into service to represent southern townsfolk. Upon return to Hollywood, interior shooting was resumed and finally completed by early October. Another month was required to edit the picture and trim it to manageable length.

On October 6, 1927, Warner Bros. had presented **The Jazz Singer** (Warners, 1927), the

Sketch for first movie show boat, constructed in Sacramento, California.

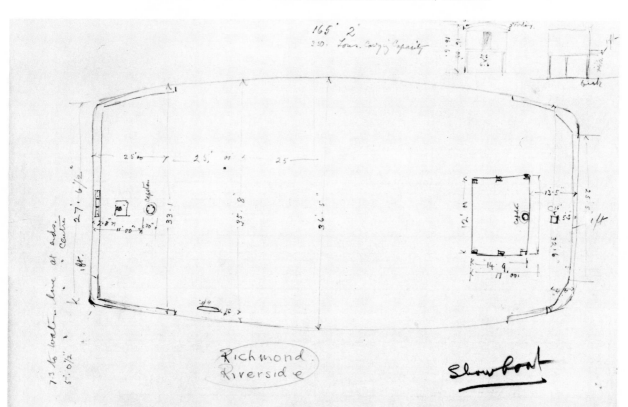

Snapshots taken by Knights Landing resident show neighbors dressed as extras. Note sun reflectors and (below) Harry Pollard's director's chair.

first feature to incorporate both songs and dialogue. Despite its enormous popularity and Warners' commitment to its sound-on-disc recording system, Vitaphone, the rest of the industry tended to scoff at the idea that talking pictures would ever last. Yet, on May 15, 1928, Paramount, MGM, and United Artists signed contracts with Western Electric for sound recording and playback equipment. Shortly after, Hal Roach and Universal joined the parade to sound. In addition to many part-talkies, Warners released the first all-dialogue feature, **Lights of New York** (Warners, 1928), on July 6, 1928. On September 19, the studio released the Al Jolson part-talkie, **The Singing Fool** (Warners, 1928), which at once became one of the biggest-grossing pictures of all times.

With the coincidence of **Show Boat**'s completion as a silent and the release of **The Singing Fool,** it was obvious that dialogue and musical sequences would have to be added to Universal's "Jewel."

Several months earlier, Universal had made arrangements with Fox to use that studio's sound-on-film Movietone system for its audible productions. Universal's hastily made all-talking quasi-musical, **The Melody of Love** (Universal, 1928), released October 1928, proved to be the first all-talking Movietone feature, predating Fox's own first all talkie, **In Old Arizona** (Fox, 1928), which was released in December, two months later.

While Universal frantically scrambled to improve its recording facilities, Negro soloists and vocal groups were swiftly engaged to supply a variety of atmospheric work songs and spirituals, including "All God's Children Got Wings" and "Joshua Fit the Battle of Jericho." The famous Billbrew Chorus, the Silvertone Quartet, and the Four Emperors of Harmony were among the groups engaged.

The task of supervising all the musical aspects of this and subsequent Universal sound productions fell to Joseph Cherniavsky, a young Russian composer who had studied with Rimsky-Korsakov. Early in 1928, Cherniavsky had been the conductor of the live pit orchestra that accompanied silent films at the Universal-leased Colony Theatre on Broadway. Whisked to the Coast, he not only had to coordinate the singing aspects of **Show Boat,** but also compose themes to fit sequences for which music could not be found by the studio's staff librarian, Nan Grant. His melody, "Love Sings a Song in My Heart," was used as a romantic theme throughout much of the film. Because Laura La Plante was not able to do her own singing, a popular Los Angeles radio singer, Eva Olivotti, was brought in to dub for her. Miss La Plante's banjo-strumming also was performed by a double.

In short, the activities at Universal in preparing an early sound picture were performed in utter chaos and confusion. And these conditions existed in every other Hollywood studio at the time, except for Warner Bros., which already had two years' experience in the sound business. The studios knew all about cinematography, editing, sets and costumes, and even a little about writing, but the use of sound threw the most experienced producers into a panic.

Not only did audible pictures require staff orchestras, composers, choreographers (for musicals), and singers, but the physical studio plants had to be entirely rebuilt to accommodate soundproofed stages. A host of new crafts were created around recording: microphone and acoustical engineers, record cutters (for those studios using sound-on-disc), mixers for controlling sound level and blending various sources, and, above all, the industry's newest tin god, the supervisor of the sound department.

At Universal, this role was filled by A. B. Heath, who was in charge of all Movietone work. Arch Heath had entered movies in 1914 to prepare promotional films for Woodrow Wilson's campaign. For years, he made serials at Pathé and comedies at MGM before coming to Universal, where he directed that studio's first, but instantly forgotten, all-talkie, **The Melody of Love.** Although **Show Boat** was directed entirely by Pollard, its sound sequences would come under the jurisdiction of Heath.

With their name derived from the popular medical fad of the day, sound sequences that were added to silent pictures were often called "goat glands." Like most surgical transplants, they were almost invariably rejected by the critics and public alike. Yet Hollywood felt that

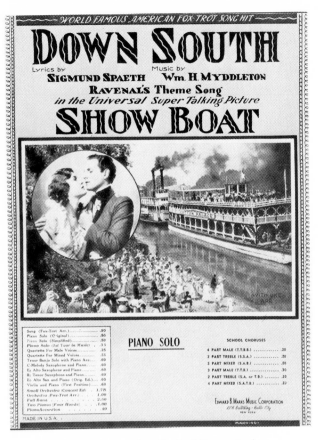

This song was used as Gaylord Ravenal's theme.

Universal's house publication heralded Helen Morgan's screen debut.

audiences were eagerly waiting to hear their favorite stars speak, so the addition of "goat gland" sequences was quite the thing during late 1928 and 1929, until the production of all-talking pictures became standard.

By late November 1928, Pollard and Supervising Film Editor Maurice Pivar had completed the silent and part-talking versions of **Show Boat.** The silent version was 10,290 feet in length, while the sound version, at 11,772 feet, was somewhat longer due to the addition of dialogue and songs. Computing the footage at the industry's standard of 90 feet per minute, the silent version ran 1 hour 54 minutes and the sound version 2 hours 11 minutes. Both had a 10-minute intermission.

It must be remembered that when Universal purchased the screen rights from Ferber back in 1926, no thought at all was given to sound. The studio had planned to produce a conventional silent picture. In the intervening two years, however, not only had sound movies arrived, but the world had come to associate **Show Boat** with the lovely songs by Jerome Kern and Oscar Hammerstein II. In fact, to the public, the work and its score had become inseparable.

Without rights to the stage score, Universal had been forced to rely on a musical hodgepodge that was bound to be rejected. With so much money already invested in this long, elaborate film, Laemmle decided his only course of action was to obtain from Ziegfeld, Kern, Hammerstein, and Ferber the rights to the theatrical version.

After several months of negotiation, a contract was finally signed on January 17, 1929, giving Universal Pictures worldwide rights to the theatre score and libretto for this filmed version of **Show Boat** and any possible remakes. The sale price was $100,000, to be divided among Ziegfeld (5/13), Kern (3/13), Ferber (3/26), Hammerstein (5/26), and their music publisher, T. B. Harms (1/13), in addition to 15% of net profits above $125,000.

With remarkable foresight, the attorneys actually included television among the various media through which the Kern-Hammerstein material could be reproduced on film. The exact phrase is worldwide rights, including "talking devices, Movietone, Vitaphone or other similar devices or by Television, radio or any other invention, device or recording apparatus for the reproduction or broadcasting of sound and/or pictures now known, invented or used, whether such synchronization and/or picture broadcasting device or devices be employed in the making. . . ."

There were a few restrictions. The songs and libretto were for the **Show Boat** property only, and the songs could not be used in any other Universal property. To protect the box office where Ziegfeld had arranged for the stage show to appear, the sound version of **Show Boat** could not be released prior to November 1, 1929, in Australia, or December 1, 1929, in Paris, nor could it be shown in Boston prior to September 1, 1929, nor in Chicago prior to January 1, 1930, unless the stage show closed in those cities prior to those dates. Edna Ferber retained the nonmusical stage rights, and television and radio rights for live performances. Further negotiations allowed Universal to utilize the services of cast members of the Ziegfeld production, which was still running after more than a year.

In anticipation of acquiring the musical-version rights, Laemmle had decided to precede the drama of **Show Boat** with an opening prologue, in which he and Ziegfeld would introduce musical highlights from the show with their original performers, accompanied by the Ziegfeld pit orchestra, conducted by Victor Baravalle. Even before contracts were signed, Heath was sent to New York to secure the Fox Movietone Studios.

At ten in the morning of Monday, January 21, 1929, rehearsals and filming of the prologue began. Ziegfeld himself introduced three of his principals: Tess "Aunt Jemima" Gardella and the Jubilee Singers singing "C'mon, Folks" and "Hey, Feller!" Helen Morgan singing "Bill" and "Can't Help Lovin' Dat Man," the latter with the chorus, and Jules Bledsoe and chorus in "Ol' Man River." Bledsoe also recorded other selections to be worked into the drama itself, including Nathaniel Shilkret and Gene Austin's "The Lonesome Road," which closes the picture. The prologue was edited to two reels by B. W. Burton.

Back in Hollywood, Pollard was busily re-

shooting as many scenes as he could to incorporate Kern music into the action of the film. For example, in the Joppers cabaret sequence, in which Magnolia first attains success by singing her river songs, her original selection, "Carry Me Back to Old Virginny," was replaced by "Ol' Man River." As she sings, images of the river are seen through double exposure; and the nostalgic effect brings tears to the eyes of the rough audience. Later, when she is seen in a concert, she sings "Can't Help Lovin' Dat Man." The moment is made particularly poignant, because the husband who has jilted and hurt her is seen watching her performance. In addition, Cherniavsky had to rescore much of the film to incorporate Kern music (particularly "Ol' Man River") as background themes.

For months, Universal had been promising that **Show Boat** would be "glamorous, glittering, glorious, and the greatest box-office property of the last decade." To bolster its barrage of publicity during the long stretches required to graft on "goat glands," the studio brought to Broadway an actual show boat acting company under the direction of Norman F. Thom, who humbly billed himself "the John Drew of the River." Thom's engagement at the Belmont Theatre began on January 21, 1929, with **The Parson's Bride,** the same melodrama depicted in **Show Boat.** The following week, the company from the floating theatre, *Princess,* offered **Shadow of the Rockies.**

Early in February, arrangements were made for Universal to lease Charles Dillingham's Globe Theatre for the New York presentation of **Show Boat.** Coincidentally, it had been in the lobby of the Globe, on the opening night of the Fred Stone show **Criss Cross,** that the meeting of Kern and Ferber, which eventually led to the stage version of **Show Boat,** took place. During Universal's negotiations with Dillingham, the stage of the Globe was occupied by **Three Cheers** (10-15-28, Globe), a musical featuring Stone's daughter Dorothy and Will Rogers. When the show closed, the house was wired for sound. It remained a movie theatre until its return to the legitimate under the name Lunt-Fontanne in 1958.

Meanwhile, Universal planned unusually festive twin world premieres for **Show Boat,** to take place Friday, March 15, 1929, in Miami at the Capitol Theatre, and Saturday, March 16, in Palm Beach at the Paramount, which, coincidentally, was designed by Joseph Urban. The premieres were scheduled to coincide with the close of the fashionable Florida winter season.

When it was learned that Kern and Ziegfeld would attend both screenings, and that the producer would allow Helen Morgan to miss all her performances from Wednesday, March 13, through the end of the week in order to be present also, all of Miami and Palm Beach high society began to schedule elaborate parties at private homes and clubs to welcome the illustrious visitors.

Five dollars top was a high price for a movie ticket in the South in 1929, even for a stylish premiere, but the Capitol Theatre was filled with its quota of millionaires and visiting celebrities, including Mrs. James J. Walker, wife of New York's mayor, Harvey Firestone, Albert Lasker, Arthur Block, W. C. Fields, Anatol Friedland, Joe Frisco, and many others.

After a delay, the manager stepped out and was forced to announce that the premiere had to be cancelled because vandals had broken into the projection room, kidnapped the operators, and smashed the equipment. After an impromptu entertainment by Miss Morgan, Fields, Frisco, and Friedland, the theatre returned $6500 to the disgruntled first-nighters.

By default, the world premiere took place the following evening in Palm Beach. Despite **Show Boat**'s unusual length of fourteen reels plus the two-reel prologue, the audience was warmly receptive. Similar tony opening nights were arranged for Salt Lake City, Dallas, Omaha, San Antonio, and other cities, in anticipation of the New York opening on Wednesday, April 17. In New York, opening night tickets sold for a whopping $11.00 top; and the film ran from 8:45 until nearly midnight.

The newspaper reviews the following morning were hardly enthusiastic. All agreed with Richard Watts Jr., who wrote in the *Herald Tribune* that the film is "a long, tedious and only occasionally attractive exhibit." Watts added "the director, Harry Pollard, must have thought

he was manufacturing great art, for he held onto his scenes, and to almost incredible length." Quinn Martin of the *The World* agreed: "There was no end of unnecessary, pointless material grafted into the running story, padding which neither sped nor smoothed the action of the narrative. This, then, may very easily be remedied, and when the Universal Company has torn into the superfluous, irrelevant, tiresome and bungling passages of the picture and eliminated them 'Show Boat' will be a picture more continuously holding, more steadily dramatic." With his customary lack of flowery phraseology, Sime Silverman, founder of *Variety*, identified the basic flaw: "execrable cutting." But, recognizing that the studio had the experience of several engagements prior to New York and yet failed to trim the picture substantially, he added, "it must have been a stubborn resistance to the necessary cutting that held back this most essential need." There is no doubt that the film was inordinately long. As finally released, the running time was 2

hours 6 minutes (11,300 feet on 12 reels), in addition to the 18-minute (1600 feet) prologue and 10-minute intermission.

As for the acting, John S. Cohen Jr. in the *New York Sun* felt "Laura La Plante, as Magnolia, aged gracefully, nobly, and often touched top peaks of emotion," a sentiment generally echoed by his colleagues. Schildkraut, however, fell victim to the infantile preparation for his most dramatic dialogue sequence and was accused by all the critics of having "overacted amazingly," in Watts' words. Mordaunt Hall describes in *The New York Times*, "there is a long and silly scene where Gaylord, after borrowing money, returns on a terribly rainy night much the worse for drink. He giggles and laughs ad infinitum, until one feels relieved when he falls asleep." Again, Sime recognized the poor editing and admitted "Schildkraut [is] quite all right when protected by cutting. He well did the dandified river man."

The most controversial performance was that

Centerfold of *Universal Weekly* (March 23, 1929, issue).

of Emily Fitzroy, whose Parthy was dismissed by Creighton Peet in *The New York Evening Post* as "a caricature." Cohen, however, felt "the mother was, on first sight, a caricature, but before long she projected a very real person." Alma Rubens,* in the brief role of Julie, was unani-

mously complimented and described by Cohen as "a forlorn figure."

The sound recording was generally received poorly. Peet writes, "not all of the picture talks—which is fortunate—for the recording is pretty bad." Hall adds, "the spoken passages are only fairly well directed. . . . Sometimes the incidental sounds are too pronounced, especially the lapping of the water as Gaylord and Magnolia elope from the *Cotton Palace*." Watts felt, "the talking sequences were written without the slightest gift for dramatic dialogue."

There were kinder words for the musical numbers. Hall commented on the "excellent

---

*A hopeless drug addict, Alma Rubens was committed by her mother on May 16, 1929 (less than a month after the New York opening of **Show Boat**), to the California Institute for the Insane, following an attack on her nurse and an attempted suicide. When the sheriff's deputies arrived, she stood on the porch of her home and brandished a butcher's knife until subdued and taken away. Although she was released several months later, Miss Rubens was never successfully cured; and she died on January 22, 1931, at the age of thirty-three.

1929—The First Film Version

Movietone rendering, supposedly by Laura La Plante, of 'Ol' Man River' and 'I Can't Help Lovin' That Man.'" Sime's observation is a bit more wicked: "Miss La Plante sang a couple of 'Show Boat's' song hits, and if she did, then perhaps the river was the Mississippi."

Although out-of-town critics were enthralled by the panchromatic presence of three top Ziegfeld stars in the prologue, the New York scribes were less enthusiastic. Peet wondered, "just what these movietone excerpts from the stage presentation indicate I am sure I can't say, but they seem out of place and not very well advised.

Can't the main film stand on its own?" Of course the Gotham critics may have been a bit jaded, for they were able to drop by any evening at the Ziegfeld Theatre and see the whole show in the flesh. While the regional critics scrambled for fresh adjectives to praise Bledsoe's "Ol' Man River," Sime commented casually, "in the prolog, Jules Bledsoe sings 'Old Man River' in perfect reproduction. Otherwise the prolog, made in New York, not so nifty in sounding or photography."

Despite the film's flaws, Quinn Martin admitted, "beauty there is in the motion picture 'Show

The *Cotton Palace* arrives in town.

87

1929—The First Film Version

Boat,' and the glamour of moonlit nights on the old Mississippi. It is this rich, romantic flavor of the silent river, this melancholy, haunting breath from out the deep mysterious waters, which makes Carl Laemmle's annual superfilm at the Globe a noteworthy and, for the greater part, a superbly managed picture play." Cohen, too, felt the "quality of sentiment, of poignancy, that the film projects in such an amazing degree. . . . Despite its faults, it is just about the best movie tribute that has been paid to 'Old Man River.'"

The film opens with the arrival of the show boat (renamed the *Cotton Palace* in the picture) and the pilot boat, *Mollie Able*, at a small Mississippi River community. As the calliope summons the townspeople, Magnolia as a child (Jane La Verne) dances gaily on the deck, her stern-visaged mother, Parthy (Emily Fitzroy), staring at her with reproach. Captain Andy (Otis Harlan) and the child then lead the band parade up the main street.

Inside the auditorium, the child is enthralled by the acting of Julie Dozier (Alma Rubens) and tells her mother she will be a great actress too some day. Parthy spanks her, and Magnolia runs

Typical show boat fare. Note the modest design of the auditorium interior as compared with later stage and screen versions.

Captain Andy (Otis Harlan) bids farewell to Julie (Alma Rubens) under the stern eye of Parthy (Emily Fitzroy).

to her room. A backwoodsman in the audience interrupts the show by demanding that a baby in the play be returned to its mother. Andy and the troupe are startled and amused.

During intermission, Julie comes to Magnolia's room to comfort the crying child by singing to her and hugging her. Magnolia says she wishes Julie were her mother. Just then, Parthy bursts into the room and shouts that she will not have her daughter corrupted by a "show boat trollop"; Julie is fired. Andy enters and escorts her off, while the child shrieks tearfully.

Time passes, and Parthy is seen paying off an actor whom she accuses of having made love to

Magnolia. Andy claims that this is the third leading man to be fired that season, but he has wired for a replacement who will be waiting at the wharf.

Looking through opera glasses, they see dapper Gaylord Ravenal (Joseph Schildkraut) tossing a coin to a porter. Although Andy notices that the young man's shoes are cracked, Parthy thinks he is not an actor but a gentleman and orders her husband to bring Ravenal on board. On the wharf, Andy tried to convince Gay what a fine Romeo he will make. When Magnolia (Laura La Plante) appears on an upper deck, and Gay learns that she plays Juliet, he needs no

1929—The First Film Version

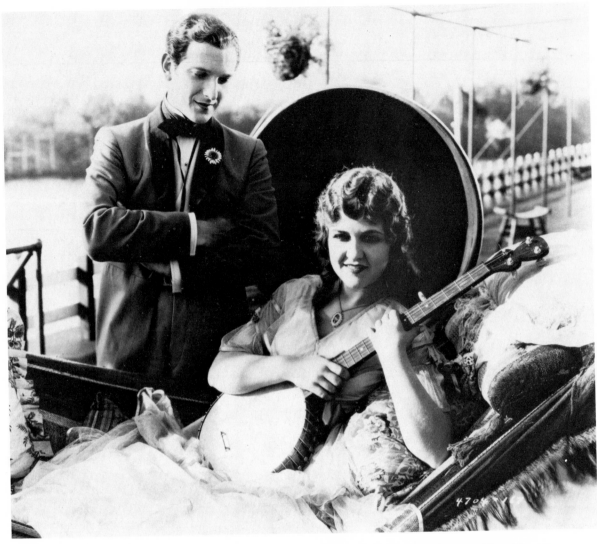

Ravenal (Joseph Schildkraut) and Magnolia (Laura La Plante) fall in love, as she sings "Deep River."

more convincing. He suavely kisses Parthy's hand, and she announces his salary at fifteen dollars a week, if he lasts a week. Alone with Andy, Gay confesses that he is a "gentleman gambler," so Andy agrees to teach him what he needs to know about acting.

With the moon shining on the river, Magnolia is seated on the deck, strumming her banjo and singing ("Deep River"). Ravenal blends his rehearsing a love scene with the real thing, when he is interrupted by Parthy.

A poster announces Magnolia Hawks supported by Gaylord Ravenal. On stage, she is singing, when the villain appears. Gay, as the parson, enters to enthusiastic applause. Every time he tries to kiss Magnolia in the play, Parthy grows increasingly irate and even tries to break into the scene, much to the amusement of the audience. Parthy fires Ravenal, but Andy, for once, vetoes his tyrannical wife.

Later, while Andy and Windy (Jack McDonald) stroll on deck, Ravenal enters and tells Magnolia that he has a minister waiting to marry them in town. Silently, they slip overboard into a rowboat, their elopement observed with amusement by Andy.

90

1929—The First Film Version

After a series of shots denoting the passage of time, during which Parthy yells continuously at her new son-in-law, there is a raging storm on the river. Andy brings aboard a doctor and announces to the audience that the river is rising. As the people all begin to leave swiftly, Andy learns that Magnolia has given birth to a girl. He calls to the departing townsfolk, "another leading lady."

The gangplank breaks as the crowd surges across it. Andy and Ravenal run along the deck watching, when suddenly a railing breaks and Andy falls into the violent water. Ravenal dives in to save him, as some men get a lifeboat to begin a search. Magnolia is in bed; when a sailor informs Parthy that her husband has drowned: she faints. When Magnolia asks about her father, Gay quietly tells her that he is sleeping after the storm. Contentedly, she falls asleep in his arms.

Another montage of Parthy's shouting at Gay indicates a nine-year passage of time. Gay, Magnolia, and their little daughter Kim (Jane La Verne) are leaving the boat. Parthy hands her daughter a draft for $20,000 but warns the girl she won't have it long—"that gambler will squander it." Parthy promises to write once a month and tells Magnolia to return when the

Hard times fall upon the Ravenals. Joseph Schildkraut, Laura La Plante, Jane La Verne.

91

money is gone. Sternly, the girl insists she will never come back. With Magnolia crying, the family leaves. Parthy stares after them and returns to the cabin.

INTERMISSION
TEN MINUTES

In turn-of-the-century Chicago, the Ravenals are driving in a carriage, when Gay points out the notorious madam Hetty Chilson. While her husband is off at a gambling emporium and hocking his prized Malacca cane, Kim and Magnolia wait in their smart Sherman House hotel room. Kim promises she will go to bed if her mother sings "I've Got Shoes." She does so, as the child dances for a moment and then falls asleep on her lap. When Ravenal returns without his cane, Magnolia learns that all the money Parthy gave her is gone.

There is a dissolve, and Kim finds herself awakening in a frowsy furnished room, which she says is ugly. Although Gay claims this will not happen again, there is a cut to a handwritten statement that he owes the Ontario House two weeks rent, $14.00, overdue. Gay enters to inform his wife cheerily that they are leaving and he has bought back all her "pretties." The sleeping Kim is again wafted to elegant quarters.

Gay buys a trotting horse, and the three go to the track to watch it in a race. All at once, the horse breaks its leg and must be destroyed: Kim cries hysterically.

Parthy receives a letter from Magnolia, who claims that all is fine. But we see the young woman in the old rooming house, as she sings "Coon Coon Coon" with her banjo. She puts her head down on the table and cries.

Gay enters to exclaim "the reformers are killing the game in this town." When he asks for Kim, Magnolia answers that she has placed the child in a convent school and plans to keep her there by going back to work as a performer. She has been hired by Schultzy (Neely Edwards) from the show boat, who is now the stage manager at Joppers, a cabaret with tables and a stage for entertainment. As they argue, the landlady brings in a telegram addressed to the Sherman House and brought over by a friend. Parthy will

be visiting them on Thursday, and they should engage a "moderately priced room" for her. Magnolia asks if Gay can borrow some money from friends, and he agrees to try.

That night, Magnolia has fallen asleep waiting for Gay to return. When Ravenal staggers in it is very late. Drunkenly, he refers to his wife and Hetty Chilson as "two good sports." He proceeds to laugh hysterically, as he hands Magnolia two thousand dollars. When he falls asleep on a couch, she stuffs the money into her purse and exits.

At Hetty Chilson's, a butler tries to close the door in Magnolia's face, but she demands to be allowed to enter. Magnolia is startled to see that Hetty Chilson is in fact her childhood friend, Julie Dozier, whose picture she continues to carry around her neck in a locket. Julie rebuffs Magnolia's embrace and denies her identity. When Magnolia returns the money and is shown out by the butler, Julie returns upstairs all alone and, looking at an old picture of Magnolia as a child, begins to cry.

Parthy has found the rooming house and delights in saying "I told you so." When Magnolia explains that Gay will return soon, Parthy shows her a letter she found when the landlady let her into the rooms. It is Gay's farewell note, expressing his feeling that he must leave because he is dragging his wife down. Magnolia is furious that Parthy seems actually glad to have him gone and claims that she will wait for him, even if it takes a lifetime. Haughtily, Parthy storms out.

At Joppers, Magnolia follows Little Egypt's undulating dance. At first, the unruly crowd yells during her song for the management to "get the hook." When Schultzy tells her to get back on the stage and sing the old songs as she used to, she picks up her banjo and begins "Ol' Man River." Visions of the Mississippi dissolve over the scene, as the misty-eyed rowdies begin to sob sentimentally. She is called upon to sing another number.

Following a success montage, we see Magnolia, smartly gowned, singing "Can't Help Lovin' Dat Man" on the stage of a huge Broadway theatre, while Ravenal, lost in the vast audience, sobs to himself. Later, at a distance, Gay

In the old rooming house, Magnolia (Laura La Plante) sings "Coon Coon Coon."

Julie, now known as Hetty Chilson (Alma Rubens), looks at a childhood picture of Magnolia and begins to cry.

Magnolia (Laura La Plante), in concert, sings "Can't Help Lovin' Dat Man."

watches Magnolia and Schultzy leave the theatre in the rain.

Parthy, on the show boat, now reads a newspaper that announces Magnolia's retirement from the stage after a long and brilliant career. As Joe and Queenie sing their old songs, Parthy envisions Magnolia as a child, dancing on the deck. The old woman wipes her eyes.

In New York, Magnolia reads a letter from Kim, now grown and married, that she and her husband, Kenneth, have decided to remain in France for another year. A telegram arrives to reveal that Parthy has died suddenly on the show boat en route to Cold Springs, Tennessee.

Magnolia leaves at once and is greeted upon her arrival by Windy. Joe is singing "The Lone-some Road." As Magnolia stands on the upper deck, images of her life pass before her. She turns to see Gay entering slowly and tossing his cane, a symbol of his gambling days, into the river below. Tenderly, he kneels at her feet, as the stirring strains of "The Lonesome Road" reach out across the river.

Charles Kenyon's scenario touches lightly on many key scenes from Ferber's novel but skims fleetingly from one event to another without ever taking the time for a situation or character relationship to develop. Magnolia and Gay have barely two scenes together, when they run off to elope.

Also, there is an excessive reliance upon coincidence throughout: the unexpected ap-

pearance of Ravenal on a wharf where an actor had been expected; the simultaneous birth of Kim and the death of Captain Andy; the twin arrivals of messages announcing a happy future for Kim and the death of Parthy; and the return of Gay after wandering for decades to the show boat at just the moment Magnolia should also return there for the first time in over twenty years.

Most extraordinary, yet curiously inventive, is the handling of the character of Julie (called Dozier in the film as in the novel). In this version, Julie is compelled to leave the show boat, not because she is part Negro, but because Parthy is jealous of the affection Magnolia as a child shows toward the actress: a plot twist intended to cater to southern theatres that might balk at booking a movie that dealt with miscegenation.

Instead of Julie's return to the story as a frail employee at Hetty Chilson's brothel as in the novel, or a drunken cabaret singer as in the musical, Julie in this film actually is the notorious harlot who services the wealthiest men in Chicago. In the book, Magnolia can hardly recognize her childhood friend, and in the musical she does not even know that Julie is the featured singer whom she replaces at the Trocadero. The reunion in this first film version, while cunningly contrived, is most affecting, with the audience's emotions wrenched first by Magnolia's showing Julie the locket, then her rejected embrace, and finally the image of Julie alone looking at Magnolia's childhood picture. Another

Magnolia (Laura La Plante), now retired from the stage, learns of the death of her mother.

95

After a separation of many years, Ravenal (Joseph Schildkraut) repentently returns to his wife (Laura La Plante) on the *Cotton Palace* deck.

creative touch is the use of the sleeping Kim to link the transition of the Ravenals from wealth to poverty and back again.

Although the scenario is so exaggerated that it is more melodrama than drama, the majestic sweep of the story itself, the quaint period costumes and settings, and the intensity of the romantic plot are all quite at home on the silent screen. Had **Show Boat** been more tightly edited, it probably would rank as a major silent drama. The problem seems to lie in the addition of sound in general, and the Kern score in particular, for the dialogue arranged by Pollard and Tom Reed and the awkward handling of the

talking sequences received the harshest criticism in the papers.

Heavy promotion on radio and in the press accompanied the film as it opened in one city after another, generally to warm reviews. Its distribution was widened in May, when M. Van Praag, the studio's general sales manager, announced that **Show Boat** would be one of the first eight features to be released by Universal with sound-on-disc (in addition to sound-on-film), for those theatres equipped for Vitaphone only. Repeating the Florida gimmick, Universal tried to arrange for every opening night to be attended by as many local members of society as

1929—The First Film Version

VOL. 29, No. 15   UNIVERSAL WEEKLY   11

"SHOW BOAT" SCENE BROADCAST TO TELEVISION FANS OF WORLD

James V. Bryson, Managing Director of European Pictures, Arranges Radio Television of "Show Boat" Scenes Over Station 2LO—London—Radiogrammed to Carl Laemmle in New York by R. C. A.

ONE of the most novel exploitation stunts ever accomplished was put over recently by James V. Bryson, managing director of European Pictures, when he arranged with officials and engineers of radio station 2 L O—London to broadcast a "Show Boat" scene to the television fans of the world. The scene shows Laura La Plante playing a banjo and singing "Ol' Man River." The broadcast of the photograph took place on a Saturday night at 11:15 Greenwich time on transmission 5 G. B. Daventry 622 Kilocycles 482.3 metres.

The stunt created big newspaper write-ups in London and was picked up in numerous countries on the continent. As it was impossible to photograph the picture received on the television apparatus, Bryson also radioed the same scene by R. C. A. to Carl Laemmle in New York City. An actual copy of the radio picture appears on this page. The mottled character of the photography, which somewhat resembles an old sampler, is due to the dot and dash transmission of light waves on the receiving apparatus.

This photograph of Laura La Plante playing a banjo as she sings "Ol' Man River" in "Show Boat" is an actual copy of the radio television picture sent over Station 2 L O—London. The stunt is typical of the modern showmanship characteristic of J. V. Bryson.

Universal Weekly (May 18, 1929, issue) proudly proclaims the historic British telecast of an excerpt from **Show Boat.** Revival playbills, before and after Ziegfeld's death in July, 1932.

possible, with advanced prices for most openings.

Other promotional points were scored when an ultramoderne 2000-seat seaside theatre was named the "Show Boat" in a New Jersey resort town. In Britain, the entire "Ol' Man River" sequence in Joppers was broadcast on television. In addition, the Rialto Theatre in Washington was reopened on April 22 after being dark for months, and the Uptown Theatre in Boston was entirely remodeled and renamed (from the St. James) on August 2, just for **Show Boat** premieres in those cities.

Despite Universal's vigorous campaign to sell its Jewel, **Show Boat** proved only a moderate success at the box office. It is perhaps the only movie to have been made in a silent version and two entirely different sound versions, although the first was never seen by the public. Its prologue captures on film three legendary Ziegfeld players at the very time their show was still running. It experienced what must rank as the most unusual world premiere in film history, and very likely it is the first feature to have been seen even partially on television.

1932
The Ziegfeld Revival

ALTHOUGH ZIEGFELD had produced five successful book shows in a row, **Rio Rita, Show Boat, Rosalie, The Three Musketeers,** and **Whoopee,** his fortunes completely reversed themselves during the middle of 1929.

He lavishly mounted J. P. McEvoy's **Show Girl** (7-2-29, Ziegfeld), which featured Ruby Keeler, Clayton, Jackson, and Durante, and Duke Ellington's Orchestra, in addition to a ballet of Gershwin's "An American in Paris," danced by Harriet Hoctor. The show lasted only three months.

In association with Arch Selwyn, he presented Noël Coward's elaborate **Bitter Sweet** (11-5-29, Ziegfeld), which failed after a mere 159 performances, having opened only seven days after the Stock Market crash on October 29, 1929. Other failures passed rapidly by: Ed Wynn and Ruth Etting in Rodgers and Hart's **Simple Simon** (2-18-30, Ziegfeld), Marilyn Miller and Fred and Adele Astaire in Vincent Youmans' **Smiles** (11-18-30, Ziegfeld), Harry Richman, Jack Pearl, Ruth Etting, and Helen Morgan in **Ziegfeld Follies of 1931** (7-1-31,

Ziegfeld), and Bert Lahr, Lupe Velez, and Buddy Rogers in **Hot-Cha!** (3-8-32, Ziegfeld). The last show, which opened during the depths of the Depression, had to be financed by mobsters, who seemed to be the only people with enough money to invest in theatre.

Not only did this overwhelming string of flops tarnish Ziegfeld's reputation as a producer, but his own personal fortune had been wiped out both through massive gambling debts and Wall Street losses.

By 1932, the once jovial man-about-town was broken in spirit and health and growing increasingly eccentric. Although seriously in debt, he continued to maintain a veneer of solvency, largely through the generosity of financier A.C. Blumenthal, who had married the Ziegfeld show girl, Peggy Fears.

The famed producer had been unable to adjust his own theatrical styles to those of changing times. Morrie Ryskind and George S. Kaufman's **Strike Up the Band** (1-14-30, Times Square), Kaufman and Moss Hart's **Of Thee I Sing** (12-26-31, Music Box), both with scores by George and Ira Gershwin, and Hart and Irving Berlin's

1932—The Ziegfeld Revival

Face the Music (2-17-32, New Amsterdam) had introduced to the American musical a new biting edge of satire, which seemed very much in tune with the rough economic times.

The critics had struggled to be kind to **Hot-Cha!** but were forced to concede that for all its physical beauty and the knockabout comedy of Bert Lahr, the show was sadly old-fashioned.

Ziegfeld's only hope for survival seemed to lie in reviving his most popular work, **Show Boat.** On February 4, 1932, Kern and Hammerstein each sent the producer a registered letter that in effect cancelled their contracts on the original production. On April 26, they signed new agreements with Ziegfeld, and the revival was officially born, although rehearsals had actually begun on April 18.

Due to hard economic times, the mortality rate of Broadway productions was high; and performers found themselves at liberty far more often than they might have cared for. Ziegfeld decided to take advantage of this by rounding up as many of his original 1927 principals as possible, with two major changes.

In place of Jules Bledsoe, Ziegfeld decided to use Paul Robeson, who had created such a personal triumph in London. Howard Marsh, despite a fine tenor voice, had been criticized as rather wooden in his acting. Dennis King, on the other hand, was an English dramatic actor who had made a startling vocal debut in Friml and Stothart's **Rose Marie** and followed this with a brilliantly swashbuckling portrayal as François Villon in Friml's **The Vagabond King** (9-21-25, Casino). For Ziegfeld, he appeared as D'Artagnan in Friml's **The Three Musketeers** both on Broadway and in London (3-28-30, Drury Lane, London). Although he was a high

"Show Boat" as Seen in Dress Rehearsal

Some of those interested in the production of the Ziegfeld revival superintend the last ultimate details of the presentation, with Charles Winninger going through his paces behind the footlights

Box Office Opens Thursday, May 12, 1932
Casino Theatre
Formerly the New Carroll Theatre
Seventh Avenue and 50th Street
Opens Thursday, May 19, 1932
ZIEGFELD PRODUCTION SHOW BOAT

COTTON BLOSSOM

SHOWBOAT

Music by Jerome Kern
Book and Lyrics by Oscar Hammerstein II
From the Novel by Edna Ferber
All Star Cast
Norma Terris — Dennis King
Helen Morgan — Edna May Oliver
Eva Puck — Sammy White
Charles Ellis — Aunt Jemima
and Charles Winninger also Paul Robeson
75 Glorified Girls   100 Jubilee Singers
Prices 50¢ to $3.00 no tax
Matinees Wednesday and Saturday, Prices 50¢ to $2.00 no tax
No Raise in Prices Opening Night
Mail Orders With Checks. Now Buy Your Seats at Box Office
Hot-Cha
Brown and Henderson Laughing Sensation with Bert Lahr and Lupe Velez
All Star Cast and 75 Glorified Girls Ziegfeld Theatre

baritone and not a tenor, King, as a fine singer-actor, was well suited for the debonair Gaylord Ravenal.

There were numerous changes in smaller roles: James Swift for Bert Chapman as Pete and Old Sport; Gladstone Waldrip for Jack Wynn as the Faro Dealer and Jeb; V. Ann Kaye for Annette Harding as the Sister; Evelyn Eaton for Eleanor Shaw as Kim the child; Pat Mann for Ted Daniels as the Man with Guitar; Gertrude Walker for Tana Kamp as Lottie; and Miss Kamp for Dagmar Oakland as Dolly.

Earl Carroll, one of Ziegfeld's principal rivals in the production of annual revues, had just built a glistening, moderne theatre on Seventh Av-

enue and 50th Street, just across the street from the Roxy. In an obvious attempt to outdo Ziegfeld's own theatre five blocks away, Carroll had spent a fortune on construction and opened with the **Earl Carroll Vanities of 1931** (8-27-31, Earl Carroll), which, with its reliance on low comedy and scantily clad show girls, proved as old-fashioned in its own way as **Hot-Cha!**

Although the show ran for almost 300 performances, Carroll could not meet his expenses, and the theatre became available for rental. With **Hot-Cha!** at his own house, Ziegfeld took over the Carroll and changed its name to the Casino. The original Casino, built in exotic Moorish design in 1882 and recently de-

molished, had been the home of some of Broadway's legendary musicals, including **Florodora** (11-10-00, Casino).

With no pre-Broadway tour, the **Show Boat** revival opened Thursday, May 19, 1932, at the newly dubbed Casino. To attract Depression audiences, Ziegfeld established a $3 top, with balcony seats scaled down so that 128 seats went for as little as 50¢. Matinees ranged from a $2 top down to 50¢. At capacity, the revival could gross $50,000 weekly.

According to *Variety*, Ziegfeld's payroll to his principals had to be higher for the revival, due to the increased professional standing of many of them since the original production. Edna May Oliver, who had become a great favorite in RKO movies and was granted a leave of absence by the studio, jumped from $750 a week to $1000. Helen Morgan's $1250, Eva Puck and Sammy White's $1250, Charles Winninger's $1000, and

Norma Terris and Tess Gardella's $500 were about the same. Dennis King received around $1000, a cut from his salary in **The Three Musketeers,** which guaranteed him $2000 a week against 10% of the gross. The greatest increase was that of Paul Robeson's $1500 over Bledsoe's $500 in the original.

Blessed by ecstatic reviews, all of which commented favorably on the addition of King and Robeson, the revival was off to a flying start. Week after week, it was the highest grosser on Broadway, which is very unusual for a revival and particularly one with such a low ticket scale.

For Ziegfeld, however, the success proved to be a last hurrah. In failing health, he left for California to be with his wife, Billie Burke, who was making the film **A Bill of Divorcement** (RKO, 1932). After a few days in her Santa Monica home, he was taken to Cedars of Lebanon Hospital, where he died of complications

Revival playbills, before and after Ziegfeld's death in July 1932.

The original 1932 cover for the first album of show music recorded in America. On the right, the 1941 Columbia repackaging.

from pleurisy at 3:45 in the afternoon of July 22, 1932.*

It is traditional for Broadway productions to lose business during the warm summer months. Early in July, **Show Boat** was affected by the

---

*It is a curious coincidence that at the time of Ziegfeld's death, Jack Kapp, recording chief of Brunswick Records, was producing the very first American record album ever made from the score of a Broadway musical: it was **Show Boat.** The set consisted of four 12″ 78 rpm discs, arranged and conducted by Victor Young. From the cast of the revival, Kapp selected Helen Morgan and Paul Robeson. Other vocalists were radio favorites, hired just for the album.

Recording began on July 20 with James Melton singing "You Are Love," followed the next day by Robeson's "Ol' Man River." On August 9, Frank Munn and Countess Olga Albani sang "Why Do I Love You?" Melton sang "Make Believe," and Helen Morgan, with Louis Alter at the piano, sang "Bill" and "Can't Help Lovin' Dat Man," the latter arrangement including an opening fragment of "Mis'ry's Comin' Aroun'." The album was completed on August 26, when Young and a chorus recorded an Overture and Finale.

Despite the set's historical interest, many of Young's arrangements are dreary, with a pretentious attempt to simulate symphonic importance. Morgan's vocals, for example, are more listless than her original February 14, 1928, recordings of the same selections, made for The Victor Talking Machine Co., during the early days of the original stage production.

CBS took over rights to the set in 1938 and on May 16, 1941, reissued it on the Columbia label with a new cover. In that form, it remained in print until supplanted by Columbia's original cast album of the 1946 Broadway revival. In 1974, Columbia issued the 1932 set on LP for the first time.

---

slump, so to keep the production going, the entire cast agreed to take a salary cut. A second cut a few weeks later trimmed the payroll by about 50%. By and large, this was an act of generosity toward the chorus people by the principals, who could have obtained other jobs.

Although attendance had dropped, the show was kept running by A. C. Blumenthal, who had taken over its management prior to Ziegfeld's death. His faith seemed justified, for the production continued to make money until its closing on Saturday, Ocotber 22, after a run of 180 (*The Beat Plays*) or 181 (*The Billboard*) performances. One of the big draws had been Edna May Oliver, who was forced to return to Hollywood, and had been replaced by Bertha Belmore.

Winninger had signed a contract to star as Captain Henry on the weekly NBC **Show Boat** radio series, sponsored by Maxwell House Coffee, to premiere on Thursday, October 6. At first, he planned to quit the stage show altogether, but he and Blumenthal worked out an arrangement in which he would be replaced by William Kent on Thursday evenings and would accept a cut in salary from $900 to $700. The conflict proved too taxing, however, and on

Monday, October 17, Kent was forced to take over the role entirely.

By closing night, Charles Ellis as Steve had been replaced by George Blackwood, Charles Winninger by William Kent, and Paul Robeson by Robert Raines of the Jubilee Singers.

Blumenthal decided to take the production on the road at once, with the assurance that Norma Terris, Helen Morgan, and Puck and White would travel. When the tour began Monday, October 24, at the Shubert in Boston, Paul Keast had replaced Dennis King, and Jules Bledsoe had resumed his original 1927 role. Tess Gardella was replaced by one of the Jubilee Singers, Angeline Lawson, the first real Negro to appear in the role in a Broadway production.

After two weeks in Boston, the tour began a series of one-week stays at the Forrest, Philadel-phia (11-7-32), National, Washington (11-14-32), Ford's, Baltimore (11-21-32), Nixon, Pittsburgh (11-28-32), and the Shubert, Cincinatti (12-4-32). Blumenthal had miscalculated the enormous expense in touring such a huge show and announced that, despite good houses, the revival would close after Cincinatti, on Saturday, December 10. It had lost $8000 since leaving Broadway, because of the need to gross more than $22,000 a week.

The only hope for survival was another salary cut. The original principals had run-of-the-play contracts and could be neither fired nor forced to accept lower salaries. Terris and Puck and White all refused. Actually, Norma Terris had come down with the flu and missed not only the final performance in Pittsburgh but the entire week in Cincinatti. Her part had been taken by Clemen-

Show Boat—

Gaylord Ravenal   Magnolia and Julie

Most New Yorkers have never had more than a fleeting glimpse of the Mississippi, but at *Show Boat* we feel that the region is homeland. Ol' Man River, though majestically indifferent to our troubles, is ours, and his children, white and dark, are our relatives and friends. It is this friendliness between the characters and the audience which gives *Show Boat* that peculiar quality of lovableness. In the present revival all the important characters save two are acted by those who appeared in the original production four years ago. The dashing gambler, Gaylord Ravenal, is played by one of the newcomers, Dennis King. But Helen Morgan as Julie still tells Magnolia (Norma Terris) that she just can't help lovin' dat man.

Elly and Frank

Joe   Captain Andy and Parthy Ann

Aunt Jemima

And Charles Winninger as Captain Andy still spats with Parthy Ann (the same Edna May Oliver as before, though now a movie star). Paul Robeson, who replaces Jules Bledsoe as Joe, fills the enormous Casino Theatre with his trombone-like baritone when he sings Ol' Man River (and the audience never gets enough of it). Eva Puck and Sammy White, the Elly and Frank, are (on this second seeing four years later there is no longer any doubt of it) two of the most engaging eccentrics on our stage. And *Show Boat* would not be quite what it ought to be if it lacked the refulgent smile of Tess Gardell's Aunt Jemima. Not since the days of the Bostonians have individual players in musical comedy been so identified with their parts.

tine Rigeau. Kent and Keast also missed performances from the near epidemic.

Although Puck and White had refused a 20% cut, they did offer to put up $10,000 for floating expenses and taking over the production on a cooperative basis. When Blumenthal refused the offer, they chose to withdraw from the cast, thereby allowing the tour to continue. They received a letter of thanks from the entire company for their generosity. The team was replaced by Harland Dixon and Peggy Cornell. Norma Terris and Jules Bledsoe were replaced by Margaret Adams and Robert Raines.

The troupe moved on to Cleveland but waited two weeks to rehearse the new principals and offer ailing cast members the chance to recover. Helen Morgan, the only original principal to stay on, decided to use the free time for a night-club engagement at Cleveland's smart Mounds Club, where she opened December 11. Unfortunately, the police raided the spot when a man claimed he was cheated of $40,000 while gambling.

When the tour resumed at Cleveland's Hanna Theatre, Monday, December 26, the Negro contingent had been cut from 60 to 16; the 24 show girls now numbered 10; and there were only 12 boys and 12 girls in the line. Salaries were approximately half that of the Broadway standard, and the touring ensemble, including crew, numbered 128.

Helen Morgan was given star billing when **Show Boat** played one week in Cleveland, one week at the Cass, Detroit (1-2-33), and three final weeks at Louis Sullivan's beautiful Auditorium Theatre, Chicago (1-8-33). A pro-

1932—The Ziegfeld Revival

From the **Show Boat** radio cast, Muriel Wilson, Lanny Ross, Molasses and January
(Pat Padget and Pick Malone), Annette Hanshaw, Charles Winninger.

A GALLERY OF CAP'N ANDYS

1. Charles Winninger—1927 Broadway
2. Otis Harlan—1929 film
3. Charles Winninger—1936 film
4. Ralph Dumke—1946 Broadway
5. Joe E. Brown—1951 film
6. Burl Ives—1954 New York City Center
7. Paul Hartman—1956 Jones Beach
8. Andy Devine—1957 Jones Beach
9. David Wayne—1966 Lincoln Center
10. Derek Royle—1971 London

 1

 2

 3

 4

 5

ANDY

 6

 7

 8

 9

 10

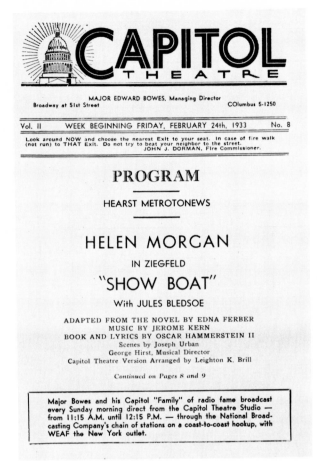

PROGRAM

HEARST METROTONEWS

HELEN MORGAN

IN ZIEGFELD

"SHOW BOAT"

With JULES BLEDSOE

ADAPTED FROM THE NOVEL BY EDNA FERBER
MUSIC BY JEROME KERN
BOOK AND LYRICS BY OSCAR HAMMERSTEIN II
Scenes by Joseph Urban
George Hirst, Musical Director
Capitol Theatre Version Arranged by Leighton K. Brill

Continued on Pages 8 and 9

posed tour through the South never took place.

Instead, Blumenthal made arrangements to have this lengthy and massive production cut down to a mere ninety minutes of running time and presented in tabloid fashion as a stage show that would accompany motion pictures in downtown movie palaces. The company would receive $12,500 a week.

Hammerstein's long-time assistant, Leighton K. Brill, was sent to Chicago to cut and restage the work, a bizarre and exacting task if there ever was one. Of course, the truncated story did not really have to make sense, because the public was actually going to see a movie, with **Show Boat** simply tossed in as an extra added attraction.

From Act One, out went the saloon exterior and the final wedding scene, and, from Act Two, the Ontario Street boarding house, St. Agatha's Convent, and the transition scene to 1927, with old Joe's reprise of "Ol' Man River." Many minor roles were eliminated: the Faro Dealer, Gambler, Landlady, Ethel, Sister, Mother Superior, Kim as a child, and Man with Guitar. The musical victims included "Life on the Wicked Stage," "Till Good Luck Comes My Way," "C'mon, Folks," "In Dahomey," "Hey, Feller!" and the reprise of "Why Do I Love You?" Remaining scenes and songs were trimmed, and the entire work was presented in one long act. At movie prices, however, patrons could hardly complain about being cheated.

Beginning at the Balaban and Katz Chicago Theatre on Friday, February 3, 1933, this curious tab show was seen playing four and five times daily, between screenings of Sally Eilers in **Second Hand Wife** (Fox, 1933).

The (no doubt) weary mummers trudged on to Cleveland, where they spent a week at the Loew's State (2-10-33) with Edmund Lowe and

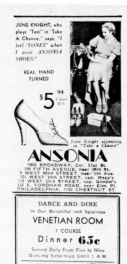
CAPITOL THEATRE

Program Continued From Page 7

CAST IN ORDER OF APPEARANCE

WINDY	PHIL SHERIDAN
STEVE	STONEY WAHL
PETE	JAMES SWIFT
QUEENIE	ANGELINE LAWSON
PARTHY ANN HAWKS	BERTHA BELMORE
CAP'N ANDY	SAM HEARN
ELLY	PEGGY CORNELL
FRANK	HARLAND DIXON
RUBBER FACE	FRANCIS X. MAHONEY
JULIE	HELEN MORGAN
GAYLORD RAVENAL	PAUL KEAST
VAILON	THOMAS GUNN
MAGNOLIA	MARGARET ADAMS
JOE	JULES BLEDSOE
BACKWOODSMAN	JACK DALEY
JEB	CHARLES SPENCER
LaBELLE FATIMA	DOROTHY DENESE
OLD SPORT	JAMES SWIFT
JAKE, PIANO PLAYER	ROBERT FARICY
JIM	JACK DALEY
CHARLIE—Doorman at Trocadero	J. LEWIS JOHNSON
LOTTIE	PEGGY STEBBINS
DOLLY	JOSEPHINE CONNOR
HAZEL	FRANCES STEWART
OLD LADY ON LEVEE	ELEANOR TIERNEY

SYNOPSIS OF SCENES

SCENE 1—The Levee at Natchez on the Mississippi—in the late eighties.
SCENE 2—Kitchen Pantry of the "Cotton Blossom"—a half hour later.
SCENE 3—Auditorium and Stage of the "Cotton Blossom"—one hour later.
SCENE 4—Box Office, on Foredeck of "Cotton Blossom"—three weeks later.
SCENE 5—Auditorium and Stage of the "Cotton Blossom"—during the Third Act of "The Parson's Bride"—that evening.
SCENE 6—The Top Deck of the "Cotton Blossom"—later that night.
SCENE 7—The Midway Plaisance, Chicago World's Fair, 1893.
SCENE 8—Rehearsal Room of the Trocadero Music Hall, about 5 p.m., 1904.
SCENE 9—Corner of Lobby—Hotel Sherman, Chicago, 8 p.m., New Year's Eve, 1904.
SCENE 10—Trocadero Music Hall, New Year's Eve, 11:30, 1904.
SCENE 11—Top Deck of the "Cotton Blossom," 1932.
SCENE 12—Levee at Natchez, the Next Night.

Continued from Page 8 and 9

MUSICAL PROGRAM

1.	Opening—"Cotton Blossom"	Entire Ensemble
2.	"Only Make Believe"	Ravenal and Magnolia
3.	"Old Man River"	Joe and Jubilee Singers
4.	"Can't Help Lovin' That Man"	Julie, Queenie, Magnolia and Joe
5.	"I Might Fall Back on You"	Elly, Frank and Girls
6.	"You Are Love"	Magnolia and Ravenal
7.	"At the Fair"	Sightseers, Dandies, Barkers, Etc.
8.	"Why Do I Love You"	Magnolia, Ravenal, Andy, Parthy and Chorus
9.	"Bill" (Lyrics by P. G. Wodehouse)	Julie
10.	"Can't Help Lovin' That Man"	Magnolia
11.	"Cake Walk"	Frank and Elly
12.	"Ol' Man River"	Old Joe
13.	Finale	Entire Ensemble

CREDITS

The entire production of ladies' costumes executed by Veronica Blythe and Charles T. Schneider. The men's costumes executed by Eaves Costume Co. Miss Adams and Miss Cornell's modern gowns personally executed under supervision of Ben Platt, Jr., through Corbeau Cie. All fabrics used in the production were executed by F. Ducharne Silk Co., Duplan-Coudurier, Fructus and Deschard, Bianchini and Stoffels.

Artificial flowers executed by George Legg. Shoes by I. Miller. Hosiery by Nat Lewis. Dancers' gowns in finale executed by Veronica Blythe and Charles Schneider. Show girls' gowns in finale executed by Bonwit Teller. Wigs by Hepner, renovated by Saul Cohen. Gentlemen's furnishings by Nat Lewis and Doyle & Black.

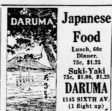

BARBARA STANWYCK
in
"LADIES THEY TALK ABOUT"
THE CAST:

NAN	BARBARA STANWYCK
DAVID SLADE	PRESTON S. FOSTER
DON	LYLE TALBOT
SUSIE	DOROTHY BURGESS
LINDA	LILLIAN ROTH
AUNT MAGGIE	MAUDE EBURNE
LEFTY	HAROLD HUBER
NOONAN	RUTH DONNELLY
THE WARDEN	ROBERT WARWICK
MISS JOHNSON	HELEN WARE
TRACY	DeWITT JENNINGS
DISTRICT ATTORNEY	ROBERT McWADE
MRS. ARLINGTON	CECIL CUNNINGHAM
BLONDIE	HELEN MANN
MARIE	GRACE CUNARD
MUSTARD	Mme. SUL-TE-WAN
DUTCH	HAROLD HEALY
BANK GUARD	HARRY GRIBBON

Based on Play by Dorothy Mackaye and Carlton Miles
Directed by Howard Bretherton and William Keighley
A Warner Brothers and Vitaphone Picture

Program Subject to Change Without Notice

Lupe Velez in **Hot Pepper** (Fox, 1933). Following a week of welcome rest, they opened on Broadway at the Capitol (2-24-33), accompanying Barbara Stanwyck in **Ladies They Talk About** (Warners, 1933). This pathetically emasculated version of the once brilliant Ziegfeld production, mercifully, played its final week in Brooklyn in the company of Lee Tracy in **Clear All Wires** (MGM, 1933), at the Loew's Metropolitan, from Friday, March 3, through Thursday, March 9, 1933.

The saga of the 1932 revival is of interest, not only because it proved to be the last production mounted by Ziegfeld, but because it exemplifies the desperate measures to which players and managers alike were subjected during the Depression.

In a way, Helen Morgan emerges as quite the heroine of this tale. Not only did she alone of the principals choose to give up more lucrative roles and nightclub engagements to remain with the tour to its bitter end, but her generosity toward her fellow players is amply documented. In addition to thoughtful Christmas presents for the entire company, Miss Morgan overheard aged Annie Hart sigh wearily after one performance. The veteran performer had always dreamed of having a chaise longue in her dressing room, ever since she saw that Lillian Russell had one. The star of **Show Boat** promptly went out the next day and bought a modern couch for Miss Hart's dressing room.

On March 25, accompanied by her mother, Helen Morgan sailed for Europe on the steamship *Paris* for a well-earned rest.

CHAPTER 5

1936
The Classic Universal Version

IN 1926, Carl Laemmle Jr. was hired by his father to join Universal Pictures as a writer on the popular two-reel comedy series, **The Collegians** (Universal, 1926–29). Junior later began to supervise their production and that of several features. In 1928, he was appointed associate producer and in this capacity produced the flamboyant screen version of **Broadway** (Universal, 1929). In 1929, Carl Laemmle Jr. was appointed general manager in charge of all studio production. Born April 28, 1908, he had barely turned twenty-one.

Despite opposition, Laemmle produced **All Quiet on the Western Front** (Universal, 1930), a daring pacifist drama told from the German point of view. The picture won an Oscar for the best film of 1930. Later that year, he mounted the ambitious all-Technicolor extravaganza, **King of Jazz** (Universal, 1930), starring Paul Whiteman and His Orchestra. Laemmle not only introduced the great Universal horror cycle with **Dracula** (Universal, 1931) and **Frankenstein** (Universal, 1931), but also championed glossy, sentimental soap operas like **Back Street** (Universal, 1932) and **Magnificent Ob-**session (Universal, 1935), the last two starring the beautiful and intelligent actress, Irene Dunne.

In August 1933, Universal announced its plan to remake **Show Boat,** possibly with Russ Columbo, the darkly suave radio crooner, as Gaylord Ravenal. In November, this project was cancelled. In June 1934, the remake surfaced again, announced for the 1934–35 season. In September, Carl Laemmle Jr. revealed that he personally would produce the picture, then planned for a January 2, 1935, starting date. Early in December, famed playwright Zoë Akins completed a continuity for the film and left for New York to participate in rehearsals for her play, **The Old Maid** (1-7-35, Empire). Production was pushed back to February 1, 1935.

Although Laemmle was dissatisfied with Miss Akins' continuity, Irene Dunne and Charles Winninger were both announced in January 1935. That June, it was revealed that **Show Boat** would be directed by the Englishman James Whale, who had first achieved screen fame with **Journey's End** (Tiffany, 1930) and had soon become Universal's pre-eminent director of horror

Announcement from *Universal Weekly* (June 29, 1935, issue).

Francis X. Mahoney, and Sammy White were signed to re-create their original stage roles. With Eva Puck now divorced from White, the role of Ellie went to Queenie Smith, another popular stage soubrette. Edna May Oliver was invited to play Parthy, but she declined, preferring to satisfy a longtime ambition to portray the Nurse in **Romeo and Juliet** (MGM, 1936), which was to be filmed at the same time. Her role went to Theatre Guild actress Helen Westley, who had recently made her screen debut in **Moulin Rouge** (UA, 1934). Hattie McDaniel, who had played Queenie in the first West Coast production in 1933,* joined those re-creating their roles for the screen.

The biggest guessing game in Hollywood was the identity of the leading man who would be selected to play Gaylord Ravenal. After dozens of screen singers had been tested and turned down, the role went at last to a young, classically trained tenor who was virtually a novice in movies: Allan Jones. After an early career in concerts, opera, radio, and recording,† Jones began to turn more to light opera. He played Ravenal for two weeks at the St. Louis Municipal Opera, beginning August 13, 1934. Jones made his screen debut in **Reckless** (MGM, 1935) and then made quite a hit in the Marx Bros. vehicle, **A Night at the Opera** (MGM,

films with **Frankenstein, The Old Dark House** (Universal, 1932), **The Invisible Man** (Universal, 1933), and **Bride of Frankenstein** (Universal, 1935). Although Whale had never directed a musical, his sensitivity and feeling for atmospheric detail made his assignment seem hardly improbable.

What did seem improbable was that Laemmle did not initially invite Oscar Hammerstein to adapt his own work for the screen, for Zoë Akins completed her third continuity on October 3, 1935; and, like two earlier versions, this too was dropped, along with her treatment for **My Man Godfrey** (Universal, 1936). Barely three weeks later, on November 1, Hammerstein's own first continuity was finished. On November 23, his completed screenplay was ready for shooting.

The third principal to be cast was Paul Robeson, who arrived in Hollywood in mid-November, following a series of concerts made during his westward trek. Soon after, Helen Morgan,

*The West Coast production was presented by (Edward) Belasco and (Homer F.) Curran, in association with Howard Lang, at the Curran Theatre, San Francisco, from Monday, October 30, 1933, through Saturday, December 2. This first California presentation of **Show Boat** was directed by Edgar J. MacGregor, with Pearl Eaton choreographer, and Herman Heller musical director.

Perry Askam, a West Coast operetta favorite, played Ravenal; and Charlotte Lansing, who had played Magnolia in the 1930 St. Louis Municipal Opera production, repeated her role. Most interesting was the casting of silent film star and former wife of Jack Dempsey, Estelle Taylor, in the role of Julie. Others in the cast included William Kent (Cap'n Andy), Cecil Cunningham (Parthy), Nina Olivette (Ellie), Billy Wayne (Frank), Kenneth Spencer (Joe), Hattie McDaniel (Queenie), and Freita Shaw's Etude Ethiopian Chorus.

Starting Monday, December 4, the production played for one week at the Mayan Theatre, Los Angeles, and then moved to the modern Hollywood Boulevard movie palace, the Pantages, where it played three performances daily without intermission from Thursday, December 14, through Wednesday, December 27. Both engagements proved disastrous for Lang, who had bought out his partners while the show was still running at the Curran.

†Allan Jones made his recording debut on an RCA Victor Red Seal album (M-138) as soloist in the Bach **St. Matthew Passion,** recorded by the St. Bartholomew Choir, March 23, 1932.

FRANCIS X. MAHONEY
as Rubber Face.

Paul Robeson with director James Whale.

113

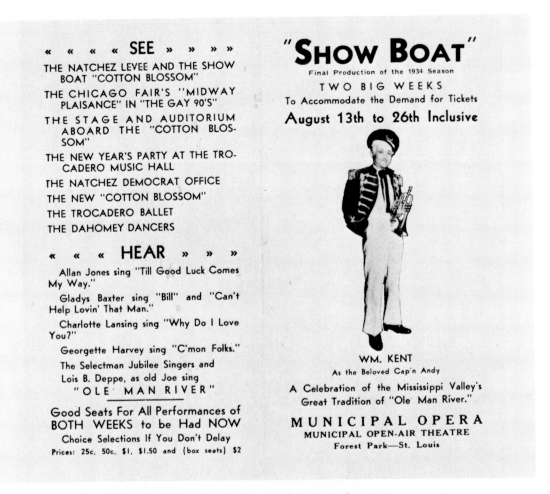

« « « « SEE » » » »

THE NATCHEZ LEVEE AND THE SHOW BOAT "COTTON BLOSSOM"

THE CHICAGO FAIR'S "MIDWAY PLAISANCE" IN "THE GAY 90'S"

THE STAGE AND AUDITORIUM ABOARD THE "COTTON BLOS-SOM"

THE NEW YEAR'S PARTY AT THE TRO-CADERO MUSIC HALL

THE NATCHEZ DEMOCRAT OFFICE

THE NEW "COTTON BLOSSOM"

THE TROCADERO BALLET

THE DAHOMEY DANCERS

« « « HEAR » » »

Allan Jones sing "Till Good Luck Comes My Way."

Gladys Baxter sing "Bill" and "Can't Help Lovin' That Man."

Charlotte Lansing sing "Why Do I Love You?"

Georgette Harvey sing "C'mon Folks."

The Selectman Jubilee Singers and Lois B. Deppe, as old Joe sing "OLE MAN RIVER"

Good Seats For All Performances of BOTH WEEKS to be Had NOW

Choice Selections If You Don't Delay

Prices: 25c, 50c, $1, $1.50 and (box seats) $2

"SHOW BOAT"
Final Production of the 1934 Season

TWO BIG WEEKS
To Accommodate the Demand for Tickets

August 13th to 26th Inclusive

WM. KENT
As the Beloved Cap'n Andy

A Celebration of the Mississippi Valley's Great Tradition of "Ole Man River."

MUNICIPAL OPERA
MUNICIPAL OPEN-AIR THEATRE
Forest Park—St. Louis

Flier for the 1934 St. Louis Municipal Opera production.

1935). On the strength of his latter appearance, he was borrowed from his home studio for Universal's **Show Boat** and was signed one week after shooting had begun on Monday, December 2, 1935.

In an endeavor to populate the film with **Show Boat** veterans, Laemmle borrowed its original conductor, Victor Baravalle, from MGM and brought its orchestrator, Robert Russell Bennett, from New York. John Harkrider, who had designed Ziegfeld's costumes, was not used in that capacity, because Whale preferred Doris Zinkeisen, an Englishwoman whom he had known. But Harkrider did provide the film's unusual titles: an animated display of paper cutout figures depicting dozens of townsfolk watching a show boat parade marching past. Little figurines carry overhead banners that contain the film's titles, and they pass the screen one by one to the offscreen beat of an actual brass band.

Although only thirty, Doris Zinkeisen was a major designer in England. Not only did her paintings hang in the Royal Academy, but, in 1935, she was given the honor of designing the Court of St. James's costumes for the Silver Jubilee of King George V. Her trip to America was being made on the maiden voyage of the *Queen Mary*, for which she had painted "Entertainoent," a thirty-foot mural in the liner's nightclub.

Danny Hall, who had designed sets for the 1929 version, repeated his task, although on a

far vaster scale than before. Five acres of backlot were transformed into a typical southern town of 1885. At one end sprang a portion of the Mississippi River, gouged out of earth by three giant steam shovels that worked for two weeks, and filled with water pumped from a dammed portion of the nearby Los Angeles River.

Although an elaborate publicity campaign was waged to explain that Universal had purchased an old show boat, beached and being used as a dance hall at Plum Point, Tennessee, the boat used in the film was a studio-made exterior only. The interiors depicting the auditorium and stage of the *Cotton Palace* were actually built in Stage Twelve. Universal's publicity department had invented a wonderfully fanciful story that, after

shooting the exteriors, a crew of carpenters sawed the "old craft" into thirds from the top deck down through the keel. The sections were then "lifted" to dry land and could be clamped together or separated, so that one or more sections could be used for filming interiors with the rear open to admit light and allow for camera movement.

Shooting began with the arrival of the *Cotton Palace* in Boonville (the name changed from Natchez), a sequence showing the excitement that the boat's arrival makes on a small waterfront community. There is a witty, briskly edited (Ted Kent, Bernard Burton) montage showing Negroes dancing on the levee, children running out of their one-room schoolhouse,

Cover of *Universal Weekly* (January 11, 1936, issue).

COSTUMES
BY
DORIS
ZINKEISEN

DORIS ZINKEISEN

carousers flowing out of a waterfront saloon, a horse running from its barn, and even a hog scurrying out of its pen, her nursing piglets following closely behind. Intercut are shots of the boat coming closer and closer, its calliope singing a siren song of welcome.

With the river scenes shot first, Robeson was the first principal dismissed; and he promptly left for London to continue his recital career. Instead of prerecording "Ol' Man River" in the huge voice that he normally used to fill theatres and concert halls, he chose instead to sing quietly, with the microphone only two feet away. This quasi-crooning interpretation imparts a gentleness that in many ways is characteristic of the atmosphere throughout the picture and, one might even say, of James Whale's overall vision of the material.

Before shooting began, Whale called together his principals, all of whom (except for Westley and Smith) had played in various stage productions of **Show Boat,** and informed them that the roles would be acted his own way, not necessarily in accordance with **Show Boat** tradition. Not only did this arouse some hostility at the time, but till this day, both Irene Dunne and Allan Jones feel that Whale was an inappropriate choice for director, primarily because he was English and could not understand fully the southern customs of the story.

While it is pointless to speculate on how the movie might have been directed, there is no doubt that, British or not, Whale's work is masterful. Perhaps more than any other musical film, **Show Boat** offers a completely accurate depiction of a bygone period. Whale manages to

1936—The Classic Universal Version

blend perfectly his finely crafted sketch of social mores, architectural and interior decor, costume design, and geographic atmosphere with the inherent conventions of the musical. Although he may have imparted a very personal tone of bittersweet softness throughout, Whale's exposition, sequence by sequence, follows Hammerstein's original 1927 libretto very closely until the modern-dress scenes toward the end.

Except for the abridgment of the opening chorus ("Cotton Blossom"), Act One, Scene One is played as on the stage. Following Andy's (Charles Winninger) ballyhoo and introduction of the troupe, come Frank (Sammy White) and Ellie's (Queenie Smith) "looking out to sea" buck-and-wing and the fight between Steve (Donald Cook) and Pete (Arthur Hohl). Whale transposes to the *Cotton Palace* deck the scene in which Parthy (Helen Westley) informs Julie (Helen Morgan) not to continue giving piano lessons to Magnolia or be friendly toward her, or Julie will be asked to leave the company. Ellie promptly seizes the opportunity to offer her own services as a leading lady, an idea that is laughed off by Andy.

The action then returns to the levee, where Ravenal (Allan Jones) saunters out of the riverboat *River Queen* onto the levee as he sings "Where's the Mate for Me?" Seeing Magnolia (Irene Dunne) on the second deck of the *Cotton Palace*, he at once begins to woo her with "Make Believe." As in the show, the sequence comes to

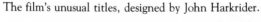

The film's unusual titles, designed by John Harkrider.

The town turns out to greet the *Cotton Palace*.

A good view of Universal's large outdoor set with the *Cotton Palace* in the distance.

Andy introduces members of his troupe. Sammy White, Queenie Smith, Charles Winninger

a stirring conclusion with "Ol' Man River," sung by Joe (Paul Robeson) and the stevedores.

Seated on a crate and leaning back against a piling at the river's edge, Joe calmly whittles on a stick while singing. The camera looks down at his right side from an angle of about 45°. In one unbroken, breathtaking movement, the camera smoothly arcs around and behind his seated figure a full 180° and moves in for a close-up of his face. By shooting first from the levee side toward the water with a corner of the *Cotton Palace* in the background, and then sweeping around and reversing his view with the camera above the water and the bustling levee in the background, cinematographer John J. Mescall provides a sense of authentic "place" that one rarely experiences in a medium as artificial as the musical.

Throughout the film, Mescall moves his camera gracefully around furniture in rooms, behind pillars in the rear of theatres, in and out of corridors, and in many other situations. By constantly shifting his angle of vision, he effectively suggests that the viewer is looking not at painted sets with only one side, but rather real places in a real time in history. Mescall's soft and sinuous

Setting up for "Make Believe." Cinematographer John Mescall is seated behind the camera, while James Whale, standing on the gangplank, leans against a piling.

"Make Believe," sung by Allan Jones and Irene Dunne. Note the bottom of the painted backdrop.

121

PAUL ROBESON
sings "Ol' Man River."

photography and Whale's delicate direction blend to create images of startling beauty and understated emotional conviction.

The action continues directly into Act One, Scene Two, the kitchen pantry, where Julie gives Magnolia advice on love by singing "Can't Help Lovin' Dat Man" and is joined by Queenie (Hattie McDaniel) and Joe. Irene Dunne's slack-jawed, eye-rolling shuffle dance is one of the unexpected joys of the movie.

Scene Three, outside a waterfront gambling saloon, is entirely omitted and with it the two songs, "Life on the Wicked Stage" and "Till Good Luck Comes My Way," both heard in-strumentally elsewhere in the picture. There is, however, a brief moment inside such a saloon, where the jilted Pete informs Sheriff Vallon (Charles Middleton), Frank, and Ellie about Julie's mixed blood.

Except for a few trimmed lines, Scene Four plays exactly as in the theatre. A rehearsal of **The Parson's Bride** is interrupted by Ellie's rushing in to inform Steve that Vallon is on his way. The miscegenation scene, the film's first dramatic highlight, is played with all stops removed. Steve's switchblade knife is produced in a startling close-up to the accompaniment of tremulous chords in the orchestra. And one can

fairly feel the incision as he draws the blade down firmly onto Julie's delicate hand to the horror of everyone standing around. Except for the change of Vallon's stage use of the word "nigger" to "Negro," the scene has been perfectly and hauntingly preserved on film, even to the black chorus' singing of "Mis'ry's Comin' Aroun'," as Windy (J. Farrell MacDonald) and the others swear that Steve has Negro blood in him.

The only slight change is that Ravenal is introduced to the troupe not by Frank, as in the show, but rather by Queenie, who breathlessly waddles down the aisle toward the stage to mention that a handsome stranger wishes to book passage to the next town. As in the show, Andy makes his daughter the leading lady and Ravenal, despite his claim to be a Tennessee gen-

tleman, her leading man. As in the show, the scene concludes with his tossing aside his script, kneeling at Magnolia's feet, and making more ardent Thespian love than Parthy thinks is proper.

In the play's Scene Five, Ellie sells a pair of tickets to the rough Backwoodsman and his friend Jeb. She and Frank discuss the sudden popularity of Magnolia and Ravenal as performers and console each other by duetting "I Might Fall Back on You." Parthy shows Andy Pete's letter with its promise to reveal something about Gay's past, and she is determined to visit Pete the following day, when the *Cotton Palace* stops at Natchez. The scene concludes with Queenie's ballyhoo, "C'mon, Folks," an attempt to rally Negro patronage for the troupe.

This scene is transposed to Ellie's dressing

"Can't Help Lovin' Dat Man," performed by Paul Robeson, Irene Dunne, Hattie McDaniel, and Helen Morgan.

Pete (Arthur Hohl) steals Julie's picture.

He takes it to Sheriff Vallon (Charles Middleton). Middleton, Sammy White, Arthur Hohl, Queenie Smith, Lloyd Whitlock

Ellie (Queenie Smith) whispers to Steve (Donald Cook) that the sheriff is coming.

Upon learning the news, Julie faints. Queenie Smith, Irene Dunne, Helen Morgan, Donald Cook, Charles Winninger

Steve produces a knife to cut Julie's hand. Helen Morgan, Donald Cook, Charles Winninger

Parthy orders Julie and Steve to leave the boat. Helen Morgan, Donald Cook, Helen Westley

Julie turns her head from Magnolia's kiss. Helen Morgan, Irene Dunne

Steve and Julie depart up the aisle. Francis X. Mahoney, Queenie Smith, Sammy White, Donald Cook, Irene Dunne, Charles Winninger, Helen Morgan, Helen Westley

Steve and Julie leave the boat. Paul Robeson, Donald Cook, Helen Morgan

Ravenal auditions for the company. Irene Dunne, Allan Jones, Charles Winninger, Helen Westley

room, where she and Frank again discuss the company's new favorite stars. They are interrupted by the moralistic Parthy, who breaks into the room and insists that as an unmarried man Frank must leave Ellie's dressing room at once. The scene is therefore cut prior to "I Might Fall Back on You," which is omitted from the movie score.

But the transposition to backstage does allow a smooth transition to a new love scene between Magnolia and Gay, as they go to their respective rooms, his on the deck above hers. Separately, they remove their make-up and costumes. She hangs her stockings on a line outside her window, while he, looking down, tenderly lifts one stocking with his cane and sings to it the film's new ballad, "I Have the Room above Her." The couple blend voices and then decide to have a secret rendezvous on the moonlit top deck.

This is followed by two surviving extracts from Scene Five, their order reversed in the film. First comes the discussion between Andy and Parthy about Pete's letter. This is followed by the comic scene in which the Backwoodsman (Stanley Fields) and his friend, renamed Zebe (Stanley J. "Tiny" Sandford), buy their tickets. Placing this scene last may seem a trifle, but it is an adroit way to set into momentum the *Cotton Palace* performance of **The Parson's Bride,** which immediately follows.

The humorous Scene Six follows without any change in text. It is here that Frank's dastardly behavior toward the melodrama's heroine, Magnolia, is challenged by the armed Backwoodsman, thereby forcing Cap'n Andy to step on stage and act out all the parts himself. At the conclusion of his routine, he introduces the olio. In the stage **Show Boat,** the act is a soft-shoe dance by Frank, now safely out of character. While this is taking place, the actress playing Magnolia is busily changing costumes for the next scene. As this problem does not exist in

ALLAN JONES
sings "I Have the Room above Her."

A wider view of the same scene.
Irene Dunne, Allan Jones

129

Veteran actress Flora Finch played a deaf theatregoer in a scene deleted from the picture. Charles Winninger, Flora Finch

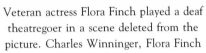

The heroine pleads for mercy.
Irene Dunne, Sammy White

moviemaking, the olio is changed to a special number for Magnolia. It is, of all things, a giddy coon song for Irene Dunne, who appears in blackface and a bushy, kinky wig, gleefully rolling her eyes, and accompanying herself on a banjo, as she struts through "Gallivantin' Around." The sight of the normally reserved and elegant Miss Dunne in a polka dot dress and blackface so startled and delighted 1936 audiences that, reputedly, this number led to her being cast in **Theodora Goes Wild** (Columbia, 1936), the first of her many major comedies.

The show's brief Scene Seven is a tryst between the lovers on the upper deck. As distant Negro voices are heard humming, Ravenal tells Magnolia he wants to marry her in Natchez the following day and claims that Andy gave him

the idea to do so. They sing "You Are Love." Except for a minor change in the dialogue, the scene plays as it does in the theatre.

Scene Eight in the show, set on the Natchez levee, opens with the first act finale, a joyous prenuptial celebration, sung by the chorus and culminating with the lilting "Happy the Day" refrain. As Gay and Magnolia are about to depart for the church, Parthy enters, armed with the information that Ravenal is a murderer. Vallon explains that the crime was committed in self-defense, and Gay was acquitted. Andy tries to top this by proudly confessing that he too once killed a man. Parthy faints, and the curtain falls on Act One as the wedding party march offstage.

Using camera freedom, the same scene is ex-

Irene Dunne sings "Gallivantin' Around." Sammy White, Queenie Smith, Charles Winninger, Helen Westley, Irene Dunne

1936—The Classic Universal Version

panded in the movie to encompass the large backlot set. Although "Happy the Day" was filmed and cut prior to release, we do see the wedding party, complete with show boat band, arrive at the church in carriages, surrounded by cheering townsfolk. Parthy arrives in time to attempt to halt the proceedings and, as in the play, learns of Andy's "sordid" past and faints. All enter the church, and we see the preacher pronounce the couple man and wife.

The lavish world's fair scene that opens the second act may provide a vivacious chorus number and colorful period vista, but its impersonality and considerable length draw interest

Irene Dunne and Allan Jones sing "You Are Love."

132

Magnolia's wedding day. Sammy White, Charles Winninger,
Irene Dunne, Allan Jones

away from the principal characters. For the film, Hammerstein improves tremendously upon his own stage narrative.

Following the wedding, there is a montage suggesting a passage of time, with Robeson's voice-over singing "Ol' Man River." The song ties Hammerstein's new scenes with life on the river. A storm raging outside causes the cancellation of a performance. However, the unconcerned Joe calmly continues to shell peas in the galley. When his wife rebukes him for laziness, Joe explains his seeming character flaw as a virtue in the wryly amusing new song, "Ah Still Suits Me," sung with Queenie.

Ellie bursts in to exclaim that Magnolia's baby is due; and she, Queenie, and Parthy will have to do all the work, because a doctor cannot be obtained in the storm. Joe quickly grabs a slicker and rushes off into the night to fetch a doctor, whom he rows back across the storm-tossed waters. This sequence not only provides the immensely popular Paul Robeson with an extra song, but, perhaps more important, it is a method of developing Joe's character and show-

Hattie McDaniel and Paul Robeson sing "Ah Still Suits Me."

ing the strength of which he is capable when necessary. Further, it is a view of the kind of happy and trusting marriage that our heroine is doomed never to know.

Possibly the film's most inspired dramatic scene is the birth of Kim, which follows. Although Magnolia's room is tiny and cozily lighted by hurricane lamps, and she is surrounded by her parents and show boat family, she calls out for Gay, who is absent. In the subtlest way, Hammerstein establishes that, although the company is always near when needed, her own husband is not. With the calm-

ing of the river the following morning, Gay arrives dapperly dressed and smug with his latest winnings. He is determined to remove his wife and take her to Chicago. Upon learning that he is a father, even this swaggering card shark runs to his fragile wife's side to comfort her.

The delicacy of this scene's writing and acting is enhanced by its remarkable visual detail. It is a small room, with simple, utilitarian furniture and a gossamer curtain around the bed, as any southern bedroom on a river might have had for protection against mosquitoes. The appropriateness of every aspect of this scene imparts a dig-

1936—The Classic Universal Version

Kim is born. Note the charming, authentic decorative detail. Gunnis Davis, Charles Winninger, Irene Dunne, Helen Westley

"Why Do I Love You?" sung by Allan Jones and Irene Dunne. With baby Patricia Barry

nity and credibility enjoyed by very few musical films.

In the montage that follows, we see the attractive young Ravenals enjoying Chicago's high life, paid for by Gay's winning streak. They live at the posh Palmer House (not the Sherman House as in all other versions), where they are dutifully saluted by doormen and servants; they always win at the races; and they even own one of those newfangled contraptions called an automobile.

With their baby Kim (Patricia Barry) seated between them, Gay and Magnolia go for a drive in the country in their dusters, caps, and goggles. Her feeling of gaiety glides into song as she begins "I'm walking on the air, dear . . ." He

turns and corrects her, "Riding." She continues to sing "Why Do I Love You?" with Gay, until the mood is humorously broken by the car's backfire. Only days before the film's opening, on May 14, 1936, the vocal was deleted to tighten the running time. It is still heard instrumentally in the background of the scene.

With resourceful indirection, Hammerstein suggests the change in the Ravenal fortunes. He might have shown Gay as broke and Magnolia valiantly struggling to care for herself and young Kim; there might have been arguments and melodrama. Instead, with utter simplicity, he changes the scene to the *Cotton Palace* deck, where Andy is reading Parthy a letter from Magnolia. It mentions that the Ravenals are think-

Ravenal bids Kim farewell. Elspeth Dudgeon, Marilyn Knowlden, Allan Jones

Helen Morgan sings "Bill." Charles Wilson, Harry Barris, Helen Morgan

ing of moving to a large apartment, because they do not like the Palmer House any more; and they are placing Kim in a convent school.

As if Hammerstein senses the audience's affection for Magnolia, he has created a tactful preparation for the next scene, which in the show is Act Two, Scene Two, the humble rooming house on Ontario Street. In the play, the Landlady, while showing the rooms to Frank and Ellie, offers a lengthy explanation that the current occupants moving out are a woman and her gambling husband, whose changing fortunes keep them shuttling back and forth between On-

tario Street and the Sherman House. The exposition proves redundant, when Magnolia is reunited with her friends and repeats the whole story. With greater confidence that his film audience will not lose the thread of his plot, Hammerstein omits the Landlady's (May Beatty) narrative, but keeps the rest of the scene intact.

In the play, Act Two, Scene Three is the Trocadero rehearsal sequence in which Julie sings "Bill," and Magnolia auditions for employment. Scene Four is Ravenal's farewell to Kim at the convent. Because the action of these scenes is simultaneous, rather than sequential,

Irene Dunne sings "Can't Help Lovin' Dat Man."

the order in which they are presented is conditioned only by a secondary technical concern: the speed with which costume and set changes can be made.

With these theatre conditions removed, Hammerstein has chosen to reverse the order. Immediately after Magnolia learns that Gay has left her and is reduced to tears, we see him similarly bidding farewell to his daughter (now played by Marilyn Knowlden). The melancholy of the rooming house scene leads naturally into the softly played convent scene, with its introductory choir vocal and its intimately sung reprise of "Make Believe," Ravenal's advice to his little girl.

Not only does Hammerstein thus dispense with Ravenal earlier, in order to get on with Magnolia's story, but the somber quality of these two scenes is sharply broken by the rinky-tink piano playing ("The Washington Post March") of Jake (Harry Barris) and humorously lumbering dancing of the chubby "beef trust" chorus line at the Trocadero.

Although slightly trimmed, the film's Trocadero scene follows the play closely. However, the character of the doorman (Clarence Muse), known as Charlie in the play and Sam in the movie, is slightly expanded. He is briefly introduced when Magnolia and Frank arrive at the cabaret for her audition. Later, while Magnolia is singing "Can't Help Lovin' Dat Man," Sam joins Julie in a conversation that does not exist in the play but adds considerable poignance to the situation.

1936—The Classic Universal Version

In the play, Julie simply steps out from her dressing room the moment she hears Magnolia begin her audition, listens in the shadows, throws the girl a kiss, and disappears. In the film, she explains to Sam that she used to know Magnolia, who was the "sweetest kid" she ever knew. She begins to speculate that perhaps Magnolia needs the job very badly, and that the manager, Jim (Charles Wilson), "never uses more than one singer in a show." Thus, instead of the audience's merely watching Julie's departure, we are allowed to share her decision to quit the club and presumably begin a downward spiral to drunken self-destruction as a sacrifice for her

Julie (Helen Morgan) silently throws a kiss to Magnolia and leaves the Trocadero.

Sammy White and Queenie Smith sing "Good-bye, Ma Lady Love."

young friend. It is an intimate moment, touchingly played by Helen Morgan, and made possible only through the flexible medium of film.

Scenes Five and Six, the lobby of the Sherman House and the Trocadero on New Year's Eve, though slightly trimmed, play almost the same onscreen as onstage. Parthy and Andy, having come to the hotel, learn that the young people no longer live there. When Parthy retires to her room, Andy finds himself with three little cuties (Dorothy Granger, Barbara Pepper, Renee Whitney), whom he escorts to the cabaret.

At the Trocadero, Andy watches Frank and Ellie perform their nimble cakewalk to "Good-

bye, Ma Lady Love" and "At a Georgia Camp Meeting." Frank joins the captain and tells him that Gay has left Magnolia, who is making her debut this very evening. When the nervous young lady's rendition of "After the Ball" begins to falter, Andy rises from his table and urges her to conquer her fear by smiling; and she is triumphant.

From this point to the end, the film's narrative is entirely original. Outside the Knickerbocker Theatre, where Magnolia is starring on Broadway, a British producer (E. E. Clive) tells Andy (now dapperly dressed in evening clothes) that his daughter is the finest artist on the New

York stage; and the producer wants her for his play in the spring. Thus we see Magnolia's name in lights on the marquee of London's His Majesty's Theatre.

With the freedom of film to suggest the passage of many years, Hammerstein could offer his director many ways to depict the theatrical rise of Magnolia and her daughter as well. In a rough first-cut of the film, Whale shot the old *Cotton Palace* tied to the shore, its paint peeling, while a modern speedboat whizzes down the river. Aging Joe and Queenie sit in front of their retirement shack, while he sings a brief reprise of "Ol' Man River." A montage of headlines and martial music herald World War One. Magnolia and Andy are seen distributing coffee and doughnuts to the boys at the front. When an officer mentions that he has been a fan of hers for years,

Magnolia produces a letter in which Kim (now being played by Sunnie O'Dea) says she has obtained a small part in her first Broadway show. The scene shifts to backstage in a Broadway theatre. Kim goes on and stumbles over her lines, but she is later reassured by Parthy, who is waiting in the wings. Then, in a luxurious apartment, we see silver-haired Magnolia playing "An Old Fashioned Wife" on the piano and making critical comments about Kim's vocal interpretation.

Kim becomes a success and, in an interview in her limousine, tells a female reporter that she owes everything to her family but has packed them off to Europe until the opening night of her new show. During one of her rehearsals, the theatre manager angrily berates a white-haired backstage doorman for leaving his post and

"Smile, Nola!"
Barbara Pepper, Renee Whitney, Sammy White, Charles Winninger, Arthur Housman

IRENE DUNNE
sings "After the Ball."

Irene Dunne sings "Can't Help
Lovin' Dat Man" in a concert
sequence deleted from the film.

Old Joe (Paul Robeson) and Queenie (Hattie McDaniel) in retirement. A scene cut from the film.

Magnolia (Irene Dunne) reads Andy (Charles Winninger) a letter from Kim, while the two are serving in World War One. A scene cut from the film.

Kim (Sunnie O'Dea) rehearses for Broadway with dance director LeRoy Prinz.

watching the performers. The doorman proves to be Ravenal, now known to the company as "Pop."

Opening night finally arrives, and Kim goes on in a glamorized version of what is billed as the same number her mother used to perform years before on the show boat. The family's attendance is delayed, however, because the ocean liner on which they are returning is slowed down in the harbor by a pea-soup fog. When it finally docks, a police escort is required to get Magnolia, Andy, and Parthy to the theatre, just in time to watch Kim's routine. In the corridor outside their box, Magnolia suddenly sees Gay and invites him to join the family, much to the consternation of the manager who has just fired Ra-

venal for deserting his stage door. The reunited couple proudly gaze down from the box, as their daughter carries on the family's theatrical tradition. The screenplay concludes with a shot of the Mississippi and the off-screen voice of Joe singing a final reprise of "Ol' Man River."

According to Universal publicity releases, James Whale was faced with cutting 300,000 feet of film (55 hours, 33 minutes) down to manageable length. Although this length seems somewhat exaggerated (to say the least), there is no doubt that as shot **Show Boat** was far too long to be released without massive cutting. In addition to the elimination of "Happy the Day" and "Why Do I Love You?" already mentioned, the modern-dress section of the film underwent

enormous change. The passage of time, suggested by the moored show boat, aging Joe and Queenie, and the world war scenes were replaced by the simple device of seeing a pair of male hands (obviously Ravenal's) pasting clippings into a scrapbook. The articles, programs, and ads chronicle both Magnolia's stardom and Kim's rise in billing.

The release print does retain Kim's brief vocal lesson built around the 1917 Kern song, "An Old Fashioned Wife," but the female reporter (Helen Jerome Eddy) now interviews Kim backstage during a rehearsal, rather than in a limousine. Thus the girl's rise to fame does not seem so improbably rapid.

Basically, the incidents relating to the opening night remain the same, except from a musical point of view. In the screenplay's early draft, Magnolia, during her blackface olio, had sung a flirtatious duet with Frank called "Got My Eye on You." By the time shooting had begun, this was replaced with "Gallivantin' Around." Because Kim's opening night routine is a re-creation of her mother's big show boat hit, the song had to be switched in the finale too. Thus "Got My Eye on You," like the songs deleted from the show prior to Broadway, joins the Kern-Hammerstein catalogue of forgotten **Show Boat** literature. The fifth song the team composed for the film, "Negro Peanut Vender's

SUNNIE O'DEA
in a musical sequence deleted from the film.

744-P-113

Ravenal and Magnolia are reunited on Kim's opening night. Allan Jones, Helen Westley, Charles Winninger, Forrest Stanley, Irene Dunne

Street Cry," did not survive even into the first draft of the screenplay.

As originally shot, "Gallivantin' Around" was an elaborate finale and depicted in somewhat rudimentary fashion the Negro influence on popular dancing. The curtain rises to reveal stage right the façade of a southern mansion. Kim, in a voluminous ante-bellum hoop skirt, appears and sings "Gallivantin' Around." She is joined by a group of young gentlemen and ladies who whirl through the graceful waltz steps of the 1860's, while a contingent of Negroes bounds somewhat more energetically into several folk steps, including clogs, taps, and sand dances.

The stage revolves to reveal a highly stylized set that depicts two contrasting street views of modern Manhattan night life. On stage right is a suggestion of a downtown nightclub, where Kim leads the white dancers in fashionable rumbas and fox trots. On stage left is a big sign reading "Heart of Harlem." Beneath it, the Negroes gyrate wildly to the Big Apple, Suzy Q, and Trucking. The stage finally revolves back to the original setting, and Kim, once more in her

hoopskirt, steps forward to announce that the public has now seen her mother's song performed both the old and new way.

By the time **Show Boat** was released, the finale was shorn of Kim's vocal, much of the Negro nineteenth-century dancing, and the entire modern sequence. Without these livelier sections for contrast, what remains is a rather overlong and listless depiction of the dainty steps of Kim and her friends in period costume; and it is hard to understand why the audience depicted in the film rises to acclaim the young girl with such fervor.

Perhaps the reason for cutting this finale was the last-minute addition of a reprise of "You Are Love" for the reunited Ravenal and Magnolia, now standing arm in arm and providing a spontaneous encore for Kim's first-nighters. This reprise was such an afterthought that it does not appear even in the final shooting script.

If it had been Hammerstein's intention to use the triumph of Kim's first night as a symbolic

The *Cotton Palace* family reunited once more. Helen Westley, Irene Dunne, Allan Jones, Charles Winninger

Kim (Sunnie O'Dea) and the dancing ensemble in a finale that traces
the development of jazz dance from the southern plantation to modern
times. The plantation scenes are shown in the order in which they appear
in the film. Because the entire modern sequence was cut out prior to
release, the stills depicting that portion of the finale may not be presented
in the proper order.

device to reunite her parents, the effect is thrown wildly off balance, first, by what little we see of her in performance and, second, by the emphasis turning back to her parents from her. In a way, the whole design of the film is weakened both by Kim's failure through harsh cutting to impress us, and by the overlong modern section of the movie itself, which tends to coarsen the delicate texture of the earlier period scenes.

As in the stage original, this film version is brilliant right up through Magnolia's success at the Trocadero. The modern scenes and the return of Ravenal, though presented in circumstances entirely different from those of the play, are equally trivial in conception. In a work in which genuine emotion and credible situations are a particular strength, it is almost laughable that old "Pop" should turn out to be the leading lady's long-lost father; and that he should just happen to be standing in a corridor outside Magnolia's box just in time for a weepy reunion. It is clear that there is simply no logical way for Ravenal to return. He should leave Magnolia and never reappear, as in the novel. This would enhance her stature as a heroine and underscore the implied theme that those who live on the river draw strength from it.

As Magnolia, Irene Dunne found one of the great roles of her career. Her gradual development from youthful innocence, through the emotional maturing forced upon her by Ravenal's irresponsibility, to dignified middle age is shaded skillfully and with great tenderness. The range of her vocals too, from a raucous coon song to the most sedate love ballads, affirms her position as one of the pre-eminent stars of musical film. Not only had Miss Dunne appeared in

Caricature of Jerome Kern by
William Auerbach-Levy.

Allan Jones relaxes on the set with producer Carl Laemmle, Jr.

two Kern shows on stage, but she became his most prolific screen interpreter. Prior to **Show Boat,** she made the film versions of **Sweet Adeline** (Warners, 1934) and **Roberta** (RKO, 1935). Later, Kern composed original scores for **High, Wide and Handsome** (Paramount, 1937) and **Joy of Living** (RKO, 1938).

Although Whale directed Allan Jones in a manner that is perhaps too demonstrably emotional for a real riverboat gambler, whose professional success depends upon masking his real feelings, the interpretation is entirely consistent with the director's near poetic vision of nineteenth-century America.

Though Dunne and Jones still feel that Whale's British heritage made him the wrong choice for director, this may be the film's greatest asset. With the objectivity of a foreigner, Whale maintains the aesthetic distance to see the simple love story as an almost mythic epic of a period and a time. And Allan Jones, with his sensitive features, flowing golden locks,

and pure tenor voice, photographed often against the sky and other striking backgrounds, is transmuted from a mere riverboat gambler to a dashing love object that could easily sweep the naïve young Magnolia off her feet.

If this picture had no other virtues, it would find its place in screen history for preserving the legendary stage performances of Charles Winninger and Helen Morgan.

Winninger's feisty sparkle, reaching its comic heights when he plays all the parts in **The Parson's Bride,** his memorable tipsy cry of "Ha-a-a-a-apy New Year," and the soft-spoken strength with which he continually pacifies his wife and assumes command of the troupe and his family are joyously blended in one of the most impressive performances in musical theatre and film literature.

While Winninger has a chance to dominate by appearing throughout the entire story of **Show Boat,** Helen Morgan succeeds in haunting the whole action in just a few brief scenes that

total barely twenty minutes in a film that runs nearly two hours. Like a wounded bird, Miss Morgan's presence suggests a beauty that has been spoiled. Her long years of brandy addiction show painfully on her puffy face and limp expression. She is a lost and lonely victim and as such elicits a swelling of compassion from the viewer, who wants to reach out to the screen and protect her.

Helen Morgan never made a film after **Show Boat.** Following a few embarrassingly insignificant road shows and several nightclub stints, she died on October 8, 1941, at the age of forty-one. At the height of her career, she possessed neither great beauty nor a strong singing voice. Yet Helen Morgan will always be remembered as one of the most brilliantly gifted musical performers of the twentieth century.

On November 1, 1935, the very day that Oscar Hammerstein completed his first continuity script for **Show Boat,** Uncle Carl Laemmle succumbed to the financial troubles that had plagued Universal for years. Unlike Fox, MGM, and Paramount, Universal had no theatre chains of its own to assure bookings of the studio's product. Universal had made its money by supplying the "B" films that filled out the second half of neighborhood double bills.

When Junior took over control of production in 1929, he began to shift the emphasis toward large, expensive, prestigious pictures, many of which lost thousands of dollars. For every **Back Street** came a dozen **Sutter's Gold**s (Universal, 1936).

On that fateful November 1, an eastern combine of businessmen, calling themselves the Standard Capital Company, took an option to buy Uncle Carl's controlling interest in Universal. On March 14, 1936, the group paid more than $1,500,000 to exercise their option; and on Thursday, April 2, 1936, the transaction was completed with another payment of $4,000,000.

On that day, the new board of directors of Universal Corporation and Universal Pictures Company elected J. Cheever Cowdin chairman, R. H. Cochrane president, and Charles R. Rogers executive vice president in charge of production. Cochrane had been a close friend and associate of Uncle Carl's since their Chicago days in 1906, and since 1922 he had been a Universal vice president.

Carl Laemmle Jr. retired from the company effective with the first public preview of his film **Show Boat.** This took place late in April at the Alexander Theatre in Glendale. Although only one week shy of his twenty-eighth birthday, Junior, despite his imagination and showmanship, was never to produce another motion picture. His father, one of Hollywood's most beloved figures, died on September 23, 1939.

When **Show Boat** opened at the Radio City Music Hall on Thursday, May 14, 1936, it received rapturous reviews. In the May 20 issue of *Variety*, editor Abel Green commented on the passing from Universal of Laemmle senior and junior. Never at a loss for a sharp phrase, Green called **Show Boat** "a fitting valedictory in celluloid."

CHAPTER 6

1946
The Post-War Revival

THE DOZEN years following the 1932 revival saw the end of the Depression and a global war that tested the endurance of Western civilization. By late 1945, life in America was returning to normal, but normal was new.

In the theatre, too, there were innovations that made musicals of the 1920's seem as antique as the Model A Ford. The operetta, that rich amalgam of romantic story and florid music, often with a strong middle-European flavor, had become all but extinct. Even the light-hearted musical comedy that combined catchy tunes, pretty girls, and a plot as transparent and fragile as cellophane was definitely on the wane.

The musical was growing up. **Of Thee I Sing** and **Face the Music** had helped to popularize topical satire in book shows. Kern and Hammerstein's **Music in the Air** (11-8-32, Alvin) demonstrated that even in a romantic musical every note of the score could be inextricably intertwined with the story. The production was presented by Peggy Fears, who, through her husband A. C. Blumenthal, had inherited the property from the Ziegfeld estate. Rodgers and Hart's

On Your Toes (4-11-36, Imperial), with choreography by George Balanchine, was one of an increasing number of shows that incorporated ballet as a strong construction element.

Hammerstein's collaboration with Richard Rodgers on **Oklahoma!** (3-31-43, St. James) and **Carousel,** (4-19-45, Majestic) ushered in a new era for the musical theatre. In these and other musicals of the mid-1940's, the story itself shaped the style and final form of the work. No longer was it necessary to have an opening chorus or even a happy ending in the traditional sense. In both works, leading characters are permitted to die, a plot feature unthinkable in 1927, when convention prevented Ravenal from disappearing, as in the Ferber novel. The phrase "musical comedy" was slowly going out of fashion, to be replaced by the seemingly more mature "musical play."

It was in 1945, during this time of change in musical theatre, that Kern and Hammerstein decided to revive **Show Boat,** although the two were separated by three thousand miles. Hammerstein was enjoying the most rewarding days of his Broadway career, while Kern was basking

154

in the Beverly Hills sun and turning out one successful movie score after another. His most recent films were the Technicolored **Cover Girl** (Columbia, 1944), in which exquisite Rita Hayworth (with the dubbed voice of Martha Mears) and Gene Kelly introduced "Long Ago and Far Away," and **Can't Help Singing** (Universal, 1944) with Deanna Durbin.

Leaving for Hollywood on Monday, September 10, 1945, and arriving back in New York on Sunday, September 16, Hammerstein spent a week with his partner to collaborate on "Nobody Else But Me," a new song for the second act, to look for casting possibilities, and to discuss with MGM the studio's financing of the revival. MGM had purchased the screen rights for **Show Boat** from Universal in 1938, and a projected remake had become a frequent topic of conversation in the Culver City studio as far back as 1942. If the revival proved popular, its success could provide the extra incentive that MGM needed in deciding to refilm the property.

The production was budgeted at $230,000 (an unusually high amount for that period), which eventually swelled by opening night to around $275,000. MGM provided 75% of the backing, in addition to three contract players for leading roles.

Jan Clayton was a promising ingenue on the studio lot, when producer Samuel Marx cast her in a supporting role in **This Man's Navy** (MGM, 1945), starring Wallace Beery. She was loaned to The Theatre Guild to make an auspicious Broadway debut as Julie Jordan in **Carousel.** Despite her great acclaim in the part, she was expected to report back to MGM on January 1, 1946, to star in another Samuel Marx picture, **Jenny Was a Lady,** based on the career of Nellie Bly, the female journalist who, in 1889, circled the globe in imitation of Jules Verne's fictional Phileas Fogg. The film was to be an elaborate one, directed by S. Sylvan Simon, with action that required the use of one song to be sung by Miss Clayton.

Around October, Kern bounded into Marx's office and said that, if the studio would allow Jan Clayton to delay her return to Hollywood and appear in **Show Boat** as Magnolia for just the first thirteen weeks of its run, he and Hammer-

Souvenir program cover.

stein would write the necessary song without charge. When Marx protested that MGM had plenty of money, Kern asked him if he had a dollar in his pocket. Marx produced the bill, which Kern took: he smiled and added, "Now I owe you a song."

With his latest film, **Centennial Summer** (20th Century-Fox, 1946), completed, and his screen biography, **Till the Clouds Roll By** (MGM, 1946), well under way, Jerome Kern arrived in New York on Friday, November 2, 1945. Not only had he come about the **Show Boat** revival, but he had agreed to compose the score for a new musical (with lyrics by Dorothy Fields) based on the career of lady sharpshooter Annie Oakley, with Ethel Merman in the title role, to be produced by Rodgers and Hammerstein.

Kern spent the weekend visiting friends and professional colleagues and the graves of his parents. On Monday, he was expected at the Zieg-

Jerome Kern's last picture, taken Friday, November 2, 1945, at Eaves Costume Co. With costume designer Lucinda Ballard (left) and her assistant Anna Hill Johnstone.

Jan Clayton tries on a costume at Eaves, under the watchful eye of Lucinda Ballard and set designer Howard Bay.

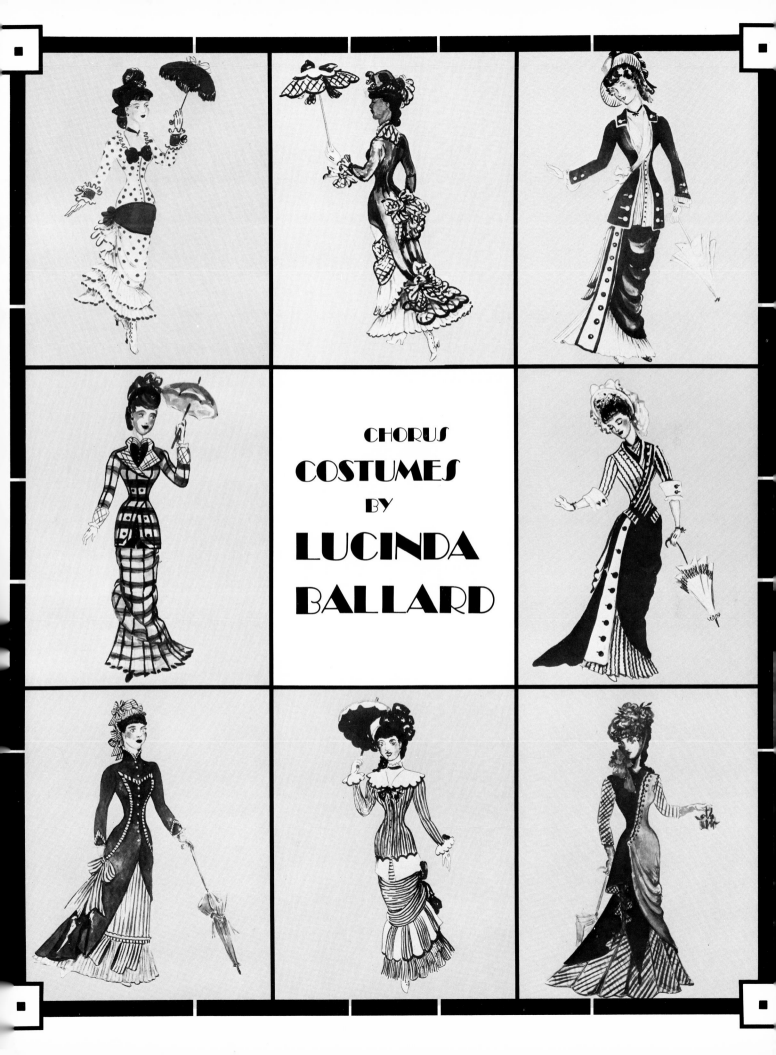

CHORUS
COSTUMES
BY
LUCINDA
BALLARD

feld Theatre in the afternoon, but he wanted to shop during the morning. Around noon, Kern suddenly collapsed on the sidewalk in front of 450 Park Avenue, near 57th Street. He was swiftly taken to a public hospital on Welfare Island, where his ASCAP membership card led to his identification and the summoning of Hammerstein to his bedside. On Wednesday, November 7, Kern was strong enough to be moved to the private Doctors Hospital, where he finally succumbed to a cerebral hemorrhage on Sunday, November 11.

Hammerstein, for the first time in his career, was now the sole producer of a Broadway show, in addition to its director and author. He engaged his brother Reginald as general stage manager and his own son, William, as Uncle Reggie's assistant.

Although the New Century and Broadway theatres had been considered earlier, **Show Boat** was finally set for the Ziegfeld Theatre, its original Broadway home, now owned by Billy Rose, whose diminutive height belied a titanic ego, energy, and imagination. Rose had produced **Carmen Jones** (12-2-43, Broadway), Hammerstein's all-Negro update of Bizet's opera **Carmen.** Howard Bay, who had won Donaldson awards for his sets for both **Carmen Jones** and **Up in Central Park** (1-27-45, New Century), was asked to mount **Show Boat.** Lucinda Ballard, a former mural painter who had designed costumes for many ballets and plays (including **I Remember Mama** (10-19-44, Music Box), which had been produced by Rodgers and Hammerstein), was selected to create the wardrobe.

As Hammerstein wrote for the liner notes to the Columbia revival cast album, "Our present production had to be built to match the enhanced glamor of the public's memory of Ziegfeld's original production." Hammerstein turned to Hassard Short, who had staged **Carmen Jones** and had a gift for working with designers and directors to help provide sparkle and excitement. Howard Bay credits "Bobby" Short with having devised the widely acclaimed color style that had given **Carmen Jones** its visual impact, and called Short "a tremendous buffer between you and business managers."

Scenic and costumes sketches had to be ap-

proved by Short, in addition to Hammerstein and choreographer Helen Tamiris; and changes were sometimes made to reflect Short's ideas about color coordination.

The original Urban settings and Harkrider costumes, used in 1927 and again in 1932, were remarkably understated for a Ziegfled production. Every effort had been made to emphasize the dramatic validity of the story by using subdued colors and fashions indigenous to the period.

Because of Hammerstein's concern that the public in 1946 had come to expect a more decorative look, there was a conscious attempt to brighten the sets and costumes. In both color and form, the mounting was intentionally theatrical and artificial, thereby setting a trend for designing **Show Boat** on stage and screen that has lasted until today.

When rehearsals began on December 3, Hammerstein directed the actors in their dramatic scenes, but Short's influence was felt in the grouping of ensembles during opening numbers and finales, for example. Although Tamiris most capably handled the actual choreography, Short's contributions embraced the overall flow and movement of the players. Jan Clayton had the exhausting task of rehearsing while appearing eight times a week in **Carousel,** in which she remained through Saturday, December 29, less than a week before previews began for **Show Boat.**

During rehearsal, Billy Rose proved himself more than merely a landlord. From his suite high atop the Ziegfeld's auditorium, he could peer down at the stage and observe rehearsals, which he frequently attended. He had, in fact, been an early co-producer but had bowed out in July. As a flamboyant showman, his opinions were often incorporated into the production.

Robert Russell Bennett recently recalled one such incident. The original 1927 overture, unlike most musical comedy overtures, is not simply a medley of the score's principal tunes. In fact, "Why Do I Love You?," which comes near the end, is one of the few recognizable airs. Bennett said that, after one of the first public previews of the revival, Rose came to him and said he noticed that the audience applauded as soon

1946—The Post-War Revival

HASSARD SHORT

BILLY ROSE

as they heard "Why Do I Love You?" He was convinced that if Bennett orchestrated a whole new overture with all the famous melodies in it, the public would applaud every one of them.

Bennett added, "I put in four or five of the main melodies of the show and made a real Broadway overture. And so we played it. Billy was delighted with it. He said, 'That's just what the doctor ordered.' Those were his words at the time. He said, 'Just what the doctor ordered.' And so they played it for the audience that night, and the audience applauded for 'Why Do I Love You?' and for nothing else."

In addition to the new overture, which is heard on the Columbia cast album, Bennett also attempted to make the overall orchestration more compatible with a 1940's theatre sound by removing the banjo and tuba and adding two trombones and a piano.

The times also demanded a major overhaul in the text. Racial attitudes had changed since **Show Boat** had been first staged, and it was feared that the use of the word "nigger" would enflame emotions. The lyric "Niggers all work on de Mississippi" in the opening chorus was changed to "Colored folks work on de Mississippi." In dialogue, the word generally became "Negro" when spoken by sympathetic characters and remained "nigger" when spoken with hostility by Pete or Sheriff Vallon.

For the theatre playbills, Hammerstein wrote, "Mr. Kern and I have kept the libretto and score of 'Show Boat' substantially as they were when originally written in 1927. We have eliminated one 'front scene' and three minor musical numbers. We have added one new song in the last scene of the play, 'Nobody Else But Me.' This takes the place of a series of imitations of stars of the Twenties performed in this spot by the original Magnolia, Miss Norma Terris."

Actually, the author's own description of his alterations is vastly oversimplified. To begin with, two scenes (not one) were entirely eliminated, and a third was so thoroughly rewritten (even in a new setting) that one might as well say three scenes were cut out.

To some extent, these cuts were made to help trim the lengthy show to a more conventional running time. More important, developments in

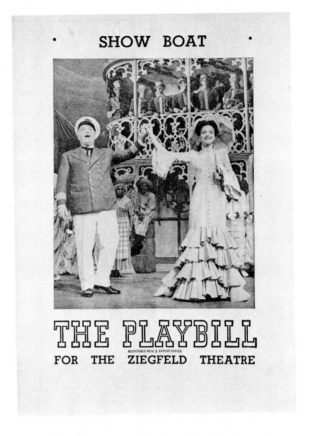

Playbill cover showing Cap'n Andy (Ralph Dumke) introducing Julie (Carol Bruce).

scenic technology permitted speedier set changes than were possible in the 1920's. In those days, a full stage set was literally assembled of many separate pieces by a fleet of stage hands, while a so-called "front scene" was being played before a drop. By the mid-1940's, medium-sized sets were pre-assembled on wheeled platforms during a previous scene; and, as one scene ended, the set for the following one could literally be rolled out, often before the audience's eyes.

All three cuts were front scenes. The first was the original Act One, Scene Three, the street in front of a gambling saloon, in which Pete goes to tell Vallon and Frank about Julie's mixed blood. Of the two songs originally heard in this scene, "Till Good Luck Comes My Way" was dropped from the revival's score, while "Life on the Wicked Stage" was moved to another scene.

With this scene cut, it became necessary for

160

the audience to be informed that Frank and Ellie are late for the rehearsal that follows, because they are in town with Pete. This information was now to be supplied by Magnolia at the start of the rehearsal scene in just a few new lines of dialogue. Actually, it is this brief piece of exposition only that justified the whole of Scene Three to begin with. The rest, including the two songs, was largely time-filler to accommodate the scene change taking place behind the drop.

Also cut were Act Two, Scene Five, the lobby of the Sherman House, in which Andy meets three attractive tarts and escorts them to the Trocadero, and Act Two, Scene Seven, in the original play the transition into 1927. It is set on a street corner, where old Joe sings a complete reprise of "Ol' Man River"; and Queenie, rather improbably dressed as a flapper, shows him the modern way to catch a man in "Hey, Feller!"

This scene was transposed to the stern of the *Cotton Blossom* in 1927. Joe puts down a sack of flour he has been carrying and starts to whittle. Queenie berates him for his laziness, with dialogue taken directly from the 1936 screenplay. He admits he has been the same for forty years and sings a partial reprise of "Ol' Man River," starting with the variant words, "New things come and ol' things go. . . ." The song, "Hey, Feller!," along with Queenie's flapper outfit, is also dropped.

In the original Act One, Scene Five, Frank offers to protect Ellie in "I Might Fall Back on

"Can't Help Lovin' Dat Man." Kenneth Spencer, Helen Dowdy, Jan Clayton, Carol Bruce.

Miscegenation scene. Ethel Owen, Jan Clayton, Francis X. Mahoney, Carol Bruce, Robert Allen, Colette Lyons, Ralph Dumke.

You." In the revival, this song is deleted. Instead, Frank and Ellie's comedy dialogue continues somewhat longer, as he tells her that he has priced a wedding ring. When he exits, five admiring girls from the town enter and ask Ellie about "Life on the Wicked Stage." Following their vocal, the girls are joined by their boy friends in a dance that incorporates an instrumental portion of "I Might Fall Back on You." Although the replacement of one song for another in the same spot requires the sacrifice of "I Might Fall Back on You," the better of the two songs is retained; and the script probably benefits from far smoother action.

In addition to the elimination of "Till Good Luck Comes My Way," "I Might Fall Back on You," and "Hey, Feller!" the three songs to which Hammerstein alludes, there were several other musical trims. In the opening chorus, the second quatrain contains the line, "Coal Black Rose or High Brown Sal...." Regarding the reference too racially questionable, Hammerstein rewrote the entire quatrain.

Queenie's ballyhoo, "C'mon, Folks," was shorn of its entire refrain, so that a brief verse leads directly into a new dance. Similarly, the latter half of the Act Two opening chorus, including the entire "Dandies on Parade" chorus,

1946—The Post-War Revival

was cut to provide more time for dancing. And dance became an integral part of the presentation of "Nobody Else But Me," the newly added, up-to-date song for Kim in the last scene.

The revival's preoccupation with dance was hardly a caprice. Balanchine's incorporation of ballet into several Rodgers and Hart musicals of the late 1930's and later Agnes de Mille's enormously influential use of ballet in **Oklahoma!, Carousel, One Touch of Venus** (10-7-43, Imperial), and **Bloomer Girl** (10-5-44, Sam S. Shubert) made ballet not only fashionable in Broadway musicals, but virtually obligatory. Helen Tamiris' beautiful Currier and Ives ballet in **Up in Central Park** led to her assignment in the **Show Boat** revival.

Because the original **Show Boat** had used dance only sparingly and in rather authentic re-creations of period steps, it was the Tamiris contribution to the revival that became its most salient feature. As if to codify the emphasis upon dance, each of Tamiris' routines was given its own name in the theatre program. For example, the dance that followed Colette Lyons' vivacious vocal of "Life on the Wicked Stage" was dubbed "No Gems, No Roses, No Gentlemen."

Even Jan Clayton's flapper dance to "Nobody Else But Me," with her partner Charles Tate, had to have a special name and was called "Dance 1927." It is interesting that the final scene, which in the Ziegfeld production had been set in modern times, was by 1946 as much a

"Life on the Wicked Stage." Colette Lyons and ladies of the ensemble.

period sequence as any in the rest of the play.

The biggest choreographic impact came from a contingent of Negro dancers, headed by the vibrant Pearl Primus. With her partner LaVerne French, the pair stopped the show nightly with their barefoot gyrations (dubbed "No Shoes"), as two young innocents lured to the show boat by Queenie's ballyhoo. Miss Primus turned up again as the Dahomey Queen in the world's fair sequence and performed her magic once more amid more decorative adornments. Two other distinguished black dancers, Claude Marchant and Talley Beatty, were featured with French in a new levee dance at the end of the first act.

Show Boat opened at the Ziegfeld Theatre on Saturday, January 5, 1946, with only a few previews and no pre-Broadway tryout. Although Hammerstein had directed the original production with great style, his shaping of the subtle values in the revival seemed somewhat uncertain.

In some ways, every change (except for the racial ones) was made in a conscious attempt to suppress the audience's comparison of the new production with the original. But it is impossible to compete with legend, and every critic without exception compared the two presentations.

Ziegfeld's principals had all brought to the original work a fine honing of their craft, based on years of performance before the public.

"No Shoes," danced by LaVerne French, Pearl Primus, and Negro ensemble. Helen Dowdy, front right.

The Parson's Bride. Ralph Dumke, Jan Clayton, Charles Fredericks, Ethel Owen, Howard Frank (Backwoodsman), Duncan Scott (Jeb).

Somehow, many of the 1946 players seemed to lack the necessary style.

This was most noticeable in the roles of Cap'n Andy and Parthy. Ralph Dumke had spent years on radio with his partner Ed East as the popular "Sisters of the Skillet." While Winninger had been small, agile, and as sprightly as a spring, Dumke was a large, portly actor whose comedy seemed deliberate. Similarly, Ethel Owen was another radio performer who had to work at being Parthy, unlike homely Edna May Oliver, who lived the part. Kenneth Spencer. though revealing a good bass voice in "Ol' Man River," lacked the magnetic stage presence of Robeson

or even Bledsoe. Except for Helen Dowdy's splendid Queenie and a return to the cast of Francis X. Mahoney and Jack Daley, the original Rubber Face and Jim, the supporting cast lacked distinction.

Characters in a drama all move at different tempi in order to best express their innate natures and to create a tapestry of interaction from one role to the next. Generally, romantic leads, particularly in period pieces like **Show Boat,** tend to be subdued and leisurely in meting out their actions, while comic characters, like Frank and Ellie, tend to skitter about like bugs on the surface of a pond.

Charles Winninger, Howard Marsh, Norma Terris, Sammy White, Eva Puck, Edna May Oliver,
Thomas Gunn, Bert Chapman.

COSTUMES BY JOHN HARKRIDER

SETTING BY JOSEPH URBAN

1946

Charles Fredericks, Jan Clayton, Ralph Dumke, Buddy Ebsen.

COSTUMES BY LUCINDA BALLARD

SETTING BY HOWARD BAY

"In Dahomey."

Buddy Ebsen's personal style, so familiar to his admirers, was leisurely in tempo and curved in design, where speed and angles might have seemed more appropriate for the role of Frank. With the elimination of "I Might Fall Back on You," Ebsen ended up with just one vocal ("Good-bye, Ma Lady Love"), the opening buck-and-wing, and his olio soft-shoe. This was hardly sufficient musical material for a player of his prominence.

A strong director could have easily solved these problems, but Hammerstein seemed to trust to fate or the instincts of his players too often. One might even say that there was too much dance where dance was not needed, and perhaps even too much color in the sets and costumes, simply as a counteraction against any possible accusation that the revival failed to live up to the original.

Of the principals, three in particular best fulfilled their potential. Perhaps none had a more difficult task than Carol Bruce, who had to live up to the audience's memory of Helen Morgan as Julie. Although the beautiful Miss Bruce revealed none of the personal dissipation that had elicited so much audience sympathy for Miss Morgan, her acting displayed such compassion, and her mellow alto singing voice such deeply felt emotion (particularly in "Bill"), that Miss Bruce was enthusiastically acclaimed a worthy successor.

The role of Ravenal hardly requires a consummate actor. The player must possess a dashing appearance and at least a certain facile charm and should have a clear tenor or high baritone voice. These conditions were generously satisfied by Charles Fredericks, who, like Jan Clayton, had been loaned by MGM. When he

"Bill." Carol Bruce, Max Showalter

"Good-bye, Ma Lady Love." Buddy Ebsen, Colette Lyons

168

"After the Ball." Ralph Dumke, Jan Clayton

Jerome Kern's last song.

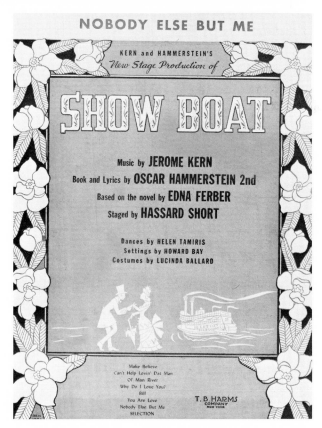

left the cast, Fredericks was replaced by another MGM contract performer, the tenor Joe Sullivan, who changed his first name to Brian when he played the male lead in Kurt Weill's **Street Scene** (1-9-47, Adelphi) the following year.

Jan Clayton brought to Magnolia a youthful freshness and a light, charming voice that were most appealing. Although she remained in the cast for only thirteen weeks (to be replaced Monday, April 15, by her understudy, Nancy Kenyon), she never returned to MGM to make **Jenny Was a Lady.** While in New York, she married Robert Lerner, younger brother of librettist Alan Jay Lerner, and temporarily retired to raise a family.

In the meantime, Richard Rodgers chose to assume Kern's obligation to supply a song for the film, so he and Hammerstein wrote a lovely ballad called "So Far." When **Jenny Was a Lady** was cancelled, they incorporated the song into their next Broadway show, **Allegro** (10-10-47, Majestic), in which it was sung by Gloria Wills.

Despite the expense and care that went into the 1946 **Show Boat** revival, the weekly operating expense of nearly $40,000 proved so high that the production, which ran 418 performances, actually lost money. However, under the banner of Rodgers and Hammerstein, the show, in somewhat truncated form, toured the country successfully until April 30, 1949, when it closed in the Hartman Theatre, Columbus, Ohio. It was this touring package that passed through New York briefly in the late summer of 1948, opening September 7 at the New York City Center.

To facilitate travel and trim the running time to avoid overtime fees for the stage hands, several cuts were made. The most enduring of these was the elimination of the adult Kim in the final scene, and with her the song "Nobody Else But Me," performed in the spot where Norma Terris had done her impersonations and, in London, Edith Day had sung "Dance Away the Night."

This cut does strengthen the reunion of Magnolia and Ravenal, and Kim has been seen in fewer and fewer revivals since 1946. Similarly, the Helen Tamiris dances, which seemed so exciting and fashionable in 1946, have been permanently deleted from all subsequent productions.

CHAPTER 7

1951
The MGM Version

AFTER OWNING the rights to **Show Boat** for seven years, MGM, in 1945, finally brought the material to the screen. Arthur Freed, who produced most of the studio's best musicals during the 1940's and 1950's, had had a lifelong adoration for the music of Jerome Kern, whom he first met in 1917, when the composer's show **Oh, Boy!** (2-20-17, Princess) was a reigning success on Broadway. In the early 1940's, several years before the vogue for songwriter biographies became a Hollywood staple, Freed had decided to film the life story of Kern. The final title, **Till the Clouds Roll By** is the name of **Oh, Boy!**'s hit song.

Although Kern's life had been surprisingly undramatic, Freed felt that the emphasis could be placed upon the composer's rich repertoire. Several years were spent in the acquisition of the Kern catalogue, and production was ready by the late summer of 1945. Kern himself had worked with the scenarists and had been present during the early days of recording and shooting, but most of his attention was diverted by the produc-

tion of **Centennial Summer,** which Otto Preminger was directing at Fox.

When Kern died suddenly on November 11, 1945, the script of **Till the Clouds Roll By** had to be rewritten to eliminate the original implication that he was still alive.

The picture opens with a grey-haired Kern, played by young Robert Walker, attending the Broadway opening night of **Show Boat.** There follows a condensation of Act One that manages to compress six songs and bits of linking business and dialogue into a bare fifteen minutes.

After a large chorus sings "Cotton Blossom," Cap'n Andy (William Halligan) steps out to introduce Steve (Bruce Cowling) and Julie (Lena Horne). Later, Tony Martin strolls onstage as Gaylord Ravenal and introduces "Where's the Mate for Me?" He spies Kathryn Grayson as Magnolia on the deck and, after a few words based on the original stage script, they duet "Make Believe." Parthy calls to Magnolia, and the pair exit. Poker-faced Virginia O'Brien as Ellie enters with a group of girls and performs "Life on the Wicked Stage," followed by Lena

Horne's seductive rendition of "Can't Help Lovin' Dat Man." The sequence concludes with "Ol' Man River," sung rather emotionally by Caleb Peterson with a mixed chorus.

Amid thunderous applause, the curtain falls on this oddly appealing abridgment. In his waiting limousine, Kern begins to reminisce with his chauffeur about the events of his life leading up to this momentous opening night. The remainder of the film is a flashback.

In many ways, this mini-**Show Boat** proved to be a dress rehearsal for MGM's later screen adaptation. Many of the same artists worked on both, not only Arthur Freed as producer and Robert Alton as choreographer, but also orchestrator Conrad Salinger and Kathryn Grayson as Magnolia. Roger Edens acted as music coordinator for both.

Perhaps because of Freed's affection for Kern, most of **Till the Clouds Roll By** possesses a credibility and charm one fails to find in most of Hollywood's songwriter biographies. Its direction by Richard Whorf is smoothly unobtrusive. But then comes the finale.

This is supposed to be a Hollywood production number being filmed for a movie biography of Jerome Kern, who, in the person of Robert Walker, is seated and watching. All the gaudy and indulgent vulgarity Whorf had suppressed throughout the picture is slopped all over the screen, as if MGM simply could not hold it in any longer.

The number is one of those overorchestrated, overmounted affairs designed to suggest the superhuman stature of contract singers and the majesty of their renditions. Each star stands atop a white, fluted Grecian column, one raised higher than the next, against a shimmering sky backdrop. Following the thematically linking "The Land Where the Good Songs Go," sung by Lucille Bremer (dubbed by Trudy Erwin), a chorus sings "Yesterdays," followed by Grayson's vocal of "Long Ago and Far Away," O'Brien's "A Fine Romance," Martin's "All the Things You Are," and Horne's "Why Was I Born?"

The orchestra then swells tremulously: there is a drum roll: our hearts are expected to pound in breathless anticipation: and there, standing atop his own little column, wearing a pure white tuxedo, and looking a bit dazed by the height, is America's bobby soxer hero, Frank Sinatra. Although his voice had been prerecorded, its frail quaver suggests that even while vocalizing, he had been picturing himself on his aerie perch, looking about as silly as anyone in the history of cinema. The spectacle of this scrawny kid in his bulky white suit singing "you and me, we sweat and strain" brought audible titters from audiences and a few well-deserved swipes from the press.

This lame-brained finale was directed by George Sidney, who was rewarded with the direction in 1950 of MGM's multimillion dollar verson of **Show Boat** (MGM, 1951).

In transferring a stage musical to the screen, it is frequently necessary to alter certain scenes to take advantage of increased visual freedom made possible by camera movement and the ability to dart from one site to another. From the earliest days of talking pictures, studios assumed these rights of alteration as inalienable. Further, because many studios owned music publishing

ARTHUR FREED

In **Till the Clouds Roll By,** Oscar Hammerstein II (Paul Langton) introduces Jerome Kern (Robert Walker) to Edna Ferber's **Show Boat.** At left is Dorothy Patrick as Mrs. Kern. Note MGM's redesigned book dust jacket with the *Cotton Blossom* as a steamboat.

In **Till the Clouds Roll By**'s **Show Boat** sequence,
Cap'n Andy (William Halligan) introduces Julie
(Lena Horne), Ellie (Virginia O'Brien), and
Steve (Bruce Cowling).

In **Till the Clouds Roll By,** Ravenal (Tony Martin) sings
'Where's the Mate for Me?'

houses, new songs were often added to provide additional revenue.

It can easily be demonstrated statistically that no studio even begins to approach MGM for its flagrant mangling (or would it be more tactful to say reconstruction) of Broadway musicals. The plots of **New Moon** (MGM, 1930), **Rose Marie** (MGM, 1936 and 1954), **The Firefly** (MGM, 1937), **The Chocolate Soldier** (MGM, 1941), **Lady Be Good** (MGM, 1941), and **The Merry Widow** (MGM, 1952), among others, bear no resemblance whatever to their stage originals.

Often stage scores too are entirely or largely replaced, as in **Flying High** (MGM, 1931), **Maytime** (MGM, 1937), **Rosalie** (MGM, 1937), **DuBarry Was a Lady** (MGM, 1943), **On the Town** (MGM, 1949), **The Belle of New York** (MGM, 1952), and **When the Boys Meet the Girls** (MGM, 1965, an alleged remake of **Girl Crazy,** MGM, 1943), to name but a few.

Generally, MGM's best musicals are those created expressly for the screen, like **Broadway Melody of 1936** (MGM, 1935), **Born To Dance** (MGM, 1936), **The Wizard of Oz,** (MGM, 1939), **Meet Me in St. Louis** (MGM, 1944), **The Harvey Girls** (MGM, 1945), **The Pirate** (MGM, 1948), **An American in Paris** (MGM, 1951), **Singin' in the Rain** (MGM,

In **Till the Clouds Roll By,** the opening **Show Boat** sequence concludes with "Ol' Man River," sung by Caleb Peterson (center stage in striped shirt), Freita Shaw's Etude Ethiopian Chorus (in foreground), and the MGM singers (in background). Although the studio designers have transformed the *Cotton Blossom* into a steamboat, the fretwork pattern on the upper deck bears a remarkable resemblance to that of the two earliest show boats pictured in Chapter One.

The finale of **Till the Clouds Roll By.** After the chorus in the foreground-left sings "Yesterdays," the camera moves from one pillar to the next to feature Kathryn Grayson ("Long Ago and Far Away"), Johnny Johnston ("Dearly Beloved"—cut prior to release), Virginia O'Brien ("A Fine Romance"), Tony Martin ("All the Things You Are"), Lena Horne ("Why Was I Born?"), and Lucille Bremer ("The Way You Look Tonight"—cut prior to release). The number and the film conclude with "Ol' Man River," sung by Frank Sinatra on the small pillar in the foreground center.

1952), **The Band Wagon** (MGM, 1953), and **Seven Brides for Seven Brothers** (MGM, 1954). The last seven were produced by Freed himself. Unfortunately, adaptations from the stage were treated as if they too were "originals" and were refashioned until they fit the acceptable MGM mould.

Freed assigned the screenplay for **Show Boat** to John Lee Mahin, who had been a staffer at MGM since the early 1930's. Either alone or in collaboration, Mahin had written some sparkling comedies, including **Red Dust** (MGM, 1932), **Bombshell** (MGM, 1933), and **The Prizefighter and the Lady** (MGM, 1933); some exciting dramas like **Treasure Island** (MGM, 1934), **China Seas** (MGM, 1935), **Captains Courageous** (MGM, 1937), and **Boom Town** (MGM, 1940); the touching **Tortilla Flat** (MGM, 1942) and the pretentious **Dr. Jekyll and Mr. Hyde** (MGM, 1941). Except for a col-

laboration with Frances Goodrich and Albert Hackett on **Naughty Marietta** (MGM, 1935), he had never written a musical.

Feeling that Hammerstein's libretto for **Show Boat** sprawls over too long a time period and leaves the reunited lovers as middle-aged, Mahin decided to reunite Ravenal and Magnolia well within the nineteenth century, while both are unchanged physically and Kim is still a small child. Although this alteration serves well to tighten the love story, it shifts the emphasis away from the more heroic theme of the river as a life force and the character of Magnolia as a woman who learns to triumph over adversity. Thus, the emphasis is placed upon domesticity rather than majesty. Inevitably, every subsequent element added to the production enhanced this abstraction.

Although Mahin chose to scrap almost all of Hammerstein's dialogue, his screenplay follows

Show Boat director George Sidney with Ava Gardner, Kathryn Grayson, Howard Keel.

the overall scenario rather faithfully up to a critical turning point in the story. As before, the *Cotton Blossom* troupe is depicted as a cozy family, headed by the martinet Parthy (Agnes Moorehead) and congenial Cap'n Andy (Joe E. Brown). Pete (Leif Erickson) still tries to lure Julie's (Ava Gardner) affections from Steve (Robert Sterling) and, following a beating from Steve, as always reports the girl's mixed blood to the local sheriff (Regis Toomey), thereby causing the tense miscegenation scene. As before, Ravenal (Howard Keel) is a small-time gambler who takes Steve's place as leading man, while Magnolia (Kathryn Grayson) takes over "temporarily" from Julie, until the boat reaches New

Orleans. Their romance inspires the usual wrath from Parthy and sympathy from Andy. In Chicago, Gay gambles away his small fortune and deserts his wife, as did all the Ravenals before him, thereby forcing Magnolia to make a triumphant cabaret debut at the Trocadero on New Year's Eve, to an audience that includes her own father.

It is here that the MGM plot becomes wholly original, with no resemblance in story or feeling to any earlier version. After Magnolia's success, instead of her going on to fame in New York and seeing her daughter Kim follow in her footsteps, Magnolia confesses to Andy that she wants to return to the *Cotton Blossom.* She is about to

"You Are Love" (right) and "Why Do I Love You?" (below) sung by Kathryn Grayson and Howard Keel.

have a child but did not have the opportunity to tell Gay this before he left her. (At this point conventionally, Kim is already enrolled in the convent school.)

In a montage, we learn that several years pass, as Gay continues to gamble on riverboats; and Kim (Sheila Clark) grows into a cute little girl, who is taught by Andy all the song-and-dance routines he had once taught Magnolia. There is a sweet feeling that show boat traditions, like the river itself, keep rolling along. On the other hand, with Magnolia now swathed in love aboard the *Cotton Blossom,* her contribution as a character is prematurely ended. The audience

now must simply wait until Ravenal decides to return to the fold for an inevitable final clinch. By eliminating any tests of endurance for Magnolia, Mahin both diminishes her stature and has inadvertently brought interest in the story to an end long before it is over. This flaw causes the final quarter of **Show Boat** to drift without direction or power.

Mahin's principal contribution is a scene that brings Julie back into the story and gives her the chance to encourage Ravenal to return to the *Cotton Blossom.* During one river voyage, Ravenal, looking quite prosperous, sees the drunken girl (whom he has never met), trying to

In a scene created for the MGM film, Julie (Ava Gardner) urges Ravenal (Howard Keel) to return to Magnolia.

Joe (William Warfield) sings the film's concluding reprise of "Ol' Man River."

encourage a piano player (Harry Seymour) to bang out "Can't Help Lovin' Dat Man." Gay recognizes the tune as one that his wife used to sing and punches Julie's surly boy friend (William Tannen), who has slapped the pathetic, fallen creature. When Gay withdraws to the deck, Julie learns his identity from the barkeep (Earl Hodgins) and joins him outside. She tells him that the *Cotton Blossom* is docked at Natchez, the riverboat's next stop, and shows him a newspaper clipping containing a photo of Andy, Magnolia, and Kim, of whose existence he is totally unaware.

Julie and her friend disbark at Natchez, and so, we learn, does Gay, who meets his daughter for the first time on the levee and is reunited with his wife. Their embrace is seen by her parents high on the top deck and is met with ardent approval. As the boat pulls away to an offscreen choir of "Ol' Man River," the lovers are locked in each other's arms on deck. From the shadows of the pier, Julie, wearing no make-up and looking worn, silently blows them a kiss.

Surely the coincidence of Gay and Julie's meeting is no more remarkable than any of the earlier devices used to reunite Ravenal and

Kathryn Grayson and Ava Gardner sing a reprise of "Can't Help Lovin' Dat Man,"
during one of the film's happiest moments.

Magnolia: they have all been equally improbable. But this version at least provides the actress who plays Julie with one more scene and, as it happens, her most touching.

Because Julie is easily the story's most interesting character, it was decided to build up this role for Judy Garland, whose own life alarmingly paralleled Julie's too closely for comfort. Like Julie, Judy spent her early years as part of a performing family (at MGM) and, because she had been turned into a drug addict and could not perform to standard, was tossed out into the wilds (like Julie) through no fault of her own. The later dissolution shared by character and performer is so close that one can only wonder

silently how moving Judy might have been in this part.

With Judy dismissed from the studio in June 1950, the role of the sweetly fragile, highly vulnerable bird who is crushed by circumstances went to (of all people) the voluptuous Ava Gardner, who appears strong enough to take on a cage of wild tigers. Not sure enough of her acting talents that were yet to develop, Miss Gardner relies on the breathy style of line delivery audiences of that period had come to expect from "sex symbols" like herself, Rita Hayworth, and others. Instead of simply speaking to other people, Miss Gardner seems always on the verge of seducing them: male or female.

1951—The MGM Version

In **The Hucksters** (MGM, 1947), **One Touch of Venus** (UI, 1948), and **The Bribe** (MGM, 1949), Ava's singing had been dubbed by soprano Eileen Wilson. For **Show Boat,** Miss Gardner was determined to sing for herself with the honest justification that Julie's two songs require as much acting ability as vocal skill. In the end, her vocals were dubbed by Annette Warren, whose singing is sultry, richly attractive, but in the film is largely devoid of dramatic feeling. Furthermore, it is far too low a voice to match Miss Gardner's own breathy speech. Gardner's own vocals are heard on the MGM soundtrack album. While they are more personal and expressive than Miss Warren's, they reflect inexperience and uncertain pitch and would have seemed feeble in a large theatre, as in fact they did during several sneak previews.

Except for the plaintive desperation Miss Gardner expresses during her final scene with Ravenal, her performance is a curious anachronism. She is a glamour queen trying valiantly to break out of her mould to become a serious actress. Yet apparently neither she nor the studio is quite sure how to manage the transition.

In the 1936 version, Helen Morgan stands quietly by an upright piano to sing "Bill." She is bleary-eyed, pudgy, ill-kempt, wearing a baggy, formless, dowdy dress; and she is magnificent. In the MGM version, Gardner slithers around the piano with her lipstick perfectly applied, her hair (except for one coyly dangling curl) impeccably sprayed, and her dress as curvy as nature and shrewd tailoring will allow. She wears a smile on her face that conflicts with the lyrics, and she even performs part of the song lounging sinu-

Glamorous Ava Gardner warbles "Bill" with the help of Annette Warren.

183

Marge and Gower Champion perform a buck-and-wing, as Ava Gardner, Robert Sterling, Joe E. Brown, and Agnes Moorehead look on.

ously across the few steps leading up to the Trocadero stage. She is as exciting as an apple core.

There has rarely been a major musical film as poorly cast. Kathryn Grayson plays Magnolia presumably just because she was under contract to the studio. In almost a decade before the cameras, she managed to learn nothing of acting and speaks with a vague quiver that suggests both heartbreak and heartburn. Her gurgly, thin, reedy soprano is almost painfully unattractive and is scarcely enhanced by the deliberate cuteness of some of her vocal mannerisms, presumably approved by Robert Tucker, the film's vocal arranger. Instead of maturing as Magnolia must under the stress of adversity, Grayson remains vapidly virginal throughout.

As a pair of hoofers who will never make big time, Sammy White and Queenie Smith of the 1936 film perfectly captured the seediness of show boat performance and managed to blend this with an irresistible vivacity and self-confident innocence that make both their acting and musical numbers creations of simple joy.

In their screen debuts as a couple, Marge and Gower Champion in the same roles are so urbanely polished, attractively groomed, and dazzlingly skillful that one wonders why on earth Frank and Ellie are not top Broadway headliners. In their two production numbers, "I Might Fall Back on You" and "Life on the Wicked Stage" (the latter refashioned into a duet), they prove the screen's most engaging song-and-dance couple since the days of Fred Astaire and Ginger

1951—The MGM Version

Rogers at RKO. Their style contains such a perfect blend of acrobatics, ballet, jazz, and comedy that the couple seems to leap from the screen and demand the audience's affection. That the Champions are utterly miscast is no fault of their own, but this is another contribution to the movie's overall ill-conception.

By contrast, Joe E. Brown was adroitly cast as Cap'n Andy. The comic had spent decades regaling audiences on stage and screen with his broad humor (and mouth) and his angular, eccentric dancing. No better successor could be found for Charles Winninger. But, oddly, the Mahin script manages to strip virtually all of Andy's funny scenes. Following a truncated opening ballyhoo, he is seen comforting the lovers from time to time, and he is provided a fleeting moment with the three tarts at the Troca-

dero; but that is all. One is grateful that Brown is allowed a brief buck-and-wing, with little Sheila Clark, as a pale hint of the spry vitality he still possessed when the film was shot. What might have been a great comic performance is drained of all impact.

In earlier versions, Parthy's dictatorial manner is tempered with tenderness and even a dash of self-parody. As written by Mahin, Parthy is simply a nasty, prim, humorless wretch, who irritates everyone and inspires no affection in either the show boat family or in the movie's audience. There is no way that charming Agnes Moorehead could possibly have made Mahin's Parthy sympathetic. Her final expression of rapture that Ravenal has returned is utterly inexplicable.

Even when she first meets Gay and has no idea that he is a gambler, Parthy disapproves of

Cap'n Andy (Joe E. Brown) teaches his granddaughter Kim (Sheila Clark) the buck-and-wing.

him. Later, when he courts and marries Magnolia, Parthy's feelings develop into overt hostility. Now that he has deserted her daughter for years and decides one day to show up again, she becomes utterly giddy with glee. As there is no clue in either writing or direction why Parthy should express such emotion, the character change seems shabbily contrived.

Of all the principals, the one most sympathetically portrayed and performed is Gaylord Ravenal. Instead of being depicted as a man driven beyond reason by his gambling obsession, and who uses others for selfish gain, Gay in this version seems never to discuss or engage in gambling from the time he first steps aboard the *Cotton Blossom* until he arrives in Chicago with

his wife. He seems truly repentant for the pain he is causing Magnolia and even tries to explain to her the curious love relationship he bears for a deck of cards. In addition, he seems more successful at cards than earlier incarnations of Ravenal, for he returns to the *Cotton Blossom* looking well-to-do and apparently once again willing and able to put the cards away. He has simply been a man engaged in a temporary affair with the Queen of Hearts and who now returns to his true love.

In one of his sturdiest performances, Howard Keel not only assumes full command of every scene in which he appears, but he transforms this bounder into a man of considerable tenderness. Although the role is usually played by a

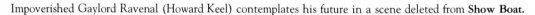

Impoverished Gaylord Ravenal (Howard Keel) contemplates his future in a scene deleted from **Show Boat.**

WILLIAM WARFIELD
sings "Ol' Man River."

tenor, Keel's resonant baritone lends a warmth that reinforces his skillfully understated performance.

The presence too of William Warfield as Joe is strongly felt, despite the brevity of his role. Warfield's face suggests a wisdom not found in his meagre dialogue. When Julie leaves the *Cotton Blossom* and walks out into the night, she stops on the foggy pier and touches Joe's face tenderly as if for strength. His slow, surging rendition of "Ol' Man River" soars over the waters and guides Julie and Steve's carriage through the night.

The departure sequence is seen through a thick, foggy haze, a mist that imparts a romantic sadness. Julie's traveling clothes are suitably somber. As Warfield sings, the key colors keep shifting the fog into varying tones of dark greens and steely blues. Inside the boat are glowing golden flames from the furnace and lamps: outside there is only the chill of the night, a foreboding of Julie and Steve's inevitable fate.

As their carriage passes the camera in a brief shot, Julie's head is bowed as if in shame. Hearing Joe's singing in the distance, she turns for

Cap'n Andy (Joe E. Brown) bids farewell, as Steve (Robert Sterling) and Julie (Ava Gardner)
prepare to drive off into the foggy night.

one last glimpse of the warm home she once shared. They ride off into the cold night with Andy tearfully looking on. The boat veers away into the river. The following morning, there is a long shot of the *Cotton Blossom* seen against a brilliantly sunny sky, with bright foliage and cheery color everywhere. The sickness of the night before has been purged.

This brief sequence, the most brilliant of the film, was directed by Roger Edens* during an illness of George Sidney. Although he had never directed before, Edens' sensitivity to emotion and color provides the film with a dignity it deserves but rarely receives elsewhere.

Mahin's script does contain some inventive

---

*One of MGM's most gifted arrangers, composers, musical supervisors, and producers, Roger Edens joined the studio in 1934 after years on Broadway. Perhaps his most famous piece of special material was "Dear Mr. Gable," sung by Judy Garland in **Broadway Melody of 1938** (MGM, 1937). He was an unbilled associate producer of **Show Boat**, unbilled composer of "Born in a Trunk" in **A Star Is Born** (Warners, 1954), producer of **Funny Face** (Paramount, 1956), and associate producer of **Hello, Dolly!** (20th Century-Fox, 1969). Roger Edens died on July 13, 1970.

moments. When Pete storms down the town's main street to locate the sheriff, he passes a saloon where, through a window, we have our first glimpse of Ravenal gambling. It is an efficient way to introduce the leading man, depict his favorite vice, and move the plot along without fuss.

To show the parallel lives being followed by Gay and Magnolia after their separation, there is a series of dissolves (created by montage director Peter Ballbusch) from an image depicting one life to one of the other. A close-up of Gay's hands holding some cards dissolves into a close-up of Magnolia's hands holding their newborn baby. As the doctor enters Kim's name into the Bible, there is a hurricane lamp on the table. Its flame is replaced by a single candle on Kim's first birthday cake. A gamblers' dice cage dissolves into a bird cage, a present for Kim. Her spinning toy top is replaced by a spinning roulette wheel. Ravenal places a cane across the wheel. Next, we see baby Kim pick up another cane that is hanging over the edge of the *Cotton Blossom* stage, as she commences a little dance with Andy.

These touches reveal that Mahin is a writer

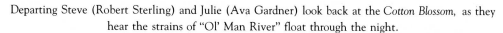

Departing Steve (Robert Sterling) and Julie (Ava Gardner) look back at the *Cotton Blossom,* as they hear the strains of "Ol' Man River" float through the night.

with a strong sense of the use of film. It is odd, however, that a man who supplied Jean Harlow and Clark Gable with some of the saltiest quips of the 1930's should remove virtually all the inherent humor from **Show Boat.** Gone entirely are the *Cotton Blossom* performances, the Backwoodsman, Cap'n Andy's playing all of the roles in **The Parson's Bride,** the lowbrow antics of Ellie and Frank, the banter between Joe and Queenie (the latter barely an extra in this version), the fun of the world's fair, and the foolish pomposity of Parthy.

If the film lacks humor on the one hand, it also lacks intense drama on the other; and for this, the blame falls largely to its director, George Sidney. For example, Mahin rather ingeniously has shifted the tense miscengenation scene from rehearsal time to an actual *Cotton Blossom* performance. While Frank and Ellie are gaily dancing out front, Julie and Steve's lives are being destroyed backstage. Instead of heightening this irony by showing Steve taking out a menacing knife, cutting his beloved's finger in front of the astonished troupe, and

MGM's ludicrous idea of what a show boat should look like. This nautical nightmare was designed by Jack Martin Smith at an alleged cost of $126,468. In addition to its spurious rigging, exterior staircase, third-deck cabin, pointed prow, and obsessively overdone gingerbread, the studio's *Cotton Blossom* has fostered the myth that show boats were steam-powered paddle wheelers with twin smokestacks.

1951—The MGM Version

Robert Sterling and Howard Keel relax by canoeing between takes. Note the camera platform on the side of the *Cotton Blossom*.

drawing the girl's blood into his mouth, Sidney so understates the action that only a viewer familiar with **Show Boat** can figure out what is happening.

Instead of a knife, Steve withdraws a tiny pin that is barely visible to both the troupe and the moviegoer. Julie's hand is discreetly lowered below the frame line of the screen, and she hardly winces when he presumably pricks her finger daintily. He lowers his mouth out of view for a moment; and to all this curious activity, there is hardly a reaction among the show boat family looking on. Naturally, Steve's claim to have Negro blood in him makes no sense at all. A major turning point of the story has been

squandered through inept direction. Sidney seems eager to get on quickly with the more picturesque aspects of his love story, rather than dwell on racial trouble.

Although one expects a certain prettiness in a musical, there is more to **Show Boat** than pure escapism. To give credence to the more serious aspects of its plot, there must be an authentic sense of time and place. This the MGM craftsmen have largely failed to provide.

The biggest anachronism is the celebrated show boat itself, which MGM claims is the largest movable prop ever made for a motion picture. Designed by the film's art director, Jack Martin Smith, the backlot *Cotton Blossom* cost

191

"I Might Fall Back on You," performed by Marge and Gower Champion.

an alleged $126,468. It is hard to imagine that the studio's research department can be blamed for this preposterous oversight, but MGM's *Cotton Blossom* was constructed as a steam-driven, back-wheel paddle boat, while in fact all show boats were simply barges with no power whatever of their own. They were pushed along by little towboats, not unlike the tugboats one sees in seaport harbors today.

Any ship with huge, 19½-foot paddles moved by massive pistons on either side would obviously have had to have its giant furnace and engine right in the middle of the ship, or exactly in the center of the show boat's auditorium. River boats with paddles, engines, and tall smokestacks were strictly for commerce or excur-

sions, the latter with, perhaps, some modest entertainment in one of the public rooms.

The twin curved staircases that join the front of the upper and lower decks of the *Cotton Blossom* are also pure MGM invention. They were designed simply to provide Robert Alton with a rising plane against which a platoon of dancers in brightly colored costumes could cavort and wave their tambourines to attract the townsfolk.

The dance does indeed provide a bright, upbeat opening for the picture and is cleverly supported by jaunty syncopation in the background scoring. But who on earth are all those dancers! Surely no show boat ever housed dozens of dancing boys and girls. And where do they disappear to after the opening number? In reality, small

The Champions sing "Life on the Wicked Stage."

touring companies of show boat actors were crammed into combination dressing and state rooms. Except for a small galley below deck, there was simply no more room aboard.

With its ludicrously inappropriate paddle wheel, twin staircases, elaborate mechanical rigging for raising and lowering its gangplanks, and obsessively overdone gingerbread detail, MGM's *Cotton Blossom* seems to have been squeezed from a pastry chef's icing bag. Its fraudulence sets a design tone for the entire film.

Alton's choreography for the Champions in "I Might Fall Back on You" is similarly resourceful but historically silly. He has Marge and Gower seated on a small garden love seat that is mounted to swivel freely on a pole running up its

center. When pushed by the Champions' feet, the seat swirls around and around. While cute perhaps, the prop is so contemporary in conception that it is yet another detail to weaken the film's sense of period.

A far more serious infraction is Alton's staging of "Life on the Wicked Stage." As Marge dances around the Trocadero stage, Gower first appears downstage right dressed as a mustachioed melodrama villain in cape and top hat. A moment later, he is downstage left with a fake theatrical beard as an old man. In another instant, he is himself, dressed in a purple cutaway. Finally, he is seen as a hunter, wearing a coonskin cap and carrying a rifle. These are amusing cinematic tricks but would not be possible before a live

1

2

3

ANDY
& HIS
3
TARTS

audience in a nightclub. Furthermore, they are too cunningly clever for a depiction of an era of innocence.

Although Walter Plunkett's costumes are so finely designed and tailored that they raise the economic level of all the characters several degrees beyond probability, they are, by and large, appropriate. There are a few exceptions. Cap'n Andy's three tarts in the 1936 version are gaudily dressed and made up for their profession: in this film they are three wholesome extra girls who might be expected at Lady Astor's in their chic finery.

But the most grotesque costume in this (or perhaps any) motion picture is the concoction thrown together seemingly out of scraps from the wardrobe department for Magnolia's cabaret debut at the Trocadero. It is a short, black bustle gown with a fluffy chartreuse trim at the lowcut neckline and hem. Swathed in ungainly fashion across the skirt are broad stripes of pink and chartreuse satin, all drawn to a bunch in the rear. Her black shoes too are decorated with big balls of chartreuse fluff. All in all, she looks rather like a deranged chicken in some bizarre fairy tale. One would have hoped for simple dignity in this gown, for Magnolia is trying to establish herself as a serious interpreter of popular song, not a female impersonator.

Visually, the film's strongest asset is its cinematography, particularly during the musical numbers and Roger Edens' departure sequence. Charles Rosher, a veteran cameraman, whose career dates back to 1912, systematically uses the color pallette of the performers' costumes and their backgrounds to create images that are strong, simple, and clearly related to mood and situation.

When Ravenal sings "Where's the Mate for Me?" while strolling along the river's edge, he is wearing a striking blue cutaway. Rosher noses his camera down at a 45° angle and provides a matching background of blue water.

While singing "Make Believe," Magnolia wears a dress with a dainty print of pink flowers. In one shot, Rosher repeats this delicate pattern by shooting a background of trees with their leaves an airy filigree. Gardner's "Can't Help Lovin' Dat Man" costume is an earthy bluish green with a bold plaid pattern. Rosher picks up the green of the river embankment behind her in one shot and then, shooting at a downward angle in another, frames Ava's beautiful face with a plane of dark green water.

Instead of aping John Mescall's more baroque camera movements in the 1936 version, Rosher is content to let his camera rest on his subject; and he relies upon John Dunning's film editing for whatever movement may be necessary. Rosher's masterfully understated window to this nineteenth-century fable earned him a well-deserved Academy Award nomination for cinematography.

As MGM had done before in many adaptations from the stage, the studio assumes the privilege of altering the structure of the musical numbers with no regard for Kern's original concepts. In the stage and 1936 film versions, "Can't Help Lovin' Dat Man," for example, is a quartet performed by Julie, Queenie, Magnolia, and Joe, with mixed chorus. The song is characterized as an old tune performed for years by Negroes on the river. In the MGM version, it has been transformed into a slow, contemplative soliloquy for Julie, with "dat man" clearly referring to her husband, Steve.

Such an interpretation may have dramatic logic, but one wonders if the adapters have a

FROM 1927 TO 1951, CAP'N ANDY'S THREE TARTS GREW INCREASINGLY LADYLIKE.

1. Tana Kamp, Charles Winniger, Dagmar Oakland, Maurine Holmes
2. Barbara Pepper, Renee Whitney, Dorothy Granger, Charles Winniger
3. Joe E. Brown with Sue Casey, Meredith Leeds, Jean Romaine

1951—The MGM Version

HOWARD KEEL
sings "Where's the Mate for Me?"

AVA GARDNER
performs "Can't Help Lovin' Dat Man."

right (other than legal) to alter a composer's conception of his material. If the quartet from **Rigoletto** is performed faithfully in MGM's operatic movies, why not the quartet from **Show Boat**!

Is all legally owned property to be reduced simply to grist for the corporate studio mill? Can Ellie's advice to local townswomen, "Life on the Wicked Stage," be turned into a cabaret set-piece with the girls simply a back-up to a specialty dance by Marge and Gower Champion?

Can all of "Ol' Man River" except for its refrain be eliminated because the deleted sections shift too much emphasis to the daily labors of Negro dock hands?

Apparently so, for an ill-informed gaggle of critics and the public alike swallowed this film, its largely inappropriate cast, its musical mutilation, its humorless script, and its empty Technicolored fripperies like a sack of sticky, sweet gumdrops. The picture grossed far more than $8,000,000.

CHAPTER 8

Recent Productions

CURIOUSLY, whenever a musical play survives long enough to be regarded as a classic, there begins a campaign to present it as part of an opera season. Opera, at least in the United States, is still regarded with a kind of awe that sets it apart from all other forms of theatre, probably because it is performed in a foreign language that Americans cannot comprehend. By reverse snobbery, if one of our home-grown products can compete with an **Aida** or a **Tannhäuser,** then it too is acclaimed great art.

Show Boat became great art in 1954. At least that is the year in which it was dignified with its first presentation by a major opera company. On Thursday, April 8, 1954, the New York City Opera presented the work at the New York City Center, the tile-decorated former Mecca Temple that looms imperiously on West 55th Street in mid-Manhattan, and which for decades offered superb seasons of legitimate theatre, ballet, and opera (both grand and light) at modest prices.

Robert Rounseville (Ravenal), Laurel Hurley (Magnolia), and Helena Bliss (Julie), all veterans of the opera company, sang superbly. But

many of the **Show Boat** roles have little or no singing, and these were played by guest performers: Stanley Carlson (Cap'n Andy), Marjorie Gateson (Parthy), Jack Albertson (Frank), and Diana Drake (Ellie) among them.

As soon as the opera season closed, **Show Boat** was transmuted back to a less lofty status and was permitted to open the City Center's Light Opera season on Wednesday, May 5. There were a few cast changes. Burl Ives took over the part of Cap'n Andy, Lawrence Winters replaced Bill Smith as Joe, Donn Driver replaced Jack Albertson as Frank, and Helen Phillips took over Queenie from Lucretia West; but most of the cast remained the same.

Both engagements were conducted by the City Center's longtime musical director, Julius Rudel, with settings by Howard Bay, costumes by John Boyt, and lighting by Jean Rosenthal.

The staging for both was by William Hammerstein, who had seen the first production of **Show Boat** as a small child and had helped his father type the screenplay of the second film version in 1935. From his stage managing of the 1946 revival until today, **Show Boat** has been an

integral part of Hammerstein's life. Not only has he directed several productions, but, working with his father until his death in 1960 and then continuing alone, William Hammerstein has shaped many of the dialogue and structural changes over the years.

Show Boat returned to the City Center on Thursday, October 28, 1954, with a cast again headed by Rounseville, Hurley, Bliss, and Winters, and newcomers Richard Wentworth (Cap'n Andy), Jean Handzlik (Parthy), and Betty Allen (Queenie).

On Wednesday, April 12, 1961, an entirely new production, directed by Dania Krupska and choreographed by Arthur Partington, was presented there with a cast starring Joe E. Brown as Cap'n Andy. The comic turns that had been denied Brown in the 1951 MGM film version were his to revel in during this final City Center revival of the work. The acrobatic dancing and loose-limbed pratfalls, the mile-wide grin, and the cocky braggadocio for which Brown was loved for half a century were offered in an exuberant and touching performance perhaps unequaled since that of Charles Winninger.

The fine supporting cast featured Rounseville once more as Ravenal, Jo Sullivan (Magnolia), Jane Kean (Ellie), Carol Brice (Queenie), Anita Darian (Julie), Richard France (Frank), Andrew Frierson (Joe), Isabella Hoopes (Parthy), and Herbert Fields (Steve).

In the early 1960's, New Yorkers witnessed the transformation of a West Side slum into Lincoln Center for the Performing Arts. The nation's most ambitious cultural complex was in time to contain an opera house, several legitimate theatres and concert halls, an outdoor band shell, and the Library and Museum of the Performing Arts.

One of the main structures, the New York State Theatre, was created to house opera, ballet, and musicals. This was the home of the Music Theater of Lincoln Center, a producing organization headed by Richard Rodgers. The policy was to offer two lavish revivals each summer. The first three seasons presented **The King and I** (7-6-64, State), **The Merry Widow** (8-17-64, State), **Kismet** (6-22-65, State), **Carousel** (8-10-65, State), **Annie Get Your Gun** (5-31-66, State), and inevitably **Show Boat,** which opened Tuesday, July 19, 1966.

For some reason, whenever **Show Boat** is treated to a major revival, there seems to be a prevailing attitude that the poor old thing is an antique from a former generation and requires plastic surgery to keep it young and fashionable. Despite the attractiveness of the score, there are many highly emotional moments that offer contrast to Kern's airy melodies. This revival was as pretty as a parade float but just as hollow.

At the outset, the task of creating emotional drama in a huge and architecturally frigid theatre like the State is a formidable one. The audience is simply too far away, and the actors are so many specks in a moving canvas. Further, the use of electronic amplification augments the dehumanization process and diminishes severely the impact of even the most heartrending performances.

But in this case, the decision to emphasize the pictorial aspects of the work, rather than its drama, seems unquestionably deliberate. From the complete removal of the Negro stevedores from the opening chorus, to the rewriting of two stanzas of "Can't Help Lovin' Dat Man" to eliminate any possible racial references, to the musical restructuring of "Ol' Man River" to cut out the middle section in which the stevedores work on the Mississippi, the performance was designed to glide along simply as pretty nostalgia.

Taking advantage of the massive State Theatre stage and its turntable, Oliver Smith whipped up a sumptuous *Cotton Blossom* that could not only arrive in port before the eyes of the audience, but could turn to allow views of its decks and interior. This gave director Lawrence Kasha (who had previously staged **Show Boat** at the Dallas Summer Musicals, August 19, 1963) the opportunity to move from one scene to the next with greater smoothness than is customary. It is, in fact, smoothness that characterizes both his direction and Ronald Field's choreography. The actors rarely came to life as real people with interrelationships, nor did the dancing brighten the mood perceptibly. Everything was meticulous but emotionally even.

As Cap'n Andy, David Wayne revealed the

Marjorie Gateson (Parthy), Laurel Hurley (Magnolia), Helena Bliss (Julie), Robert Gallagher (Steve), and Burl Ives (Cap'n Andy) pose for the miscegenation scene in the lobby of the New York City Center, 1954.

Barbara Cook (Magnolia), Eddie Phillips (Frank), and David Wayne (Cap'n Andy) perform **The Parson's Bride** in the 1966 Lincoln Center revival.

difference between an actor trying to be comic, and a comic trying to act. Everything Wayne did was rationally appropriate and appealing, but he never sparkled or seemed outrageously funny. Barbara Cook (Magnolia) and Stephen Douglass (Ravenal) sang well but seemed curiously indifferent to each other. The fire of Miss Cook's "Glitter and Be Gay" in **Candide** (12-1-56, Martin Beck) had become a mere spark, while wooden Mr. Douglass's southern accent kept drifting in and out like the tide.

From a musical point of view, the production held some uncomfortable surprises. Despite an augmented orchestra of 43 musicians, fifteen more than is customary on Broadway, the new orchestrations by Robert Russell Bennett tended to lack the beguiling grace, delicacy, and innocence of his earlier work. The seven musical themes comprising his new overture too often seemed artificially linked, with little regard to the overture's overall form.

Despite his normally fine musicianship, musical director Franz Allers conducted the familiar songs with an almost startling eccentricity in tempo. "Can't Help Lovin' Dat Man," for example, was taken at a frantic speed; and the "Dandies on Parade" chorus was so rapid that it was drained of its natural lilt. On the other hand, "Life on the Wicked Stage" opened and closed so slowly, with such indifference to its

Oliver Smith's imaginative setting for the world's fair sequence in the 1966 Lincoln Center revival.

"Why Do I Love You?" sung by Barbara Cook and Stephen Douglass. The splendid Lincoln Center costumes by Stanley Simmons blend authentic period style with considerable theatrical charm.

CONSTANCE TOWERS
sings "Bill."

BARBARA COOK
sings "Can't Help Lovin' Dat Man."

Allyn McLerie and Eddie Phillips perform "Good-bye, Ma Lady Love" in the 1966 Lincoln Center revival.

being a comedy song, that only Allyn McLerie's spirited performance as Ellie prevented it from sounding like a dirge.

"Ol' Man River" was entirely restructured as a one-refrain solo, with the choral group reduced simply to humming in the background. While this format provided a stunning frame for William Warfield's powerful voice, it was a needless alteration of the song as originally laid out by Kern himself.

Undoubtedly, the production's most memorable musical moment was the singing of "Bill" by Constance Towers, a striking blonde soprano, who performed the role of Julie in a dark wig. She sang the first chorus perched traditionally on her piano, then strolled offstage. Amid applause, she returned as if to retrieve a purse she had forgotten. Then she ambled to the wings to lean against the proscenium and offer the second chorus. Accompanied by a solo piano, Miss Towers' voice rang clearly through the cavernous State Theatre in an impressive display of vocal art and showmanship.

Of all the performers, those who came closest to playing their roles in an appropriate style were Margaret Hamilton (Parthy), whose sour expression suggested that she ate green apples before each scene, and Eddie Phillips (Frank) and Allyn McLerie, whose cakewalk was one of the rare joys of the production.

Rosetta Le Noire (Queenie) provided considerable spirit in her acting and musical ballyhoo, but her solo section in "Can't Help Lovin' Dat Man" was sabotaged by an ill-advised rewrite. The original lyrics:

Mah man is shiftless
An' good for nothin' too,
He's mah man jes' de same.
He's never round here
When dere is work to do.
He's never roun' me
When dere's workin' to do.
De chimley's smokin',
De roof is leakin' in,
But he don' seem to care,
He can be happy
Wid jes' a sip of gin.
Ah even loves him
When his kisses got gin.

were replaced by:

Mah man's a dreamer.
He don't have much to say.
He's mah man just the same.
Instead of workin',
He sits and dreams all day.
Instead of workin',
He'll be dreamin' all day.
De chimney's smokin',
De roof is leakin' in,
But he don't seem to care.
He only looks at
The things he wants to see
An' how I love him
When he's lookin' at me.

These new words not only fail to fit the music, but their banality weakens the entire character of the song.

Much musical tampering also took place in the London production that Harold Fielding presented at the Adelphi Theatre on Thursday, July 29, 1971. Directed and choreographed by Wendy Toye, the work was extensively edited by Benny Green, with the addition of a new scene and thereby a new song for England's popular cabaret singer, Cleo Laine, in the role of Julie. Miss Laine had agreed to play the part only if she could sing three songs, so an extra scene in a St. Louis bar was added just before the wedding scene finale of Act One to provide a situation for her slow, sultry version of "Nobody Else But Me." All of Miss Laine's vocals were performed in her throaty, intimate style; and, despite her musical liberties, the overall effect proved most effective.

"Dance Away the Night," normally Kim's flapper song in British productions, was given to Frank, who was played by the stylish American song-and-dance man, Kenneth Nelson, recently seen as a dramatic actor in **The Boys in the Band** (4-15-68, Theater Four). Another musical curiosity was the cutting of "Life on the Wicked Stage" in favor of "I Might Fall Back on You."

New orchestrations were composed by Keith Amos in the tawdry, ricky-ticky style typical of background music in bad British movies of the 1960's. The conducting by Ray Cook also reflected a surprisingly independent attitude to-

Ad for the long-running 1971 London revival.

CLEO LAINE

ward traditional **Show Boat** musical disciplines of tempo and stress.

Further, there was a weird crazy quilt of accents. In addition to the native British contingent of soloists, Ravenal was played by André Jobin, a Canadian with a pronounced French accent and a painfully strained upper register. Ena Cabayo (Queenie) and many of the Negro singers had a strong West Indian cadence that seemed oddly alien to America's Midwest. In addition to Kenneth Nelson, there were two other Americans with fine voices, Lorna Dallas (Magnolia) and Thomas Carey (Joe). Cap'n Andy was played by Englishman Derek Royle.

205

DEREK ROYLE
as Cap'n Andy in the 1971 London revival.

The *Cotton Blossom* arrives in town, London, 1971. Note the paddle wheel, undoubtedly influenced by the MGM film.

Recent Productions

André Jobin (Ravenal) and Lorna Dallas (Magnolia) in the
1971 London revival.

Perhaps the most enthusiastic acclaim went to a young Puerto Rican dancer, Miguel Godreau, who, in the role of a world's fair Knife Thrower, was described by Ronald Bryden in *The Observer* as "a grinning Bacchic faun."

Despite the British reputation for being "mod," their theatregoers are basically a very sentimental lot. A 1943 revival of **Show Boat** had played for 264 performances. The 1971 Fielding revival managed to attain 910 performances, by far the longest run of the work anywhere in the world.

Show Boat continues to be presented all over America. During the 1976 Bicentennial year, it was offered at the St. Louis Municipal Opera with Gale Gordon (Cap'n Andy), Ron Husmann (Ravenal), and Shirley Jones (Magnolia). Guy Lombardo presented another outdoor production at the Jones Beach Theatre in Wantagh, Long Island. Other productions appear regularly in summer theatres every year.

That **Show Boat** is the solitary American musical of the 1920's to continue in standard repertoire is a matter of no small fascination. The

Recent Productions

American Negro Thomas Carey takes London by storm, as Paul Robeson had done forty-three years earlier.

Ena Cabayo (Queenie) rouses the townsfolk with "C'mon, Folks."

standard 1920's musical presented an opening number in which a glistening chorus of boys and girls sang about the fun of a weekend on Long Island, or the fun of college life, or the fun of being glorified by Flo Ziegfeld.

Imagine the shock on the evening of December 27, 1927, when the curtain rose on **Show Boat** at the magnificent Ziegfeld Theatre, and a chorus of Negroes, lugging huge cotton bales, turned to the audience and sang:

Niggers all work on de Mississippi,
Niggers all work while de white folks play—
Loadin' up boats wid de bales of cotton,
Gittin' no rest till de Judgment Day.

This quatrain—terse, powerful, and precisely to the point—not only stunned the audience, but brilliantly prepared it to spend the next three hours watching a spectacular portrait of the Old South from the 1880's to what was then the present. **Show Boat** made history, not only because of Kern's beautiful score, but also because the characters and situations were interesting and genuine enough to sustain the forty-year time span of the story.

In a very real sense, it is the Mississippi River, which "jes' keeps rollin' along," that is the hero of the play; for the river is the focal point around which revolve the lives of all the characters; and whether they travel to Chicago or New York, they always return to the river.

The Negroes, who load boats with cotton bales, remain the most vital and dignified characters in the play, as if constant proximity to the river supplies them with a perpetual life force. They are depicted as simple, hardworking, and pious people, who are content with their lot and possess no fanciful illusions about the future.

MIGUEL GODREAU,
hit of the 1971 London revival, as a world's fair knife thrower.

Recent Productions

Jan Hunt (Ellie) and Kenneth Nelson (Frank) enliven proceedings at the Trocadero with "How'd You Like To Spoon with Me?" London, 1971.

By contrast, the white characters in **Show Boat** create a sugary fantasy world for themselves. It is Ravenal who sings to Magnolia:

In this sweet, improbable and unreal world
Finding you has given me my ideal world.

WHY DO I LOVE YOU?

It is the incapacity of the whites in **Show Boat** to sustain this ideal that causes their lives and dreams to crumble like dried frosting on an an-cient cake, while the Negroes and their river "jes' keep rollin' along."

Much of the strength of **Show Boat** depends upon librettist Hammerstein's skill for using words that ring true for each given situation. He effectively establishes the fantasy love of Magnolia and Ravenal through their excessively repeated observations that love is an idyllic state quite removed from daily realities ("Make Believe," "Why Do I Love You?," "You Are Love"), while his use of the word "nigger" is not a white writer's attempt to be derogatory or flip-

210

pant, but rather an unashamed expression of artistic honesty; for the term was and, in some cases, still is used in the South by whites and Negroes alike.

Unfortunately, the honest use of this term has grown unpopular in the last few decades (even when no derogation is implied), not only in **Show Boat,** but in all American literature. Some of Mark Twain's finest novels, many of Stephen Foster's best songs, and **Show Boat** alike have fallen victim to a bleaching process that has drained them of that ineffable quality of truth that occurs only when the right word is chosen for the right situation.

In the case of **Show Boat,** the use of "nigger" as the very opening word serves superbly to shock an audience from its complacency and cause it to consider (at least subconsciously) the servile condition to which southern Negroes were subjected nearly a century ago. The word is therefore an indictment against those times and conditions, not against the Negro race.

Thus the progression of euphemistic alterations to which this opening line has been subjected is almost ludicrous. First it was "*Niggers* all work on de Mississippi," in the 1936 film it was "*Darkies* all work on de Mississippi," in the 1946 revival it was "*Colored folks* work on de Missis-

The prop *Cotton Blossom*, wired for sound, rounds into view in the lagoon at the outdoor Jones Beach Theatre, 1976. The side panel bearing the name of the boat opens to reveal the auditorium.

The world's fair setting at Jones Beach.

sippi," in **Till the Clouds Roll By** it was "Here *we all* work on de Mississippi," and by the 1966 revival, it was—*Nobody* works on de Mississippi, because the Negro chorus was omitted altogether from the opening number.

Perhaps the alteration of this line would not seem so significant were it not so conspicuously placed at the very opening of the play. Somehow, "Here we all work..." is so devoid of potency that it seems almost apologetic, as if the producers preferred that Kern's score had been written for a musical set at a Wellesley tea dance, instead of the Old South.

With an increasing tendency to minimize the drama of the miscegenation scene, and with the omission of "I Might Fall Back on You," "Till Good Luck Comes My Way" (Ravenal's effective expression of his philosophy of life), and other songs, there is increasing reliance upon reprises, as if the production is merely a vehicle to show off a half-dozen standards by Kern and Hammerstein.

Although the show's earliest alterations were made by Hammerstein himself as a method of keeping the work vital to a changing audience, the trend was begun to permit the show to follow whatever theatrical vogue might have been fashionable. Like an older building that has been "modernized" through the elimination of its distinctive architectural details, **Show Boat** has been left without its original form and with only diluted dramatic impact.

It is curious that, unlike other major American musicals, **Show Boat** has no official script

at all. When one sees **Oklahoma!** or **Carousel** today, it is exactly the same show that was first viewed in the mid-1940's. Today's critics who assail **Show Boat**'s book and praise only its score, lamentably, are not viewing the genuine article.

While it is true that **Show Boat** has survived all these years because it was altered to reflect what was believed to be changing aesthetic and racial attitudes, its endurance has made the work a classic. As such, it exists far beyond fleeting artistic and social fashions.

Just as there is now a tendency to perform Bizet's **Carmen** without the recitatives composed by another man, and just as the deleted portions of George Gershwin's **Porgy and Bess** (10-10-35, Alvin) have recently been restored, perhaps the time has come to re-create **Show Boat** in the form that inspired *New York Telegram* critic Robert Garland to call it on opening night simply "an American masterpiece."

APPENDICES A, B, AND C

Appendices A, B, and C contain listings of all the principal roles and their players given in the order of appearance on the original Broadway opening night. Over the years, many roles (frequently the Faro Dealer, Gambler, Old Sport, and Hazel) have been eliminated. In such cases, blank spaces are left. In addition, many playbills for regional productions provide only incomplete information, thereby adding to the number of blank spaces.

Appendix A is a complete list of all twelve New York City area productions: Broadway, New York City Center, Lincoln Center, Randall's Island, and Jones Beach included. Appendix B contains all three London productions. It should be noted that Jim, the manager of the Trocadero, was called Max in the 1928 and 1943 productions. Appendix C contains all ten productions of the St. Louis Municipal Opera and all four from both the Los Angeles Civic Light Opera and Dallas Summer Musicals. These three organizations are among the country's leading producers of summer musicals. In addition, there is an entry for the historic first West Coast production in 1933.

Appendices A, B, and C also provide the names of principal production staff members. In some regional productions, the names of costume designers are omitted, because the costumes in those cases were usually rented.

APPENDIX A—NEW YORK CITY AREA STAGE PRODUCTIONS

Opening Date	December 27, 1927	May 19, 1932	June 29, 1938
Closing Date	May 4, 1929	October 22, 1932	July 16, 1938
Theatre	Ziegfeld	Casino	Municipal Stadium, Randall's Island
Length of Run	575 performances	181 performances	16 performances
Producer	Florenz Ziegfeld	Florenz Ziegfeld	San Carlo Opera Company: Fortune Gallo Shubert Productions: John Shubert
Director	Oscar Hammerstein II (uncredited), Zeke Colvan (credited)	Oscar Hammerstein II (uncredited)	Edward J. Scanlon Robert Alton
Choreographer	Sammy Lee	Sammy Lee (uncredited)	Watson Barratt
Settings	Joseph Urban	Joseph Urban	———
Costumes	John Harkrider	John Harkrider	Giuseppe Bamboschek
Musical Director	Victor Baravalle	Oscar Bradley	———
Choral Director	Will Vodery (uncredited)	Will Vodery (uncredited)	
WINDY	Allan Campbell	Allan Campbell	Jack Richards
STEVE	Charles Ellis	Charles Ellis	James Farrell
PETE	Bert Chapman	James Swift	William Lilling
QUEENIE	Tess ("Aunt Jemima") Gardella	Tess ("Aunt Jemima") Gardella	Mary Dyer
PARTHY ANN HAWKS	Edna May Oliver	Edna May Oliver	Zella Russell
CAP'N ANDY	Charles Winninger	Charles Winninger	William Kent
ELLIE	Eva Puck	Eva Puck	Nina Olivette
FRANK	Sammy White	Sammy White	Harry K. Morton
RUBBER FACE	Francis X. Mahoney	Francis X. Mahoney	———
JULIE	Helen Morgan	Helen Morgan	Natalie Hall
GAYLORD RAVENAL	Howard Marsh	Dennis King	Guy Robertson
VALLON	Thomas Gunn	Thomas Gunn	Franklyn Fox
MAGNOLIA	Norma Terris	Norma Terris	Bettina Hall
JOE	Jules Bledsoe	Paul Robeson	Lansing Hatfield
FARO DEALER	Jack Wynn	Gladstone Waldrip	———
GAMBLER	Phil Sheridan	Phil Sheridan	———
BACKWOODSMAN	Jack Daley	Jack Daley	Fred Mannatt
JEB	Jack Wynn	Gladstone Waldrip	Wesley Bender
LA BELLE FATIMA	Dorothy Denese	Dorothy Denese	———
OLD SPORT	Bert Chapman	James Swift	———
ETHEL	Estelle Floyd	Estelle Floyd	———
LANDLADY	Annie Hart	Annie Hart	Hannah Toback
SISTER	Annette Harding	V. Ann Kaye	———
MOTHER SUPERIOR	Mildred Schwenke	Mildred Schwenke	———
KIM (child)	Eleanor Shaw	Evelyn Eaton	———
JAKE	Robert Faricy	Robert Faricy	Roger Stearns
JIM	Jack Daley	Jack Daley	Fred Mannatt
MAN WITH GUITAR	Ted Daniels	Pat Mann	———
CHARLIE	J. Lewis Johnson	J. Lewis Johnson	———
LOTTIE	Tana Kamp	Gertrude Walker	———
DOLLY	Dagmar Oakland	Tana Kamp	Gracie Worth
HAZEL	Maurine Holmes	Maurine Holmes	———
KIM (young woman)	Norma Terris	Norma Terris	———
OLD LADY ON LEVEE	Laura Clairon	Laura Clairon	
			Fokine Ballet

Appendix A

January 5, 1946	September 7, 1948	April 8, 1954	May 5, 1954
January 4, 1947	September 19, 1948	October 31, 1954	May 16, 1954
Ziegfeld	New York City Center	New York City Center	New York City Center
418 performances	18 performances	5 performances in repertory (April 17, May 2, October 28, October 31)	15 performances
Kern and Hammerstein	Richard Rodgers and Oscar Hammerstein II	New York City Opera	The New York City Light Opera Company: William Hammerstein
Oscar Hammerstein II, Hassard Short	Oscar Hammerstein II, Hassard Short	William Hammerstein	William Hammerstein
Helen Tamiris	Helen Tamiris	John Butler	———
Howard Bay	Howard Bay	Howard Bay	Howard Bay
Lucinda Ballard	Lucinda Ballard	John Boyt	John Boyt
Edwin McArthur	David Mordecai	Julius Rudel	Julius Rudel
Pembroke Davenport, Will Vodery	Pembroke Davenport, Will Vodery		
Scott Moore	George Spellman	Arthur Newman	Arthur Newman
Robert Allen	Fred Brookins	Robert Gallagher	Robert Gallagher
Seldon Bennett	Gerald Prosk	Michael Pollock	Boris Aplon
Helen Dowdy	Helen Dowdy	Lucretia West	Helen Phillips
Ethel Owen	Ruth Gates	Marjorie Gateson	Marjorie Gateson
Ralph Dumke	Billy House	Stanley Carlson	Burl Ives
Colette Lyons	Clare Alden	Diana Drake	Diana Drake
Buddy Ebsen	Sammy White	Jack Albertson	Donn Driver
Francis X. Mahoney	Gordon Alexander	———	Thomas R. Powell
Carol Bruce	Carol Bruce	Helena Bliss	Helena Bliss
Charles Fredericks	Norwood Smith	Robert Rounseville	Robert Rounseville
Ralph Chambers	Fred Ardath	Leon Lishner	Lawrence Haynes
Jan Clayton	Pamela Caveness	Laurel Hurley	Laurel Hurley
Kenneth Spencer	William C. Smith	William C. Smith	Lawrence Winters
———	———	———	———
———	———	———	———
Howard Frank	Howard Frank	Benjamin Plotkin	Arthur Newman
Duncan Scott	Gerald Prosk	Arthur Newman	Lawrence Haynes
Jean Reeves	Sylvia Myers	———	Ann Barry
Willie Torpey	Robert Fleming	———	Roland Miles
Assota Marshall	Assota Marshall	Gloria Wynder	Gloria Wynder
Sara Floyd	Sara Floyd	Sara Floyd	Sara Floyd
Sheila Hogan	———	———	Barbara Ford
Iris Manley	Lorraine Waldman	———	Ellen Gleason
Alyce Mace	Alyce Mace	Adele Newton	Adele Newton
Max Showalter	King Brill	Milton Lyon	Milton Lyon
Jack Daley	Seldon Bennett	Michael Pollock	Boris Aplon
Thomas Bowman	Albert McCary	Charles Kuestner	Charles Kuestner
William C. Smith	Walter Mosby	Walter P. Brown	William C. Smith
Nancy Kenyon	Sara Dillon	———	Marilyn Bladd
Lydia Fredericks	Elaine Hume	———	Dorothy Mirr
———		———	———
Jan Clayton	———	———	Greta Thormsen
Frederica Slemons	Ann Lloyd	Sara Floyd	Sara Floyd
Pearl Primus, LaVerne French, Claude Marchant, Talley Beatty, Charles Tate	Gloria Smith, La Verne French		

Appendix A

Opening Date	June 21, 1956	June 27, 1957	April 12, 1961
Closing Date	September 3, 1956	September 7, 1957	April 23, 1961
Theatre	Jones Beach Marine Theatre	Jones Beach Marine Theatre	New York City Center
Length of Run	68 performances	70 performances	14 performances
Producer	Guy Lombardo: John Kennedy	Guy Lombardo: John Kennedy	The New York City Center Light Opera Company: Jean Dalrymple
Director	Reginald Hammerstein	Reginald Hammerstein	Dania Krupska
Choreographer	Lee Sherman	Lee Sherman	Arthur Partington
Settings	Albert Johnson	Albert Johnson	Howard Bay
Costumes	Michael Travers	Michael Travis	Stanley Simmons
Musical Director	Fred Dvonch	Fred Dvonch	Julius Rudel
Choral Director			William Jonson
WINDY	Scott Moore	Scott Moore	Scott Moore
STEVE	Evans Thornton	Evans Thornton	Herbert Fields
PETE	Michael Dominico	Donald Farnworth	William Coppola
QUEENIE	Helen Dowdy	Helen Dowdy	Carol Brice
PARTHY ANN HAWKS	Helen Raymond	Helen Raymond	Isabella Hoopes
CAP'N ANDY	Paul Hartman	Andy Devine	Joe E. Brown
ELLIE	Marie Foster	Marie Foster	Jane Kean
FRANK	Hal LeRoy	Lou Wills Jr.	Richard France
RUBBER FACE	Henry Lawrence	Henry Lawrence	J. Patrick Carter
JULIE	Helena Bliss	Helena Bliss	Anita Darian
GAYLORD RAVENAL	David Atkinson	David Atkinson	Robert Rounseville
VALLON	Charles Massinger	Charles Massinger	John J. Martin
MAGNOLIA	Gloria Hamilton	Gloria Hamilton	Jo Sullivan
JOE	William C. Smith	William C. Smith	Andrew Frierson
FARO DEALER	——	——	——
GAMBLER			
BACKWOODSMAN	Walt Calhoun	Richard Wentworth	Norman A. Grogan
JEB	David Kurlan	David Kurlan	Feodore Tedick
LA BELLE FATIMA	Lillian D'Honau	Judy Sargent	——
OLD SPORT	David Smith	James J. Fox	Jack Rains
ETHEL	Dolores Murden	Dolores Murden	Alyce Webb
LANDLADY	Sara Floyd	Sara Floyd	Claire Waring
SISTER	——	——	
MOTHER SUPERIOR	——	——	Miriam Lawrence
KIM (child)	——	——	Bridget Knapp
JAKE	Buddy Brennan	Buddy Brennan	William Coppola
JIM	David Kurlan	David Kurlan	Henry Lawrence
MAN WITH GUITAR	James Stevenson	Ray Cook	J. Patrick Carter
CHARLIE	Theodore Hines	Theodore Hines	Ned Wright
LOTTIE	Judy Rawlings	Ethel Madsen	Helen Guile
DOLLY	Adrienne Angel	Barbara Saxby	Mara Wirt
HAZEL	——	——	
KIM (young woman)	——	——	Jo Sullivan
OLD LADY ON LEVEE	Sara Floyd	Sara Floyd	Sara Floyd
	Geoffrey Holder		

Appendix A

July 19, 1966	July 1, 1976
September 10, 1966	September 5, 1976
New York State, Lincoln Center	Jones Beach Marine Theatre
104 performances	67 performances

Music Theater of Lincoln Center: Richard Rodgers   Guy Lombardo: Arnold Spector

Lawrence Kasha	John Fearnley
Ronald Field	Robert Pagent
Oliver Smith	John W. Keck
Stanley Simmons	Winn Morton
Franz Allers	Jay Blackton
	Robert Monteil
David Thomas	Robert Pagent
William Traylor	Bob Slater
Bob Monroe	Ralph Vucci
Rosetta Le Noire	Alyce Webb
Margaret Hamilton	Lizabeth Pritchett
David Wayne	Max Showalter
Allyn McLerie	Connie Day
Eddie Phillips	Lee Roy Reams
Bob La Crosse	Jimmy Rivers
Constance Towers	Beth Fowler
Stephen Douglass	Robert Peterson
Barton Stone	John Dorrin
Barbara Cook	Barbara Meister
William Warfield	Edward Pierson
———	———
———	———
Neil McNelis	Lee Cass
Jess Green	Dale Muchmore
Sally Neil	Irma Rogers
	———
Joyce McDonald	———
Helen Noyes	Irma Rogers
Frances Haywood	———
Mary Manchester	Elaine Bunse
Maureen McNabb	Karen DiBianco
Clyde Walker	Kevin Wilson
Barton Stone	Lee Cass
Paul Adams	Don Bonnell
Edward Taylor	Eugene Edwards
Martha Danielle	———
Trudy Wallace	———
———	
———	
Helen Noyes	Irma Rogers

APPENDIX B—THREE LONDON PRODUCTIONS

Opening Date	May 3, 1928	April 17, 1943	July 29, 1971
Closing Date	March 2, 1929	September 18, 1943	September 29, 1973
Theatre	Theatre Royal Drury Lane, London	Stoll, London	Adelphi, London
Length of Run	350 performances	264 performances	910 performances
Producer	Alfred Butt	Prince Littler: Frank C. Marshall	Harold Fielding
Director	Felix Edwardes	James Moran	Wendy Toye
Choreographer	Max Scheck	Max Rivers	Wendy Toye
Settings	Joseph and Phil Harker	James Needle	Tim Goodchild
Costumes	Irene Segalla	Charles H. Fox	Tim Goodchild
Musical Director	Herman Finck	Reginald Burston, Albert W. Leggett	Ray Cook
Choral Director	John Payne		John McCarthy
WINDY	Jack Martin	J. P. Kennedy	Len Maley
STEVE	Colin Clive	Robert Elson	John Larson
PETE	Fred Hearne	Gaylord Bryan	Brian Gidley
QUEENIE	Alberta Hunter	Lucille Benstead	Ena Cabayo
PARTHY ANN HAWKS	Viola Compton	Hester Paton Brown	Pearl Hackney
CAP'N ANDY	Cedric Hardwicke	Mark Daly	Derek Royle
ELLIE	Dorothy Lena	Sylvia Kellaway	Jan Hunt
FRANK	Leslie Sarony	Leslie Kellaway	Kenneth Nelson
RUBBER FACE	Henry Thomas	W. S. Percy	Albin Pahernik
JULIE	Marie Burke	Pat Taylor	Cleo Laine
GAYLORD RAVENAL	Howett Worster	Bruce Carfax	Andre Jobin
VALLON	Percy Parsons	Ralph Tovey	Michael Napier-Brown
MAGNOLIA	Edith Day	Gwyneth Lascelles	Lorna Dallas
JOE	Paul Robeson	"Mr. Jetsam"	Thomas Carey
FARO DEALER	William Wallace	Albert Digney	———
GAMBLER	Alec J. Willard	Wilfred Brandon	———
BACKWOODSMAN	Roy Emerton	Albert Digney	Ron Rich
JEB	Gordon Crocker	W. S. Percy	Stanley Fleet
LA BELLE FATIMA	Lenore Gadsden	Malvina Fraser	Nicky Migden
OLD SPORT	Cecil Dereham	Roy Neilson	———
ETHEL	Kathleen Thomas	Sadie Hopkins	Marcedes Kirkwood
LANDLADY	Margaret Yarde	Georgina De Lara	Margo Cunningham
SISTER	———	———	———
MOTHER SUPERIOR	Maud Cressall	———	———
KIM (child)	Helen Moore		
JAKE	Michael Cole	Albert Digney	Ray Cook
JIM	Will Stuart	W. S. Percy	Michael Napier-Brown
MAN WITH GUITAR	Walter Webster	———	———
CHARLIE	Norris Smith	Mathias Vroom	Eddie Tagoe
LOTTIE	Nancy Brown	Anna Pollak	Beatrice Aston
DOLLY	Peggy Lovat	Helen Grindley	Rae Delarosa
HAZEL	Ann Barbour	———	Kelly Wilson
KIM (young woman)	Edith Day	Valerie Hay	Yvonne Peters
OLD LADY ON LEVEE	Maud Cressall	———	Margo Cunningham
			Miguel Godreau

220

APPENDIX C—AMERICAN REGIONAL PRODUCTIONS
(A Selective Listing)

Opening Date	August 11, 1930	October 30, 1933	August 13, 1934
Closing Date	August 24, 1930	December 2, 1933	August 26, 1934
Theatre	Municipal Opera, St. Louis	Curran, San Francisco	Municipal Opera, St. Louis
Length of Run	14 performances	40 performances	14 performances
Producer	The Municipal Theater Association: Milton I. Shubert	(Edward) Belasco and (Homer F.) Curran, in association with Howard Lang	The Municipal Theatre Association of St. Louis
Director	Lew Morton	Edgar J. MacGregor	Zeke Colvan
Choreographer	Marie Peterson	Pearl Eaton	Palmere Brandeaux
Settings	Herbert Moore	Leo Atkinson	Watson Barratt
Costumes	John Harkrider, Orry Kelly	———	Ernest R. Schrapps
Musical Director	Giuseppe Bamboschek	Herman Heller	Oscar Bradley
Choral Director		Freita Shaw	
WINDY	Hal Forde	Norman Fusier	Robert Long
STEVE	Leonard Ceeley	Victor Adams	Leonard Ceeley
PETE	Frank Horn	Philip Dare	Frank Horn
QUEENIE	Mammy Jinny	Hattie McDaniel	Georgette Harvey
PARTHY ANN HAWKS	Maude Ream Stover	Cecil Cunningham	Maude Ream Stover
CAP'N ANDY	W. C. Fields	William Kent	William Kent
ELLIE	Eva Puck	Nina Olivette	Doris Patston
FRANK	Sammy White	Billy Wayne	Sammy White
RUBBER FACE	William Blanch	Robert Dale	Truman Gaige
JULIE	Margaret Carlisle	Estelle Taylor	Gladys Baxter
GAYLORD RAVENAL	Guy Robertson	Perry Askam	Allan Jones
VALLON	George Anderson	John Clifford	Joseph Macaulay
MAGNOLIA	Charlotte Lansing	Charlotte Lansing	Charlotte Lansing
JOE	Lois B. Deppe	Kenneth Spencer	Lois B. Deppe
FARO DEALER	Edgar Hill	Al Walton	Herbert Weber
GAMBLER	———	Charles Schroeder	Sam Thomas
BACKWOODSMAN	Robert Long	Fred Peters	Victor Casmore
JEB	Nelson Zimmer	LeGrande Anderson	Frederic Persson
LA BELLE FATIMA	———	Annabelle Gammage	Marie Starner
OLD SPORT	A. W. Hempelmann	William Hardwick	Truman Gaige
ETHEL	Edith Wright	Freita Shaw	Aquila McKay
LANDLADY	Maude Odell	Ann Kingsley	Edith King
SISTER	Sylvia Saunders	———	Marvel Conheeny
MOTHER SUPERIOR	Alice Fischeles	Alta Bush	Elizabeth Crandall
KIM (child)	Elsie Doleres	Betty Kendig	Frances Belz
JAKE	Frederick Persson	Bob McCoy	Frederic Persson
JIM	George Anderson	Norman Fusier	Victor Casmore
MAN WITH GUITAR	Edgar Hunt	Noel Stafford	Herbert Weber
CHARLIE	———	Oris Corporal	Sam Thomas
LOTTIE	Dorothy Doll	Lillian Reticker	Marie Starner
DOLLY	Dassa Mackintire	Aileen Covington	Helen Eck
HAZEL	Betti Davis	Macha Vance	Sheila Harling
KIM (young woman)	Charlotte Lansing	Charlotte Lansing	Charlotte Lansing
OLD LADY ON LEVEE	Edith Wright	Ann Kingsley	Elizabeth Crandall
	Fisk University Male Octet	Freita Shaw's Etude Ethiopian Chorus	

Opening Date	August 15, 1938	May 13, 1940	August 17, 1942
Closing Date	August 28, 1938	May 18, 1940	August 30, 1942
Theatre	Municipal Opera, St. Louis	Philharmonic Auditorium, Los Angeles	Municipal Opera, St. Louis
Length of Run	14 performances	8 performances	14 performances
Producer	The Municipal Theatre Association of St. Louis: Richard H. Berger	Los Angeles Civic Light Opera Association: Edwin Lester	The Municipal Theatre Association of St. Louis: Richard H. Berger
Director	Zeke Colvan	Zeke Colvan	John Kennedy
Choreographer	Theodor Adolphus, Al White Jr.	Ada Broadbent	Theodor Adolphus, Dan M. Eckley
Settings	Raymond Sovey	Kate Drain Lawson	Watson Barratt
Costumes	Billi Livingston	Kate Drain Lawson	Ernest Schrapps
Musical Director	George Hirst	Oscar Bradley	Jacob Schwartzdorf (Jay Blackton)
Choral Director		Leon Rosebrook	
WINDY	Al Downing	Norman Fusier	Vincent Vernon
STEVE	Earle MacVeigh	Victor Adams	John Tyers
PETE	Jerry Sloane	Edward Fisher	Al Downing
QUEENIE	Minto Cato	Bertha Powell	Minto Cato
PARTHY ANN HAWKS	Helen Raymond	Winifred Harris	Helen Raymond
CAP'N ANDY	George Rasely	Guy Kibbee	Jed Prouty
ELLIE	Vicki Cummings	Helen Lynd	Vicki Cummings
FRANK	Jack Sheehan	Sammy White	Sammy White
RUBBER FACE	———	Francis X. Mahoney	———
JULIE	Margaret Carlisle	Helen Morgan	Gladys Baxter
GAYLORD RAVENAL	Ronald Graham	John Boles	Bob Lawrence
VALLON	Joseph Macaulay	Jack Rutherford	Frederic Persson
MAGNOLIA	Norma Terris	Norma Terris	Norma Terris
JOE	Kenneth Spencer	Paul Robeson	Kenneth Spencer
FARO DEALER	———	Jim Boudwin	———
GAMBLER	———	———	———
BACKWOODSMAN	Frederic Persson	Jack Daley	Joseph Cochran
JEB	Gladstone Waldrip	Don Kent	Lyndon Crews
LA BELLE FATIMA	Mary Louise Crowe	Janet Graves	———
OLD SPORT	———	Edward Fisher	———
ETHEL	———	Evelyn Burwell	———
SHOWBOAT 8	Marcella Uhl	Kathleen Smith	Ruth Urban
SISTER	Annamary Dickey	———	———
MOTHER SUPERIOR	Jeanne Gustavison	Ava Josette	Jeanne Gustavison
KIM (child)	Anita Heinrichsemeyer	Babs Savage	Jacqueline Stemmler
JAKE	John Blaine	Le Roy Pryor	Frederic Persson
JIM	Jack Carr	Jack Daley	Al Downing
MAN WITH GUITAR	Larry Siegle	Rugby Curtis	———
CHARLIE	———	Jester Hairston	———
LOTTIE	———	Muriel Goodspeed	———
DOLLY	———	Marguerite Merlin	———
HAZEL	———	Lucille Dale	———
KIM (young woman)	Norma Terris	Norma Terris	Norma Terris
OLD LADY ON LEVEE	———	Kathleen Smith	———
		Hall Johnson Singers	

Appendix C

<table>
<tr><td>

May 8, 1944
May 20, 1944
Philharmonic Auditorium,
Los Angeles
16 performances

</td><td>

June 16, 1947
June 22, 1947
Starlight Operetta, Dallas

7 performances

</td><td>

August 18, 1947
August 31, 1947
Municipal Opera, St. Louis

14 performances

</td><td>

June 5, 1952
June 15, 1952
Municipal Opera, St. Louis

11 performances

</td></tr>
<tr><td>

The Los Angeles Civic Light
Opera Association: Edwin Lester
Zeke Colvan
Aida Broadbent
Adrian Awan
Walter J. Israel
Heinz Roemheld

</td><td>

State Fair of Texas: Charles
R. Meeker Jr.
Roger Gerry
Maurice Kelly
Peter Wolf
———
Giuseppe Bamboschek

</td><td>

The Municipal Theatre Association
of St. Louis: John Kennedy
Robert E. Perry
Dan M. Eckley, Virginia Johnson
Watson Barratt
Ernest Schrapps
Edwin McArthur

</td><td>

The Municipal Theatre Association
of St. Louis: John Kennedy
Morton Da Costa
Ted Cappy
Albert Johnson
Andrew Geoly
Edwin McArthur

</td></tr>
<tr><td>

Herbert Evans
Wilton Clary
Edward Bushman
Edith Wilson
Bertha Belmore
Gene Lockhart
Colette Lyons
Sammy White
Johnny Silver
Carol Bruce
Lansing Hatfield
Jack Rutherford
Marthe Errolle
Todd Duncan
Jack Saunders
Leland Ledford
Jack Daley
Frank Breneman
Diane Meroff
Michael Austin
Evelyn Burwell
Marian Douglas
Leonne Hall, Marie Hubert
Elaine Haslett
Carol Field
David Smith
Jack Daley
Jack Garland
George Bryant
Leonne Hall
Marie Hubert
———
Marthe Errolle
Marian Douglas

</td><td>

Rollin Bauer
Wilton Clary
Fred Brookins
Helen Dowdy
Louise Lorimer
Harlan Briggs
Clare Alden
Chick Chandler
John Lipscomb
Maxine Adams
Norwood Smith
Joseph Macaulay
Pamela Caveness
William C. Smith
———
Fred Brookins
Craig Timberlake
Jane Ellen Dempsey
John Lipscomb
———
Mary Dyer
———
Beverly Kirk
Ann Duke
Harry Holton
Joseph Macaulay
———
———
———
———
Pamela Caveness
Mary Dyer

</td><td>

Stanley Simmonds
Leroy Busch
Robert Davis
Helen Dowdy
Helen Raymond
Edwin Steffe
Nina Olivette
Sammy White
Arnold Knippenberg
Marthe Errolle
Wilbur Evans
G. Swayne Gordon
Evelyn Wyckoff
William C. Smith
———
John Patrick Hickey
Arthur Breyfogle
Doris O'Brien
———
Christine Morgan
Sara Floyd

Marjorie Stormont
Margaret McGrath
John Sacco
Joseph Cusanelli
Robert Childers
Chester Bridges
Shirley Faith
Carla Caldwell
———
Evelyn Wyckoff
Sara Floyd

</td><td>

Vince Vernon
William Olvis
Edward Krawll
Bertha Powell
Mary Wickes
Edwin Steffe
Marie Foster
Hal Le Roy
Arthur F. Gibbs
Mariquita Moll
Donald Clarke
Jack Rutherford
Iva Withers
William C. Smith
———
Jack Rutherford
Joseph Cusanelli
Mary Jo Goodson
———
Clara Etta Smith
Sara Floyd

Julanne Conrad
Janet Dunphy
Rene Wiegert
Joseph Cusanelli
Ernest Thompson
Chester Bridges
Jean Kraemer
Gratia Christie
———
Iva Withers
Sara Floyd

</td></tr>
</table>

Opening Date	August 13, 1956	June 5, 1958	August 15, 1960	August 19, 1963
Closing Date	August 26, 1956	June 15, 1958	September 24, 1960	September 1, 1963
Theatre	State Fair Auditorium, Dallas	Municipal Opera, St. Louis	Philharmonic Auditorium, Los Angeles	State Fair Music Hall, Dallas
Length of Run	14 performances	11 performances	48 performances	14 performances
Producer	State Fair Musicals: Charles R. Meeker Jr.	The Municipal Theatre Association of St. Louis: John Kennedy	The Los Angeles Civic Light Opera Association: Edwin Lester	Dallas Summer Musicals: Tom Hughes
Director	George Schaefer	Edward M. Greenberg	Edward M. Greenberg	Lawrence Kasha
Choreographer	Donald Saddler	Anthony Nelle, Ted Cappy	Ernest Flatt	Toni Beck
Settings	Peter Wolf	Paul C. McGuire	Howard Bay	Peter Wolf
Costumes	Joe Crosby	Michael Travis	Dorothy Jeakins	Joe Crosby
Musical Director	Franz Allers	Edwin McArthur	Louis Adrian	James Leon
Choral Director			Edith Gordon, Jester Hairston	
WINDY	Tommy Carter	Charles Sherwood	Clarence Nordstrom	Eugene Cole
STEVE	William Le Massena	Edmund Lyndeck	Thomas Gleason	Glenn Bridges
PETE	John Grigas	Walter Richardson	Grant Griffin	Jon Vance McFadden
QUEENIE	Bertha Powell	Helen Dowdy	Virginia Capers	Rosetta LeNoire
PARTHY ANN HAWKS	Margaret Hamilton	Margaret Hamilton	Helen Raymond	Lulu Bates
CAP'N ANDY	Stanley Carlson	Andy Devine	Joe E. Brown	Charlie Ruggles
ELLIE	Joan Mann	Dorothy Keller	Ruta Lee	Betty Linton
FRANK	Tom Avera	Hal Le Roy	Eddie Foy Jr.	William Skipper
RUBBER FACE	Robert Eckles	Peter Messineo	Robert Vanselow	Forrest Lorey
JULIE	Betty Colby	Marion Marlowe	Julie Wilson	Rosalind Elias
GAYLORD RAVENAL	William Tabbert	Jim Hawthorne	Richard Banke	Richard Fredricks
VALLON	Joseph Macaulay	Eustace Fletcher	Irwin Charone	Bill Black
MAGNOLIA	Shirley Jones	Gloria Hamilton	Jacquelyn McKeever	Jacquelyn McKeever
JOE	Lawrence Winters	William C. Smith	Lawrence Winters	Brock Peters
FARO DEALER	———	———	———	———
GAMBLER				
BACKWOODSMAN	Joseph Macaulay	Joseph Cusanelli	Gordon Ewing	Norman Grogan
JEB	Norman Grogan	Vernon Shinall	Dick Hilleary	Neal Pock
LA BELLE FATIMA	Jackie Ebeier	Susan Rapp	Rachelle Reyes	Hazel Rippe
OLD SPORT	———	———	Dick Warren	———
ETHEL	Norma J. Hughes	Clara Etta Smith	Margaret Hairston	———
SHOWBOAT 8	Sadie French	Sara Floyd	Belle Mitchell	Sadie French
SISTER				
MOTHER SUPERIOR	Sadie French	June Magruder	Nancy Bramlage	Carol Kirkpatrick
KIM (child)	Joyce Ann Boyd	Betty Rae Sztukowski	Christy Lynn	Lesli Glatter
JAKE	John Jones	Rene Wiegert	Dick Hilleary	Joe Harrell
JIM	Joseph Macaulay	Joseph Cusanelli	Irwin Charone	Eivie McGehee
MAN WITH GUITAR	Mel Marshall	Carroll Wayham	Grant Griffin	———
CHARLIE	Norman Grogan	Chester Bridges	Walter Hinton	Donald Hall
LOTTIE	Phyllis Stewart	Caroline Worth	Diane Doxee	Sue Erdmann
DOLLY	Joy-Lynne Cranford	Lucille Smith	Nancy Foster	Janice Baxter
HAZEL	———		———	———
KIM (young woman)	Shirley Jones	Gloria Hamilton		Sandy Duncan
OLD LADY ON LEVEE	Sadie French	Sara Floyd	Belle Mitchell	Sadie French

Appendix C

June 22, 1964	September 19, 1967	August 5, 1968	July 26, 1976
June 28, 1964	November 4, 1967	August 11, 1968	August 1, 1976
Municipal Opera, St. Louis	Dorothy Chandler Pavilion of the Los Angeles Music Center	Municipal Opera, St. Louis	Municipal Opera, St. Louis
7 performances	56 performances	7 performances	7 performances
The Municipal Theatre Association of St. Louis: John Kennedy	The Los Angeles Civic Light Opera Association: Edwin Lester	The Municipal Theatr Association of St. Louis: Glenn Jordan	The Municipal Theatre Association of St. Louis: Edward M. Greenberg
Dan M. Eckley	Edward M. Greenberg	Crandall Diehl	Forrest Carter
Ronald Field, Mavis Ray	Lee Theodore	Zachary Solov	John Montgomery
Paul C. McGuire	Oliver Smith	Paul C. McGuire	Grady Larkins
Bill Hargate, Andrew Gec	Stanley Simmons	Don Foote	Donald Chan
Edwin McArthur	Louis Adrian	Leo Kopp	Kenneth Billups
Kenneth Billups	Lawrence Brown, Jester Hairston	Kenneth Billups	
Charles Sherwood	Ted Stanhope	Bill Atwood	James Harwood
Paul Brown	Seth Riggs	Robert (Buzz) Barton	Bill Boss
William Bentley	Michael J. Zaslow	Paul Barby	James Anthony
Rosetta Le Noire	Virginia Capers	Theresa Merritt	Venida Evans
Mary Wickes	Audrey Christie	Mary Wickes	Helen Noyes
Andy Devine	Pat O'Brien	Arthur Godfrey	Gale Gordon
June L. Walker	Sandra O'Neill	Diaan Ainslee	Betty Ann Grove
Jack Goode	Eddie Foy Jr.	Ray Becker	Geoffrey Webb
———	Robert E. Webb	———	Bill Atwood
Jean Sanders	Gale Sherwood	Jean Sanders	Kelly Garrett
William Lewis	John Tyers	Frank Porretta	Ron Husmann
Jack Murdock	Grandon Rhodes	Truman Gaige	James Paul
Wynne Miller	Eileen Christy	Judith McCauley	Shirley Jones
LeVern Hutcherson	Robert Mosley	Edward Pierson	Bruce Hubbard
———	———	———	———
———	———	———	———
Robert Eckles	Alan V. Aric	John Messana	James Anthony
———	Tom Ingram	James Paul	Garrett Conner
———	Maris O'Neill	———	Lee Nolting
———	———	———	———
———	Jean Sewell	———	Jeanette Bush
Sara Floyd	Barbara Perry	Mary Margaret Heitm:	Margaret Jeffries
———	———	———	———
———	———	———	Beth Spencer
———	Lisa Eilbacher	———	Renee Schumer
Jonathan Dudley	Lawrence Brown	Gordon Bovinet	Robert Marks
———	Benny Baker	———	James Paul
———	Robert Delaney	———	John Patrick Sundine
———	John Hawker	———	Bill Atwood
———	Joy Zaccaro	———	———
———	Anita Hile	———	———
———	———	———	———
———		———	———
———	Belle Mitchell	———	Margaret Jeffries

APPENDIX D—THE STAGE SCORE

As many songs have been added and eliminated from the **Show Boat** score since its world premiere in Washington, D. C., in November 1927, the graph in Appendix D allows the reader to see at a glance which engagement contained which songs. Notice in particular how many long-forgotten songs were used briefly prior

	11-15-27 National Washington	11-21-27 Nixon Pittsburgh	11-28-27 Ohio Cleveland	12-5-27 Erlanger Philadelphia	12-12-27 Erlanger Philadelphia	12-19-27 Erlanger Philadelphia

ACT ONE

Opening: ——

Cotton Blossom ——

Cap'n Andy's Ballyhoo ——

Where's the Mate for Me? ——————————————————————————————————————

Make Believe ——

Ol' Man River ——

Musical Scena ————————————————

Can't Help Lovin' Dat Man ——

Life on the Wicked Stage ——————————————————————————————————————

Till Good Luck Comes My Way ————————————————————————————————————

Mis'ry's Comin' Aroun' ————————————

r. Ol' Man River ——

I Would Like To Play a Lover's Part ————————

Be Happy, Too —————— I Might Fall Back on You ——————————————————

C'mon, Folks ——

You Are Love ——

Finale ——

ACT TWO

Opening: ——

At the Fair ——

Dandies on Parade ——

Cheer Up ——————————— Why Do I Love You? ————————————————————————

Specialty ——————————————————————————

In Dahomey ——————————————————————————

My Girl ——————————————————————————————

Bill ——

r. Can't Help Lovin' Dat Man ————————————————————————————————————

a) Coal Black Lady, ————————————————————
b) Bully Song ——————————————————————————

Service and Scene Music ——

r. Make Believe ————————————————————————

Trocadero Ballet ————————————   Trocadero Ballet ——————————————————

Apache Dance ——————————————————————

Hello, Ma Baby —————————————— Good-bye, Ma Lady Love ————————————————

After the Ball ——

r. Ol' Man River ——

Hey, Feller! ————————————————————————————————————

r. You Are Love ————————

It's Getting Hotter in the North ———————— Why Do I Love You? ——————————

Eccentric Dance ——————————

Tap Dance ——

Finale: Ol' Man River ——

to the Broadway opening. Notice too that the London productions replace "Good-bye, Ma Lady Love" with "How'd You Like To Spoon with Me?" and the reprise of "Why Do I Love You?" with "Dance Away the Night," in addition to dropping the convent scene altogether. It is interesting also to follow the repositioning of "Life on the Wicked Stage," following the elimination after the 1932 revival of Act One, Scene Three, in which it originally appeared.

12-27-27 Ziegfeld New York City	5-3-28 Drury Lane London	5-19-32 Casino New York City	1-5-46 Ziegfeld New York City	7-19-66 New York State New York City	7-29-71 Adelphi London
				Mis'ry's Comin' Aroun'	
		Life on the Wicked Stage	I Might Fall Back on You		
		Dance: No Gems, No Roses, No Gentlemen			
		Dance: No Shoes	Life on the Wicked Stage		
				Nobody Else But Me	
		Cakewalk			
		Service and Scene Music			
		r. Make Believe			
	How'd You Like To Spoon with Me?	Good-bye, Ma Lady Love			How'd You Like To Spoon with Me?
					Good-bye, Ma Lady Love
					r. Ol' Man River
		Hey, Feller!			
	Dance Away the Night	Why Do I Love You?	Nobody Else But Me		Dance Away the Night
		Eccentric Dance	Dance 1927		
		Tap Dance			

APPENDIX E—FILM CASTS AND SCORES

Virtually complete production and casting information is given for all three film versions. The cast of the 1929 movie was taken from the screenplay and files at Universal. The cast listings for the 1936 and 1951 versions were taken from the Call Bureau Cast Service, which listed all featured and even bit players. Many of these performers were, however, deleted by the time of final release. As it would be nearly impossible to determine exactly which of the minor players were edited out, it was decided to leave the lists intact, with the addition, in fact, of a few more names.

It is interesting to note that there was no star billing (name above the title) for any of the three films.

Because no sound print of the 1929 version is known to survive, it has been impossible to determine the precise running order of the musical numbers and who sings them, except in the prologue. Musical programs are, however, complete for the 1936 and 1951 versions.

Information about a short subject based on the **Maxwell House Show Boat** radio program has been included also.

1929 VERSION

CARL LAEMMLE
In Association with
FLORENZ ZIEGFELD
Presents a Musical Prologue of
"SHOW BOAT"
Selections presented by the original cast from "Show Boat" as produced by Florenz Ziegfeld at the Ziegfeld Theatre, New York City
Prologue directed by Arch Heath with the original Ziegfeld orchestra, Victor Baravalle, conducting
Music by Jerome Kern, Lyrics by Oscar Hammerstein II

THE PLAYERS

MASTER OF CEREMONIES	Otis Harlan	TESS ("AUNT JEMIMA")	
HELEN MORGAN	Herself	GARDELLA	Herself
JULES BLEDSOE	Himself	THE JUBILEE SINGERS	Themselves

also Carl Laemmle, Florenz Ziegfeld

MUSICAL PROGRAM

C'MON, FOLKS	Gardella, Jubilee Singers
CAN'T HELP LOVIN' DAT MAN	Morgan, Jubilee Singers
HEY, FELLER!	Gardella, Jubilee Singers
BILL	Morgan
OL' MAN RIVER	Bledsoe, Male Jubilee Singers

CARL LAEMMLE PRESENTS
SHOW BOAT
by Edna Ferber
A Harry A. Pollard Production

Continuity	Charles Kenyon	Cinematographer	Gilbert Warrenton
Story Supervision	Edward J. Montagne	Art Director	Charles D. Hall
Dialogue Arranged by	Harry A. Pollard, Tom Reed	Unit Art Director	Joseph C. Wright
Titles	Tom Reed	Make-Up	Jane Rene
Supervising Film Editor	Maurice Pivar	Costumes	Johanna Mathieson
Film Editors	Daniel Mandell, Edward Cahn	Synchronization and Score	Joseph Cherniavsky
Assistant Director	Robert Ross		

Based upon the music in Florenz Ziegfeld's stage production by Jerome Kern and Oscar Hammerstein II

Recording Supervision	C. Roy Hunter	Direction	Harry A. Pollard

Movietone System

228

Appendix E

World Premiere: Saturday, March 16, 1929. Paramount Theatre, Palm Beach, Florida.
New York City Premiere: Wednesday, April 17, 1929. Globe Theatre.

MAGNOLIA	Laura La Plante	STEVE	George Chesebro
GAYLORD RAVENAL	Joseph Schildkraut	MEANS	Harry Holden
PARTHENIA ANN HAWKS	Emily Fitzroy	MRS. MEANS	Blanche Craig
CAPTAIN ANDY HAWKS	Otis Harlan	UTILITY WOMAN	Grace Cunard
JULIE	Alma Rubens	UTILITY MAN	Max Asher
WINDY	Jack McDonald	BUTCHER	Scott Mattraw
MAGNOLIA (as a child)	Jane La Verne	OLD TRAGEDIAN	Joe Mills
KIM		NEGRO BOSS	Richard Coleman
SCHULTZY	Neely Edwards	DRUM MAJOR	James V. Ayres
ELLY	Elise Bartlett	THE KILLER	Ralph Yearsley
JOE	Stepin Fetchit	STAGEHAND	Jim Coleman
QUEENIE	Gertrude Howard	WHEELSMAN	Carl Herlinger
FRANK	Theodore Lorch*	POLICEMAN	Tom McGuire

The voices of the Billbrew Chorus, Silvertone Quartet, Claude Collins, Four Emperors of Harmony, Jules Bledsoe
*Howard Chase played the role of FRANK during early location shooting but was soon replaced by Theodore Lorch.

MUSICAL PROGRAM

This part-talkie contains many spirituals and atmospheric southern songs performed off-screen by the various Negro soloists and vocal groups listed above. During the action, Laura La Plante (her singing voice dubbed by Eva Olivotti) "sings" several songs: "Deep River," "I've Got Shoes," "Coon Coon Coon," "Ol' Man River," and "Can't Help Lovin' Dat Man." The off-screen voice of Jules Bledsoe, singing "The Lonesome Road," is heard at the film's conclusion.

"CAPTAIN HENRY'S RADIO SHOW" PARAMOUNT, 1933

One-reel short subject featuring cast members of the **Maxwell House Show Boat** radio series. Annette Hanshaw, Molasses (Pat Padget) and January (Pick Malone), Don Voorhees and His Orchestra, The Show Boat Four, announcers Tiny Ruffner and Kelvin Keech, Muriel Wilson as Mary Lou, and Lanny Ross.

MUSICAL PROGRAM

HERE COMES THE SHOW BOAT	Show Boat Four, Voorhees Orch.
COME ON DOWN SOUTH	Show Boat Four, Voorhees Orch.
PLEASE	Ross, Wilson, Voorhees Orch.
RUNNING WILD (partial)	Voorhees Orch.
RUNNING WILD (partial)	Voorhees Orch.
WE JUST COULDN'T SAY GOODBYE	Hanshaw, Voorhees Orch.
LOOK WHO'S HERE	Show Boat Four, Voorhees Orch.
HERE COMES THE SHOW BOAT	Show Boat Four, Voorhees Orch.

1936 VERSION

Carl Laemmle Presents
Edna Ferber's
SHOW BOAT
Starring Irene Dunne
A James Whale Production
Allan Jones, Charles Winninger, Paul Robeson, Helen Morgan, Helen Westley
Produced by Carl Laemmle Jr.
Stage Play, Screen Play, Lyrics by Oscar Hammerstein II
Music by Jerome Kern

Cinematographer	John J. Mescall, A. S. C.	Costumes Executed by	Vera West
Special Cinematographer	John P. Fulton	Assistant Director	Joseph A. McDonough
Art Director	Charles D. Hall	Dance Numbers Staged by	LeRoy Prinz
Musical Director	Victor Baravalle	Technical Director	Leighton K. Brill
Costumes Designed by	Doris Zinkeisen	Sound Supervisor	Gilbert Kurland

Appendix E

Film Editors	Ted Kent, Bernard Burton	Musical Arrangements	Robert Russell Bennett
Editorial Supervisor	Maurice Pivar	Title Art	John Harkrider
Sound Recorders	Mike McLaughlin (music) William Hedgecock (production)		

Noiseless Western Electric Recording
Directed by James Whale
Copyright © May 13, 1936, by Universal Productions Inc.
World Premiere: Thursday, May 14, 1936. Radio City Music Hall, New York City

MAGNOLIA	Irene Dunne	MOTHER	Anna Demetrio
GAYLORD RAVENAL	Allan Jones	FAT GIRLS	Artye Folz, Barbara Bletcher
CAP'N ANDY HAWKS	Charles Winninger	MRS. BRENCENBRIDGE	Helen Hayward
JOE	Paul Robeson	BIT GIRL	Kathleen Ellis
JULIE	Helen Morgan	JAKE	Harry Barris
PARTHY ANN HAWKS	Helen Westley	FAT WOMAN	Maude Allen
ELLIE	Queenie Smith	GAMBLER	Lloyd Whitlock
FRANK	Sammy White	DEALER	Frank Whitson
STEVE	Donald Cook	DEAF WOMAN	Flora Finch
QUEENIE	Hattie McDaniel	GAMBLERS	Eddy Chandler, Lee Phelps,
RUBBER FACE	Francis X. Mahoney		Frank Mayo, Edward Peil Sr.,
KIM (as a child)	Marilyn Knowlden		Edmund Cobb, Al Ferguson
KIM (at sixteen)	Sunnie O'Dea	MAID	Daisy Bufford
PETE	Arthur Hohl	CHORUS GIRLS	Dorothy Granger, Barbara Pepper,
VALLON	Charles Middleton		Renee Whitney
WINDY	J. Farrell MacDonald	DRUNK	Arthur Housman
SAM	Clarence Muse	THEATRE MANAGER	Forrest Stanley
JIM	Charles Wilson	HOTEL CLERK	Selmer Jackson
KIM (as a baby)	Patricia Barry	YMCA WORKER	George Hackathorne
BACKWOODSMAN	Stanley Fields	SOLDIERS	Max Wagner, James P. Burtis
ZEBE	Stanley J. "Tiny" Sandford	BIT BOYS	Billy Watson, Delmar Watson
LANDLADY	May Beatty	RACE FANS	Ernest Hilliard, Jack Mulhall,
MOTHER	Maidel Turner		Brooks Benedict
DAUGHTER	Mary Bovard	MOTHER SUPERIOR	Elspeth Dudgeon
YOUNG MAN	William Alston	ENGLISHMAN	E. E. Clive
YOUNG GIRL	Marguerite Warner	REPORTER	Helen Jerome Eddy
LOST CHILD	Bobs Watson	PRESS AGENT	Don Briggs
MRS. EWING	Jane Keckley	DANCE DIRECTOR	LeRoy Prinz
COMPANION	Isabelle LaMal	OFFICE BOY	Harold Waldridge
BIT GIRLS	Betty Brown, June Glory	SCHOOL TEACHER	Georgia O'Dell
BIT WOMAN	Helen Dickson	BIT BOY	Harry Watson
MINISTER	Tom Ricketts	OLD NEGRO	George H. Reed
DOCTOR	Gunnis Davis	YOUNG NEGRO	Eddie "Rochester" Anderson
POSTMASTER	Harold Nelson	BIT MAN	D'Arcy Corrigan
BANJO PLAYER	Patti Patterson	SIMON LEGREE	Theodore Lorch
TALL GIRL	Betty Roche	BARTENDER	Matthew Jones
MOTHER	Grace Cunard	JUVENILE	Jack Latham
LITTLE GIRL	Maralyn Harris	CHORUS GIRLS	Alma Ross, Jeanette Dixon
YOUNG MAN	Jimmy Jackson	STAND-IN (Dunne)	Katherine Stanley
OLD WOMAN	Ricca Allen	STAND-IN (Jones)	Jack Latham
THIN GIRL	Maxine Cook	STAND-IN (Morgan)	Mary Stewart
OLD MAN	Monte Montague	EXTRA	Sarah Schwartz
SMALL GIRL	Lois Verner		

MUSICAL PROGRAM

COTTON BLOSSOM	chorus
CAP'N ANDY'S BALLYHOO	Winninger, danced by Smith, White
WHERE'S THE MATE FOR ME?	Jones
MAKE BELIEVE	Jones, Dunne
OL' MAN RIVER	Robeson, Negroes
CAN'T HELP LOVIN' DAT MAN	Morgan, McDaniel, Robeson, Negroes, danced by Dunne, Negroes
MIS'RY'S COMIN' AROUN' (partial)	chorus (humming)
I HAVE THE ROOM ABOVE HER	Jones, Dunne
GALLIVANTIN' AROUND	Dunne, chorus
reprise: OL' MAN RIVER (partial)	Robeson, Negroes (humming)

230

Appendix E

YOU ARE LOVE	chorus, Jones, Dunne
reprise: OL' MAN RIVER	Robeson
AH STILL SUITS ME	Robeson, McDaniel
reprise: AH STILL SUITS ME (partial)	Robeson
SERVICE AND SCENE MUSIC	girls
reprise: MAKE BELIEVE	Jones
WASHINGTON POST MARCH	danced by girls
BILL	Morgan, Barris (piano)
reprise: CAN'T HELP LOVIN' DAT MAN	Dunne
reprise: CAN'T HELP LOVIN' DAT MAN (partial)	Dunne, danced by White, Barris (piano)
GOOD-BYE, MA LADY LOVE introducing AT A GEORGIA CAMP MEETING	Smith, White dancing by Smith, White
AFTER THE BALL	Dunne, chorus
reprise: MAKE BELIEVE	Jones
AN OLD FASHIONED WIFE (partial)	O'Dea
reprise: GALLIVANTIN' AROUND	Negroes (humming), danced by Negroes, O'Dea, dancers
reprise: YOU ARE LOVE	Dunne, Jones
reprise: OL' MAN RIVER	Robeson

Original songs written for this film by Jerome Kern and Oscar Hammerstein II:
I Have the Room above Her, Gallivantin' Around, Ah Still Suits Me, Got My Eye on You (unused), Negro Peanut Vender's Street Cry (unused).

1951 VERSION

Metro Goldwyn Mayer
SHOW BOAT
starring
Kathryn Grayson   Ava Gardner   Howard Keel
Joe E. Brown, Marge and Gower Champion, Robert Sterling, Agnes Moorehead, Leif Erickson, William Warfield

Screenplay   John Lee Mahin
Based on the Immortal Musical Play "Show Boat" by Jerome Kern and Oscar Hammerstein II. From Edna Ferber's novel.

Dances	Robert Alton	Recording Supervisor	Douglas Shearer
Associate Producer	Ben Feiner Jr. (credited)	Set Decorations	Edwin B. Willis
	Roger Edens (uncredited)	Associate	Richard A. Pefferle
Musical Direction	Adolph Deutsch	Special Effects	Warren Newcombe
Orchestrations	Conrad Salinger	Montage Sequences	Peter Ballbusch
Vocal Arrangements	Robert Tucker	Costumes	Walter Plunkett
Director of Photography	Charles Rosher, A. S. C.	Hair Styles	Sydney Guilaroff
Technicolor Color Consultants	Henri Jaffa, James Gooch	Make-Up Creator	William Tuttle
Art Directors	Cedric Gibbons, Jack Martin Smith	Producer	Arthur Freed
Film Editor	John Dunning	Director	George Sidney
Additional Orchestrations	Alexander Courage		

Copyright © June 11, 1951, by Loew's Inc.
World Premiere: Thursday, July 19, 1951. Radio City Music Hall, New York City.

MAGNOLIA	Kathryn Grayson	KIM	Sheila Clark
JULIE	Ava Gardner	DRUNK SPORT	Ian MacDonald
GAYLORD RAVENAL	Howard Keel	JAKE	Fuzzy Knight
CAP'N ANDY HAWKS	Joe E. Brown	GEORGE (Calliope Player)	Norman Leavitt
ELLIE	Marge Champion	COTTON BLOSSOM GIRLS	Anne Marie Dore
FRANK	Gower Champion		Christina Lind
STEVE	Robert Sterling		Lyn Wilde
PARTHY ANN HAWKS	Agnes Moorehead		Marietta Elliott
PETE	Leif Erickson		Joyce Jameson
JOE	William Warfield		Bette Arlen
CAMEO McQUEEN	Adele Jergens		Helen Kimbell
WINDY	Owen McGiveney		Tao Porchon
QUEENIE	Frances Williams		Mitzie Uehlein
VALLON	Regis Toomey		Judy Landon
MARK HALLSON	Frank Wilcox		Nova Dale
HERMAN	Chick Chandler		Mary Jane French
JAKE GREEN	Emory Parnell		Marilyn Kinsley

Appendix E

COTTON BLOSSOM GIRLS (*continued*)	Alice Markham	ELEVATOR OPERATOR	Allan Ray
COTTON BLOSSOM BOYS	Michael Dugan	BELLHOP	Robert Stebbins
	Robert Fortier	HOTEL CLERK	John Crawford
	George Ford	DOORMAN	Jim Pierce
	Cass Jaeger	LANDLADY	Marjorie Wood
	Boyd Ackerman	BIT GIRL	Carol Brewster
	Roy Damron	MAN WITH JULIE	William Tannen
	Joseph Roach	BIT MAN	Len Hendry
DEALER	George Lynn	SEAMSTRESS	Anna Q. Nilsson
PICKANINNY	Melford Jones	THREE CUTIES	Sue Casey
DABNEY	Louis Mercier		Meredith Leeds
RENEE	Lisa Ferraday		Jean Romaine
AD LIBS	Al Rhein	DRUNK	Bert Roach
	Charles Regan	DOCTOR	Frank Dae
	Carl Sklover	PIANO PLAYER	Harry Seymour
CROUPIER	Peter Camlin	BOUNCER	William "Bill" Hall
PLAYER	Gil Perkins	BARTENDER	Earle Hodgins
HOTEL MANAGER	Edward Keane	DECKHAND	Dan Foster
TRAINER	George Sherwood	LITTLE OLD LADY	Ida Moore
BELLBOY	Tom Irish	HEADWAITER	Alphonse Martell

MUSICAL PROGRAM

COTTON BLOSSOM, introducing CAP'N ANDY'S ENTRANCE	chorus
BUCK AND WING FINALE ACT ONE	danced by the Champions
WHERE'S THE MATE FOR ME?	Keel
MAKE BELIEVE	Keel, Grayson
CAN'T HELP LOVIN' DAT MAN	Gardner*
reprise: CAN'T HELP LOVIN' DAT MAN (partial)	Grayson, Gardner*
I MIGHT FALL BACK ON YOU	Gower and Marge Champion
reprise: BUCK AND WING FINALE ACT ONE	danced by the Champions
OL' MAN RIVER (partial)	chorus (humming)
MIS'RYS' COMIN' AROUN'	chorus (humming)
OL' MAN RIVER	Warfield, chorus
reprise: MAKE BELIEVE	chorus
YOU ARE LOVE	Grayson, Keel
WHY DO I LOVE YOU?	Grayson, Keel
BILL	Gardner*
reprise: CAN'T HELP LOVIN' DAT MAN	Grayson
C'MON, FOLKS	background for acrobats
LIFE ON THE WICKED STAGE	Marge and Gower Champion, girls
AFTER THE BALL	Grayson, chorus, danced by Grayson, Brown
AULD LANG SYNE	chorus
reprise: BUCK AND WING FINALE ACT ONE	danced by Brown, Clark
reprise: CAN'T HELP LOVIN' DAT MAN (partial)	Gardner
reprise: MAKE BELIEVE (partial)	Keel
reprise: OL' MAN RIVER	chorus, Warfield

*Ava Gardner's singing voice dubbed by Annette Warren.

APPENDIX F—RADIO

During the days of live radio in America, **Show Boat** was a favorite among broadcasters. Several hour and half-hour presentations were offered, sometimes in truncated dramatic form, sometimes simply as a concert of isolated musical numbers.

Because the documentation of early radio is so sketchy, there is probably no way to compile a definitive listing of such broadcasts, but the information in Appendix F gives an ample suggestion of the richness and variety of American radio at a time when broadcasters still respected the taste and civility of their audience. Notice that many programs utilize performers from stage and screen versions of **Show Boat.**

In addition to one-time presentations of the work, three different radio series were in fact built around Charles Winninger's identity as a riverboat captain. Although these programs had little to do with **Show Boat** in content, they too are documented in Appendix F, along with an important BBC version broadcast in London.

With all series, the premiere and final dates of the series are given, along with the specific broadcasts of **Show Boat.** The sponsors and networks are also provided.

It should be pointed out that through 1941, NBC maintained two separate networks, the red and blue. When the federal government forced the company to drop one, the Blue Network became an independent company, and this in turn evolved into the American Broadcasting Company. Thus there are references to the NBC Red Network, the NBC Blue Network, the Blue Network alone, and finally ABC.

Ziegfeld Radio Show — CBS

Series: Sunday, April 3, 1932, through Sunday, June 26, 1932.
Sponsor: Chrysler Corporation.

Ziegfeld himself hosted this half-hour series until just weeks before his death on July 22, 1932. Guests included Mrs. Ziegfeld (Billie Burke), their daughter Patricia, Will Rogers, John Steel, Lupe Velez, Helen Morgan, Jack Pearl, Leon Errol, Paul Robeson, Ray Dooley, Fanny Brice, Ruth Etting, Frances White, and other Ziegfeld stage headliners.

On May 1 and June 12, the program featured **Show Boat** music with Helen Morgan, Paul Robeson, Jean Sargent, and Charles Carlile.

Maxwell House Show Boat — NBC Red Network

Series: Thursday, October 6, 1932, through Thursday, October 21, 1937.
Sponsor: Maxwell House Coffee.

One of the most popular variety shows of the 1930's, the series was originally built around Charles Winninger's characterization of Captain Henry, a role clearly inspired by Cap'n Andy. The format at first offered a slender fictional plot with continuing characters: Captain Henry (Charles Winninger), Lanny (Lanny Ross), Mary Lou (Mabel Jackson, soprano), Annette (Annette Hanshaw, crooner), Molasses and January (Pat Padget and Pick Malone—also known as Pick and Pat), Hall Johnson Choir, Jules Bledsoe, and Don Voorhees and His Orchestra. When Winninger left the cast in 1934 to return to Broadway in **Revenge with Music** (11-28-34, New Amsterdam), veteran performer Frank McIntyre took his place in the role of Henry's brother George.

Later, there was increased reliance upon guest celebrities, who included Nelson Eddy, Pickens Sisters, Conrad Thibault, Ben Bernie, Vaughn de Leath, Billy Jones and Ernest Hare, Jessica Dragonette, Helen Jepson, John Charles Thomas, Gloria Swanson, Walter Hampden, Eddie East and Ralph Dumke (Sisters of the Skillet), Helen Morgan, Dale Carnegie, Amelia Earhart, Lillian Gish, Gertrude Lawrence, Thomas L. Thomas, Jane Froman, Hildegarde, Lucy Monroe, Cornelia Otis Skinner, Hattie McDaniel, Mary Boland, and Jack Haley.

Every few weeks, the program featured a capsule version of an operetta or musical with cast regulars and guests. On three occasions, including the final broadcast of the series, **Show Boat** was presented: July 19, 1934; May 14, 1936; and October 21, 1937. The final broadcast featured Thomas L. Thomas, Nadine Connor, Virginia Verrill, Hattie McDaniel, Alma Kruger, Warren Hull, Eddie Green, and Meredith Willson's Orchestra.

Show Boat — BBC

National program, Monday, December 10, 1934. Repeated on the regional program, Wednesday, December 12, 1934.

Adapted for radio by Henrik Ege. Directed by John Watt. Musical direction by Stanford Robinson.

| STEVE | Frank Tully | QUEENIE | *Alberta Hunter | CAP'N ANDY | ***Percy Parsons |
| PETE | C. Denier Warren | PARTHY ANN HAWKS | **Margaret Yarde | ELLIE | Mabelle George |

Appendix F

FRANK	Sydney Keith	VALLON	W. G. Ellwanger	LANDLADY	Mary O'Farrell
JULIE	Florence McHugh	MAGNOLIA	*Edith Day	CHARLIE	Morris Hansard
GAYLORD RAVENAL	****Michael Cole	JOE	Ike Hatch	KIM (young woman)	*Edith Day

     *created role in original London production
    **created role of Landlady in London production
   ***created role of Vallon in London production
  ****created role of Jake in London production

Gulf Headliners   CBS
Series: Sunday, October 7, 1934, through Sunday, September 22, 1935.
Sponsor: Gulf Refining Company

Will Rogers was the original host of this musical variety half-hour series. Starting Sunday, February 10, 1935, he was replaced by Charles Winninger as Captain Bill. The program featured Frank Parker (tenor), Pickens Sisters, The Revelers (male quartet), and Frank Tours and His Orchestra. Winninger's last appearance in the series was on March 24, after which Rogers returned. James Melton, tenor of The Revelers, was the final host.

Uncle Charlie Winninger's Ivory Tent Show   NBC Red Network
Series: Sunday, June 9, 1935, through Sunday, September 8, 1935.
Sponsor: Ivory Soap.

This third radio series based on Winninger as a riverboat captain was an outgrowth of the popular **The Gibson Family,** a most unusual musical situation comedy that featured original songs composed every week by Arthur Schwartz and Howard Dietz. To vary the domestic theme, a tent show background was introduced with its locale changed each week from one town to the next.

Winninger appeared with Conrad Thibault, Jack and Loretta Clemens, Lois Bennett, and Don Voorhees and His Orchestra from the original cast of **The Gibson Family,** in addition to newcomers Ernest Whitman and Eddie Green (Sam and Jerry) and the Six Spirits of Rhythm.

Campbell Playhouse   CBS
Series: Friday, December 9, 1938, through Friday, June 13, 1941.
Sponsor: Campbell Soup Co.

An outgrowth of the **Mercury Theatre on the Air,** this weekly dramatic series presented adaptations of famous novels, arranged by Orson Welles. On Friday, March 31, 1939, an hourlong dramatic version of **Show Boat,** directed by Welles, was presented with original music by Bernard Herrmann and the following remarkable cast:

MAGNOLIA	Margaret Sullavan	GAYLORD RAVENAL	William Johnstone
JULIE	Helen Morgan	WINDY	Ray Collins
CAP'N ANDY	Orson Welles	SCHULTZ	Everett Sloane
PARTHY ANN HAWKS	Edna Ferber	KIM	Grace Coppin

Author Edna Ferber was interviewed.

DuPont Cavalcade of America   CBS, later NBC Red Network
Series: Wednesday, October 9, 1935, through Tuesday, March 31, 1953.
Sponsor: DuPont Chemical Co.

After four seasons on CBS, this series, a tribute to American history, moved to the Red Network. On Tuesday, May 28, 1940, it presented a dramatic version of **Show Boat** with John McIntire, Frank Readick, Ted Jewitt, Bill Pringle, Kenny Delmar, Jeanette Nolan, Ray Collins, Edwin Jerome, Agnes Moorehead, Ian MacAllister, Basil Ruysdael, and announcers Karl Swenson and William Johnstone.

Lux Radio Theatre   NBC Blue Network, later CBS, NBC
Series: Sunday, October 14, 1934, through Tuesday, June 7, 1955
Sponsor: Lux Soap

One of the best loved programs in the history of American broadcasting, the **Lux Radio Theatre** originated at first from New York City, with major theatrical stars in adaptations of Broadway plays. Its first season was on the Blue Network, but the program shifted to its familiar Monday night spot on CBS on July 29, 1935.

On Monday, June 1, 1936, Cecil B. DeMille became the producer and host, when the series moved to Hollywood and began to offer hourlong versions of motion pictures, often with their original stars. DeMille remained through January 22, 1945, and was later replaced by director William Keighley. The final broadcast for CBS was on Monday, June 28, 1954, after which the series was heard on Tuesday nights on NBC for one last season: September 14, 1954, through June 7, 1955.

Two of **Show Boat**'s most important radio versions were heard on this series, on June 24, 1940, and on February 11, 1952. The cast on Monday, June 24, 1940:

MAGNOLIA	Irene Dunne	STEVE	Kristam Poppin
GAYLORD RAVENAL	Allan Jones	VALLON	Earle Ross
CAP'N ANDY	Charles Winninger	JAKE	Edward Marr
PARTHY ANN HAWKS	Verna Felton		Barbara Jean Wong
FRANK	Hal K. Dawson		Arthur Q. Bryan
ELLIE	Ynez Seabury		James Eagles
JULIE	Gloria Holden		Sarah Selby

Musical Director   Louis Silvers

The cast on Monday, February 11, 1952:

JULIE	Ava Gardner
MAGNOLIA	Kathryn Grayson
GAYLORD RAVENAL	Howard Keel
JOE	William Warfield
CAP'N ANDY	Jay C. Flippen

Great Moments in Music   CBS

Series: Wednesday, January 7, 1942, through Wednesday, June 26, 1946.

Sponsor: Celanese Corp. of America.

This popular half-hour music program featured Jean Tennyson (soprano), Jan Peerce (tenor), Robert Weede (baritone), and George Sebastian and His Orchestra and Chorus.

On Wednesday, December 30, 1942, and Wednesday, June 16, 1943, music from **Show Boat** was featured. Tennyson and Peerce duetted "Make Believe" and "You Are Love," with solos of "Bill" and "Can't Help Lovin' Dat Man" sung by Tennyson, "Why Do I Love You?" by Peerce, and "Ol' Man River" by Weede.

Radio Hall of Fame   Blue Network

Series: Sunday, December 5, 1943, through Sunday, April 28, 1946.

Sponsor: Philco Corporation.

This prestigious hourlong variety series featured Paul Whiteman and His Orchestra, with Deems Taylor as master of ceremonies. Major stars and casts from Broadway musicals were selected by *Variety* editor Abel Green.

On Sunday, December 31, 1944, *Show Boat,* adapted for radio by Mort Lewis and produced by Tom McKnight, was featured with Kathryn Grayson as Magnolia for the first time.

MAGNOLIA	Kathryn Grayson
GAYLORD RAVENAL	Allan Jones
JULIE	Helen Forrest
PARTHY ANN HAWKS	Elvia Allman
JOE	Ernest Whitman
CAP'N ANDY; narrator	Charles Winninger

The New York Philharmonic Symphony   CBS

Series: Sunday, October 5, 1930, through Saturday, May 25, 1963.

Sponsors: U. S. Rubber Co., Standard Oil of New Jersey, Willis Overland Motors Inc., Willis Motors Inc.

During its Sunday, February 10, 1946, broadcast, the Philharmonic, conducted by Artur Rodzinski, performed Kern's "Scenario for Orchestra."

The Railroad Hour   ABC; later NBC

Series: Monday, October 4, 1948, through Monday, June 21, 1954.

Sponsor: Association of American Railroads.

Gordon MacRae starred in this immensely popular series, in which Broadway musicals and operettas were shrewdly condensed to a half hour, generally by singer-actress-writer Jean Holloway, with scripts by playwrights Jerome Lawrence and Robert E. Lee. The director was Fran Van Hartesfeldt, the conductor Carmen Dragon and the choral director Norman Luboff.

The series offered **Show Boat** on five occasions, all starring MacRae with different leading ladies listed below:

ABC May 2, 1949	Lucille Norman
NBC October 3, 1949	Lucille Norman, Dorothy Kirsten
NBC October 30, 1950	Lucille Norman, Dorothy Kirsten
NBC January 19, 1953	Dorothy Kirsten
NBC October 12, 1953	Dorothy Warenskjold

APPENDIX G—A SELECTED DISCOGRAPHY

It is ironic that despite its superb score and beloved role in the American Musical Theatre, there has never been a complete recording of **Show Boat,** nor even a recording with its original 1927 orchestrations or original overture. Only three members of its original cast ever made commercial recordings of their songs. Helen Morgan recorded both "Bill" and "Can't Help Lovin' Dat Man" first in 1928 and again in 1932. Tess Gardella also recorded "Can't Help Lovin' Dat Man," and Jules Bledsoe recorded "Ol' Man River" in England. Howard Marsh recorded only a few Irish songs during the early 1920's and later some Gilbert and Sullivan, but not a note of his three celebrated stage vehicles: **Blossom Time, The Student Prince in Heidelberg,** and **Show Boat.** Neither Norma Terris, Eva Puck, nor Sammy White made any commercial records at all. Thus the original interpretation of the score has been lost forever.

Because the 1936 film version does employ the talents of many original cast members, in addition to conductor Victor Baravalle and orchestrator Robert Russell Bennett, the soundtrack of this film is perhaps the closest surviving approximation of the original score, though many songs were eliminated from the film and the orchestrations augmented for the screen.

Because of the vast number of American and British **Show Boat** singles and albums, Appendix G is a highly selective discography. The first section contains those single recordings (arranged by label) made during the original Broadway and London runs. The next section contains single discs (listed more or less in the order of their recording) made from 1930 through the early 1950's. Notice that very few song titles are repeated over and over in a wide variety of interpretations.

Song titles in parenthesis are not from **Show Boat,** and information in brackets was not supplied on label copy but seemed important enough to include. Initials "vr" denote a vocal refrain on a dance record. All singles are 10″ 78's unless otherwise noted.

The last section of album listings does not include song titles because of the monotony of repetition. There are some variations, however; and a diligent collector can assemble a fairly complete score by taking "C'mon, Folks" and "In Dahomey" from the 1928 album, "Till Good Luck Comes My Way" and Opening Act Two from Victor LM-2008, Finale Act One from Columbia OS 2220, and so on. Only "Hey, Feller!" has never been recorded vocally.

78's ISSUED DURING ORIGINAL BROADWAY RUN

Victor

21215	Can't Help Lovin' Dat Man	vr Franklyn Baur
	Nathaniel Shilkret and the Victor Orchestra	
	Why Do I Love You?	vr Franklyn Baur
21218	Ol' Man River	vr Bing Crosby
	Paul Whiteman and His Orchestra	
	Make Believe	vr Bing Crosby
21238	Can't Help Lovin' Dat Man	
	Helen Morgan [orchestra conducted by Victor Baravalle]	
	Bill	
21241	Ol' Man River	
	The Revelers [Lewis James, Elliott Shaw, James Melton, Wilfred Glenn; Frank Black, piano]	
	(Oh! Lucindy)	
35912 12″	Ol' Man River	Paul Robeson
	Paul Whiteman and His Concert Orchestra and Mixed Chorus	
	Selections: Why Do I Love You?, Can't Help Lovin' Dat Man, You Are Love, Make Believe	

Columbia

1284-D	Ol' Man River	vr Wilfred Glenn
	Don Voorhees and His Orchestra	
	Can't Help Lovin' Dat Man	vr Vaughn de Leath

236

Appendix G

1304-D	{ Can't Help Lovin' Dat Man Ol' Man River	Aunt Jemima Goodrich Silvertown Quartet

Brunswick

3766	{ Ol' Man River "Kenn" Sisson and His Orchestra Why Do I Love You?	vr Irving Kaufman vr Franklyn Baur
3808	{ Can't Help Lovin' Dat Man Ben Bernie and His Hotel Roosevelt Orchestra Make Believe	vr Vaughn de Leath vr Harold "Scrappy" Lambert
3864	{ (Varsity Drag) Zelma O'Neal Can't Help Lovin' Dat Man	
3867	{ Ol' Man River Al Jolson with William F. Wirges and His Orchestra (Back in Your Own Back Yard)	
20064 12″	{ Ol' Man River Ben Bernie and His Hotel Roosevelt Orchestra (Soliloquy)	vr Bob Schafer

Edison Diamond Discs

52223	{ Why Do I Love You?
	    B. A. Rolfe and His Palais D'Or Orchestra
	Can't Help Lovin' Dat Man
			52358	{ Ol' Man River
				    The Rollickers
				(Crazy Rhythm)

His Majesty's Voice (HMV) (British)

B 2741	{ (Together)
	    Melville Gideon
	Can't Help Lovin' Dat Man
			B 2862	{ Make Believe
				    Edward O'Henry (Organist of Mme. Tussaud's Cinema)
				Why Do I Love You?

B 2749	{ (The Girl Is You, and the Boy Is Me)
	    Morton Downey
	Make Believe
			B 5475	{ Can't Help Lovin' Dat Man
				    Jack Hylton and His Orchestra
				Ol' Man River

B 2764	{ Can't Help Lovin' Dat Man
	    Fray and Braggiotti (pianos)
	(My Blue Heaven)
			C 1531 12″	{ Selection Part One
				    New Mayfair Orchestra
				Selection Part Two

B 2858	{ Ol' Man River Peter Dawson (The Banjo Song)			

Columbia (British)

DB 4900	{ Why Do I Love You?
	    Piccadilly Players, directed by Al Starita
	Make Believe
			DB 5037	{ Ol'Man River
				    Albert Sandler and His Park Lane Orchestra
				(Japansy)

DB 4916	{ Can't Help Lovin' Dat Man Layton and Johnstone Ol' Man River			

The following 1928 British cast recordings are all accompanied by the Drury Lane Theatre Orchestra, conducted by Herman Finck.

9426 12″	{ Ol' Man River Vocal Gems: Cotton Blossom, Queenie's Ballyhoo, In Dahomey, Can't Help Lovin' Dat Man	Norris Smith, The Mississippi Chorus The Mississippi Chorus
9427 12″	{ Bill Can't Help Lovin' Dat Man	Marie Burke Marie Burke, The Mississippi Sextet
9428 12″	{ Make Believe Why Do I Love You?	Edith Day, Howett Worster
9429 12″	{ Dance Away the Night You Are Love	Edith Day, Chorus Edith Day, Howett Worster
9430 12″	{ Selection: Cotton Blossom, Make Believe, Ol' Man River, Misery, Can't Help Lovin' Dat Man Selection: Misery, You Are Love, Why Do I Love You?, Hey, Feller!, Finale	Drury Lane Theatre Orchestra

237

unissued 12″ { Ol' Man River   Paul Robeson, The Mississippi Chorus
           { In Dahomey   The Mississippi Chorus

Note: Records 9427, 9428, 9429 and "Cotton Blossom" and Queenie's Ballyhoo ("C'mon, Folks") from 9426 were reissued in 1976 on World Records Limited SH 240, a mono 12″ LP. This album, which combines the **Show Boat** collection with British cast recordings of Jerome Kern's **Sunny,** also contains the first release of "Ol' Man River," sung by Robeson and The Mississippi Chorus, and "In Dahomey," sung by the chorus alone.

LATER SINGLE RECORDS (78rpm UNLESS OTHERWISE NOTED)

HMV   (My Old Kentucky Home)
                Paul Robeson
B-3653   Ol' Man River

Victor   "Show Boat" Medley: Ol' Man River, Make Believe (Robert Simmons), Can't Help Lovin' Dat Man, Why Do I Love You?
L-16014   (Frances Langford), Ol' Man River   Jesse Crawford (organist)

Note: Beginning in 1931, RCA Victor issued for several years a series of ten and twelve-inch recordings, cut at 33 1/3rpm, with a standard three-mil groove (as in contrast to the microgroove cut of later LP's). Known as Program Transcriptions, these recordings were issued both single and double faced. This **Show Boat** medley was recorded on one side only.

Decca (British)   { (Dear Old Southland)
                       Jules Bledsoe
K.631 12″   { Ol' Man River

HMV   { Ol' Man River   Paul Robeson
B-8497   { Ah Still Suits Me   Paul Robeson, Elisabeth Welch

Victor   { Make Believe
                       Allan Jones, orchestra conducted by Lou Bring
4555   { Why Do I Love You?

Mercury   { Make Believe
                       Tony Martin, Al Sack's Orchestra
5027   { (All the Things You Are)

Columbia   { Ol' Man River
                       Frank Sinatra, orchestra conducted by Axel Stordahl
55037 12″   { (Stormy Weather)

HMV   { Selection Part One
                       Melachrino Orchestra
C4103 12″   { Selection Part Two

Columbia (British)   { Vocal Gems: Make Believe (Lizabeth Webb, Steve Conway), Can't Help Lovin' Dat Man (Adelaide Hall), Why Do I Love You? (Webb, Conway)
                       Orchestra and chorus directed by Philip Green
DX1771 12″   { Vocal Gems: Bill (Hall), You Are Love (Webb, Conway), Ol' Man River (Bryan Johnson)

ALBUMS (78rpm AND LP)

1928 London Cast
Edith Day, Paul Robeson, Marie Burke, Howett Worster, The Mississippi Chorus, Drury Lane Theatre Orchestra, conducted by Herman Finck
    A 1976 LP reissue of (British) Columbia single records, combined with 1926 London cast selections from **Sunny**
    World Records Limited   12″ mono LP

1932 Broadway Revival
Helen Morgan, Frank Munn, Paul Robeson, Countess Olga Albani, James Melton, Victor Young and the Brunswick Concert Orchestra
    See page 103 for details.

Brunswick	unnumbered set	4-12″ 78's
Columbia	C-55	4-12″ 78's
Columbia	AC 55	12″ mono LP

"Scenario for Orchestra"
The Cleveland Orchestra, conducted by Artur Rodzinski.
Commissioned by Artur Rodzinski, this short orchestral adaptation of **Show Boat** themes was composed by Jerome Kern in Hollywood, during July and August, 1941. The scoring by Charles Miller was completed in September. The premiere took place at Severance Hall, Cleveland, on Thursday, October 23, 1941.

Columbia   M-495   3-12″ 78's

Appendix G

1946 Broadway Revival

Jan Clayton, Carol Bruce, Colette Lyons, Helen Dowdy, Charles Fredericks, Kenneth Spencer, orchestra conducted by Edwin McArthur

Columbia	M/MM-611	5-12" 78's
Columbia	ML/OL 4058	12" mono LP

Studio Recording

Bing Crosby, Lee Wiley, Kenny Baker, Frances Langford, Tony Martin

Decca	A-610	4-10" 78's

Till the Clouds Roll By Soundtrack

Show Boat selections performed by Kathryn Grayson, Tony Martin, Virginia O'Brien, Lena Horne, Caleb Peterson, MGM orchestra conducted by Lennie Hayton

Except for a few earlier Walt Disney collections, this is the first soundtrack album issued from a Hollywood movie.

MGM	1	4-10" 78's
MGM	E-501	10" mono LP

Studio Recording

Tommy Dorsey and His Orchestra with Peggy Mann, Stuart Foster, Sy Oliver, and The Sentimentalists

RCA Victor	P-152	4-10" 78's

Studio Recording

Dorothy Kirsten, Robert Merrill, orchestra conducted by John Scott Trotter

RCA Victor	DM-1341	4-10" 78's
RCA Victor	LM-9002	12" mono LP

1951 Soundtrack

Kathryn Grayson, Ava Gardner, Howard Keel, Marge and Gower Champion, William Warfield, MGM orchestra conducted by Adolph Deutsch

Ava Gardner sings on this album, although her vocals were dubbed by Annette Warren in the film itself.

MGM	84	4-10" 78's
MGM	E-559	10" mono LP

Studio Recording

Carol Bruce, Helena Bliss, John Tyers, William C. Smith, orchestra conducted by Lehman Engel

Four selections from **Show Boat** were combined with four selections from Kern's **The Cat and the Fiddle** on this little album.

RCA Victor	LPM-3151	10" mono LP

Studio Recording

Robert Merrill, Patrice Munsel, Risë Stevens, Katherine Graves, Janet Pavek, Kevin Scott, orchestra conducted by Lehman Engel

RCA Victor	LM-2008	12" mono LP

Studio Recording

Gogi Grant, Howard Keel, Anne Jeffreys, Henri René and His Orchestra

RCA Victor	LOP-1505	12" mono LP
RCA Victor	LSO-1505	12" stereo LP

Studio Recording

John Raitt, Barbara Cook, William Warfield, Anita Darian, Fay De Witt, Louise Parker, The Merrill Staton Choir, orchestra conducted by Franz Allers

Columbia	OL 5820	12" mono LP
Columbia	OS 2220	12" stereo LP

1966 Lincoln Center Revival

Barbara Cook, Constance Towers, Stephen Douglass, David Wayne, William Warfield, Rosetta Le Noire, Eddie Phillips, Ann McLerie, orchestra conducted by Franz Allers

RCA Victor	LOC-1126	12" mono LP
RCA Victor	LSO-1126	12" stereo LP

1971 London Revival

Andre Jobin, Cleo Laine, Thomas Carey, Kenneth Nelson, Derek Royle, Pearl Hackney, Jan Hunt, Ena Cabayo, Lorna Dallas, orchestra conducted by Ray Cook

In Britain, this album was issued on a single LP. Additional selections were added to the American release, which is on two records.

Columbia (Britain)	SCX 6480	12" stereo LP
Stanyan (America)	10048	2-12" stereo LP's

INDEX

In the following alphabetical index, there are special groupings listed under BOATS (show boats unless noted), BOOKS, FILMS, MUSICAL NUMBERS, PERIODICALS, STAGE PLAYS AND MUSICALS, and THEATRES (New York City and elsewhere).

Numbers set in italic refer to illustrations.

DATE DUE

GAYLORD   PRINTED IN U.S.A.